# Inside
## the Voyage of the
## Dawn Treader

# Books by Devin Brown

*Inside Narnia*

*Inside Prince Caspian*

*Inside the Voyage of the Dawn Treader*

# Inside

## the Voyage of the

# Dawn Treader

### A Guide to Exploring
### the Journey beyond Narnia

## Devin Brown

**BakerBooks**

*a division of Baker Publishing Group*
Grand Rapids, Michigan

Published by Baker Books
a division of Baker Publishing Group
P.O. Box 6287, Grand Rapids, MI 49516-6287
www.bakerbooks.com

Printed in the United States of America

Library of Congress Cataloging-in-Publication Data
Brown, Devin.
    Inside The voyage of the Dawn Treader : a guide to exploring the journey beyond Narnia / Devin Brown.
        p.   cm.
    Includes bibliographical references (p.     ).
    ISBN 978-0-8010-7165-2 (pbk.)
        1. Lewis, C. S. (Clive Staples), 1898–1963. Voyage of the Dawn Treader.
    I. Title.
    PR6023.E926V6933 2010
    823'.912—dc22                                                              2010021501

Scripture is taken from the Holy Bible, New International Version®, NIV®. Copyright © 1973, 1978, 1984 by Biblica, Inc.™ Used by permission of Zondervan. All rights reserved worldwide. www.zondervan.com

Twenty-two brief quotes (648 words) from *Companion to Narnia* by Paul F. Ford and illustrated by Lorinda B. Cauley. Text copyright © 1980 by Paul F. Ford. Illustrations copyright © 1980 by Lorinda Bryan Cauley. Reprinted by permission of HarperCollins Publishers.

10   11   12   13   14   15   16          7   6   5   4   3   2   1

# Contents

# Preface

I would like to welcome those of you who have read my earlier books—*Inside Narnia* and *Inside Prince Caspian*—and to say that with *Inside the Voyage of the Dawn Treader*, I hope to provide the same sort of commentary as before. I would also like to welcome new readers and briefly explain my approach.

I teach a class on C. S. Lewis at Asbury University, where I am an English professor. In that class, as we explore Lewis's works, we look at all aspects of them. Sometimes we may focus on a literary aspect; sometimes we may focus on something more devotional. Our goal is to investigate everything that warrants a closer look. In my books on Narnia, I take this same approach.

My position is that while the Chronicles of Narnia can be read and thoroughly enjoyed by children, they can also be read more seriously by older readers because they are rich with meaning. Some of this meaning will be discovered just by spending time with the text and paying close attention to what Lewis has written. Further meaning will be found by making connections: connections to other passages within the Chronicles, to events in Lewis's life, and to other works by Lewis and the authors who influenced him. I maintain that this kind of careful study yields not only greater understanding but also greater delight.

In addition to my own analysis, I include many comments from the world's foremost Lewis scholars. My hope is to provide the kind of lively discussion that Lewis himself would have enjoyed.

Readers can track down any quotation they would like to examine on their own by looking up the source in the reference list. When quoting another work, I indicate the source or author within the text and then give the page number in parentheses. To keep citations to a minimum, when I have two or more quotes within the same paragraph from the same page of any source, I include the page number for only the first quotation.

For their valuable suggestions and encouragement, I would like to thank Marvin Hinten, Jonathan Rogers, Rich Platt, Karen Koehn, and Sharon Brown. I would also like to thank Bob Hosack, Jessica Miles, and all the other wonderful folks at Baker Books.

# Introduction

Sometime around November 1949, a fifty-one-year-old English professor living just outside Oxford in Headington Quarry, England, picked up his pen, and in a little under three months—from start to finish—he completed a remarkable story about the crew of a small sailing ship and their two-part adventure: to find seven exiled lords and then to sail to the end of the world.

That English professor was C. S. Lewis. The story he completed in less than ninety days was *The Voyage of the Dawn Treader*.

In keeping with the plan to release one new Narnia book each year, *The Voyage of the Dawn Treader* would not get published for three years. In September 1952, it took its place as the third Chronicle of Narnia after *The Lion, the Witch and the Wardrobe* (October 1950) and *Prince Caspian* (October 1951).

While Lewis was alive, the books were always listed in their original order of publication. Seventeen years after Lewis's death, the Chronicles of Narnia were given a new numbering by their publisher. Beginning with the set issued by Collins's Fontana Lions imprint in 1980 and continuing to the present, *The Magician's Nephew*—the next-to-last book during Lewis's time—has been listed first because the events it depicts occur first. The rest of the stories have likewise been rearranged in chronological order. This reordering was done, the publishers claim, in accordance with the author's wishes.

In fact, there is little evidence that Lewis wanted the series renumbered and much to suggest that he liked it the way it was. If he had wanted it renumbered, surely during his lifetime he could have requested that the order be changed. Most Lewis scholars prefer the original order because (1) it allows us to walk *with* the children, not ahead of them, as they enter Narnia in *The Lion, the Witch and the Wardrobe*, and (2) it gives much more resonance to read about how Narnia, the lamp-post, and the wardrobe came to be—events depicted in *The Magician's Nephew*—*after* we have come to know them. It is interesting and perhaps significant that the filmmakers have returned to the original order.

## A Story about Learning and Growth

In a letter dated March 5, 1961, nine years after the novel's release, Lewis explained that his main focus in writing *The Voyage of the Dawn Treader* was "the spiritual life" (*Collected Letters*, Vol. 3, 1245). While the various stages of spiritual life are seen throughout the ensemble cast in this third adventure, Lewis further noted that this focus is seen "specially in Reepicheep," because by the end of the story, the noble mouse reaches the highest goal of development, where all personal goals are subordinate to a longing for his true spiritual home.

In *The Way into Narnia*, Peter Schakel includes a chapter titled "Longing and Learning in *The Voyage of the 'Dawn Treader'*." Schakel maintains that these two topics—longing and learning—are the story's "central themes" (60). Longing has already appeared as an important theme in *Prince Caspian* and will be equally important in *Dawn Treader*, especially near the end. But what about learning? If Narnia can be said to be a school of sorts, its goal is to mature all those who are in attendance. If, as noted, the maturation process in *The Voyage of the Dawn Treader* will reach its highest point in Reepicheep, it will have its most dramatic illustration in

Eustace Clarence Scrubb. Eustace, like Edmund in the first book, has taken a wrong turn—partly due to his upbringing, partly due to his schooling, and partly due to his own choices—and is about to undergo a radical reeducation.

This is not to imply that Lucy and Edmund will not also have something more to learn this time around—they do. In fact, since they are not essential to this adventure, as they were to the earlier ones, it could be argued that the main reason they are called back into Narnia this third time is so they can continue the education they began earlier. Regarding their comparative irrelevance for the plot, Doris Myers has proposed that if Lucy and Edmund had not been included on the voyage, "the only incident that would have had a different outcome is the recovery of visibility by the Dufflepuds" (140).

So, along with Eustace, Caspian, the Duffers, and Coriakin, Lucy and Edmund will once again take their place in Aslan's classroom. And this term will be a semester at sea. Even after the close of this adventure, even after they reach the very end of the world, Edmund and Lucy will have more to learn. And it is partly because of this that they must return to England rather than enter Aslan's country with Reepicheep. Once back home, the two will begin a different kind of lesson. As Aslan will tell Lucy in the final chapter, "There I have another name. You must learn to know me by that name" (247).

What is the overall mission of Aslan's school for the soul? In *The Silver Chair*, the next book in the series, readers will be told that the masters who run Experiment House take the view that boys and girls "should be allowed to do what they liked" (3), and unfortunately, what the biggest boys and girls like best is bullying the others. Aslan takes a very different view. His educational philosophy could be stated as the belief that boys and girls should be encouraged to do what is best for them. In Aslan's view, this means living a virtuous life, one filled with a commitment to the greater good rather than merely to one's self—for this is the only path that will lead to joy and fulfillment.

As Edmund discovered in *The Lion, the Witch and the Wardrobe*, Aslan's goal is to help each of his students to get past "thinking about himself" (141) or—in the case of Susan, Lucy, Jill, Aravis, and Polly—about herself. Getting past thinking about himself will be a particularly important lesson for Eustace here in *The Voyage of the Dawn Treader*. When those Aslan has taken on as students refuse to learn the lesson he has put before them, as Eustace initially will, their refusals will have consequences. But the correction Aslan metes out is an indication that, unlike the masters at Experiment House, he truly cares about his pupils.

## A Different Kind of Book

In some ways this third Chronicle follows patterns seen in the first two books. Once again children from England suddenly find themselves in Narnia. While there, they must help on a quest, and in the end they return home better because of their experiences. However, in two other ways *The Voyage of the Dawn Treader* represents a major departure from the previous books.

First, this is the first book without Peter and Susan. At the close of *Prince Caspian*, Peter shared part of what Aslan told him and Susan, saying, "He says we're getting too old" (221). What exactly Aslan meant by this statement is a bit unclear since King Frank and Queen Helen, both adults, were allowed not only to come but to stay in Narnia. Presumably it was simply time for Peter and Susan to begin to know Aslan by another name in their own world.

Second, *The Voyage of the Dawn Treader* will be the first and, as it turns out, the only book that does not take place in Narnia at all. In *The Silver Chair*, the next story in the series, Eustace will declare, "I don't know whether this is Narnia" (36), and Jill is surprised. "Thought you said you'd been here before," she comments. Part of Jill's confusion may be due to the fact that the name Narnia, while typically used to refer to the country, can also mean the world. At the end of *Prince Caspian*, Aslan implied that Peter and Susan were too old to return to Narnia but that Edmund and Lucy would return one day. Here in the opening chapter of *The Voyage of the Dawn Treader*, the narrator says, "A promise, or very nearly a promise, had been made them in Narnia itself that they would some day get back" (6). Edmund and Lucy do get back. Yet they, along with Eustace, are sent not to the country of Narnia but to the world.

One reason behind Lewis's decision to move his third story out of Narnia was the dilemma all authors of a series face: the problem of making each succeeding book different while at the same time keeping some aspects the same. This was a problem Lewis initially encountered with *Prince Caspian*. In that book, while keeping the same geographic location, he moved the second story thirteen hundred years after the first. In this third Chronicle, Lewis does the opposite. He keeps the same general time period—Caspian tells Edmund that they have been gone "exactly three years" (19)—but moves the story out to sea.

Tolkien faced similar challenges in *The Lord of the Rings*. After writing *The Hobbit*, Tolkien at first tried to write a second book about Bilbo, but soon found he was being repetitive. In a letter written to his publishers, Tolkien reported, "The *Hobbit* sequel is still where it was, and I have only the vaguest notions of how to proceed. Not ever intending any sequel, I fear I squandered all my favorite motifs and characters on the original" (*Letters* 29). Tolkien finally found that he needed to bring in a new protagonist and change the focus to Frodo, Bilbo's nephew.

Each successive Chronicle will have this same need to be somewhat different as well. The action of *The Silver Chair*, while staying relatively close in time to the third book, will be set in the lands north of Narnia and in Underland. *The Magician's Nephew* will again take place in Narnia, in the area around the lamp-post, but Lewis will add two additional locations for the action: the land of Charn and England itself. Also, he will use not one but two new time settings. In England, we go back in time to the days when the professor was a boy. In Narnia, we go back to the very start of time when Narnia was created.

In his essay titled "On Science Fiction," Lewis observes that the desire to write a story set in "strange regions" with "gods, ghosts, ghouls, demons, fairies, monsters, etc." is "an imaginative impulse as old as the human race" (63). He speculates that while at one time these stories might have taken place on our own world, due to our "increasing geographical knowledge" of Earth, writers have increasingly been driven to write about other worlds to find this strangeness. Lewis explains, "The less known the real world is, the more plausibly your marvels can be located near at hand. As the area of knowledge spreads, you need to go further afield: like a man moving his house further and further out into the country as the new building estates catch him up." Perhaps after the extensive travels made by the Pevensies in *The Lion, the Witch and the Wardrobe* and *Prince Caspian*, Lewis decided that the geography of Narnia was so well known to readers that in order to find the marvels he wanted to include, he had to move the third book somewhere new.

## A Look Back at the Second Film

Before we moving on to explore *The Voyage of the Dawn Treader*, here is a brief look back at the recent movie adaptation of *Prince Caspian*.

While *The Lion, the Witch and the Wardrobe* culminated with a grand coronation scene, Andrew Adamson's second Narnia film, *The Chronicles of Narnia: Prince Caspian*, never gets around to officially making the young prince into a king. Nor did Lewis's original. And this is as it should be since this second adventure is about people who are more like us and about life in a world more like our own.

When a movie is made of a book that has been a beloved children's classic, reviews often end up being little more than a list of what has been left out, added, or changed. In the case of a film that is part of a series, another kind of comparison is also common. Here the reviewer provides a list of favorite elements from the first movie that are then measured against their presence or absence in the second.

After I had watched about a minute of the most recent Narnia movie, neither of these two kinds of lists seemed very important to me. Andrew Adamson's *Prince Caspian* is a captivating work. And once it starts, the viewer is caught up in the same kind of storytelling wizardry that is so abundant in C. S. Lewis's original.

Some film critics have complained that the villain in *Prince Caspian*, King Miraz, is less interesting than the White Witch and that the Narnia the Pevensies return to is less enchanting. Both claims are true, and both changes were intentional on Lewis's part. There is not supposed to be anything very special about Caspian's uncle. He is a two-bit dictator and not particularly bright or imaginative, the kind of self-seeking tyrant who can be found in every world. Like his type everywhere, what he wants he steals in a cowardly and underhanded way—in this case, his brother's crown.

Though it is unlikely we will ever have to face a villain like the White Witch in our own lives, we will all surely come up against a Miraz or two. It is fitting that, unlike the witch, who was dramatically killed by Aslan, Miraz is done in by a stab in the back from one of his own creepy henchmen.

The repression Miraz has imposed on Narnia, while harsh, is as dull and joyless as he is. We learn that he has driven into exile or underground all the enchantment that so characterized Narnia the first time. Without the talking animals, dwarfs, mythological creatures, and spirits of the trees and streams, the land has a mundane feel, not a magical one. Again, it should be noted, this more ordinary feeling is intentional.

In his sermon "The Weight of Glory," Lewis asks, "Do you think I am trying to weave a spell? Perhaps I am; but remember your fairy tales. Spells are used for breaking enchantment as well as for inducing them. And you and I have need of the strongest spell that can be found to wake us from the evil enchantment of worldliness which has been laid upon us for nearly a hundred years" (31). The Narnia we find at the start of *Prince Caspian*—much like our own civilization, Lewis would claim—is under the spell of materialism, the belief that physical matter is the only reality and there is nothing beyond what we can see and touch. The once magical land has become disenchanted, and the four children have been summoned to help break the spell and return Narnia to its proper state.

been drawing on Peter's conflict with Edmund in the previous story as well. In *The Lion, the Witch and the Wardrobe*, when Aslan was told that Edmund had gone to the White Witch to betray them, Peter confessed, "That was partly my fault, Aslan. I was angry with him and I think that helped him to go wrong" (128).

Finally, what about the film's famous kiss? While in Lewis's original, Caspian and Susan never kiss or even hold hands, can it be argued that Andrew Adamson was keeping with the spirit of the Chronicles in adding this kiss? Perhaps. At the end of *The Lion, the Witch and the Wardrobe*, readers were told, "Susan grew into a tall and gracious woman with black hair that fell almost to her feet and the kings of the countries beyond the sea began to send ambassadors asking for her hand in marriage" (183–84). This linking of Susan and romance will be continued in *The Horse and His Boy*, where Susan's courtship by Prince Rabadash is something she initially relishes. Her focus is made clear in *The Last Battle*, where Jill will claim that Susan is "interested in nothing nowadays except nylons and lipstick and invitations" (154).

If, then, we can say that Susan is the kind of girl who might be interested in a kiss, what about Caspian? In a scene late in *The Voyage of the Dawn Treader*, when Caspian meets Ramandu's daughter, his future wife, he himself will bring up the story of the prince who wakes a sleeping kingdom. He will point out to her, "In that story he could not dissolve the enchantment until he had kissed the Princess" (203). When Ramandu's daughter tells him he cannot kiss the princess until after he breaks the enchantment of the three sleepers, he is quick to reply, "Then, in the name of Aslan, show me how to set about that work at once." At the start of *The Voyage of the Dawn Treader*, Caspian will be distinctly uninterested in the daughter of the Duke of Galma, but clearly—given the right girl—Caspian seems to look favorably on kissing.

These three examples all raise the same point. While director Peter Jackson had to shrink Tolkien's huge trilogy down to movie length, Andrew Adamson had modest-sized books that allowed him to expand and extend some elements. A wonderful illustration of this expansion in the first film was the way we were shown the bombing raid on London, which was the catalyst for sending the children to the professor's. So how can we judge whether these expansions or additions are in keeping with the spirit of Lewis's original? If we look at what is present not just in the book itself but in the other Chronicles as well, we can decide what might have been in character for each of the protagonists. While we will certainly disagree on some minor elements, we may expect to agree on the major ones. For example, no one has suggested that Edmund should have done any kissing!

And now on to *The Voyage of the Dawn Treader*!

ONE

# The Picture
# in the Bedroom

## The Dedication

Fans of the Narnia stories may recall that *The Lion, the Witch and the Wardrobe* was dedicated to Lucy Barfield. Lewis dedicated *The Voyage of the Dawn Treader* to Lucy's foster brother Geoffrey, who was born in 1940 and thus was twelve when the book was released. Lewis and Owen Barfield met as undergraduates at Oxford and became lifelong friends, so it is not surprising that Lewis would dedicate two of his books for young people to his dear friend's adopted daughter and foster son. With a generosity typical of him, Lewis also paid for Geoffrey's school fees.

Geoffrey did not take his foster parents' last name until 1962. Because of this, early editions of *The Voyage of the Dawn Treader*—those printed prior to 1962—are dedicated to Geoffrey Corbett.

## Eustace Clarence Scrubb

Charles Dickens began *A Tale of Two Cities* with the unforgettable statement, "It was the best of times, it was the worst of times" (1). Jane Austen started *Pride and Prejudice* with the famous claim, "It is a truth universally acknowledged, that a single man in possession of a good fortune, must be in want of a wife" (1). Lewis's friend J. R. R. Tolkien opened *The Hobbit*, his story about the adventures of Bilbo Baggins, with the delightful announcement, "In a hole in the ground there lived a hobbit" (11).

After using the fairy-tale opening "Once there were four children" for his first two Narnia books, Lewis chose to begin the third with the statement, "There was a boy called Eustace Clarence Scrubb, and he almost deserved it" (3), a line that *American Book Review* has ranked as number forty-seven in its list of "The 100 Best First Lines from Novels."

Eustace Clarence Scrubb almost deserves his name, for at the start of *The Voyage of the Dawn Treader*, he behaves in a manner his priggish, snobby name suggests. As Bruce Edwards says, in naming "the spoiled and selfish brat Eustace Clarence Scrubb," Lewis chose a combination of names that conveys "a sense of conceited self-satisfaction" (93).

The resemblances in the tone and the initials of the name Eustace Clarence Scrubb and those of Clive Staples Lewis hint that there may be further similarities between the character and his creator. Lewis, who disliked his given name so much that he went by "Jack" all his life, shared Eustace's sharp intellect as well as his lack of physical prowess. The Eustace we meet here in chapter one is truly the "record stinker" that Edmund will call him (5), and so was Lewis himself for a time during his youth. Lewis documents this phase in his autobiography *Surprised by Joy*, confessing that at one point, his prime motivation was the craving for glitter, swagger, and distinction, and the desire to be "in the know" (68). Lewis goes on to describe his descent into a world of self-centeredness as he worked hard to make himself into "a fop, a cad, and a snob." In *The Silver Chair*, the next book in the series, Eustace will look back at his former self and exclaim, "Gosh! What a little tick I was" (5), a statement Lewis could very well have made about the corresponding period in his own youth.

It may be significant that in *The Silver Chair*, more often than not Lewis will refer to Eustace by his family name, Scrubb, suggesting perhaps that in the next story Eustace will become someone who no longer deserves his old name as he does here, or at least will not deserve it nearly as much.

## Vegetarians, Nonsmokers, and Teetotalers

Here in the first paragraph of *The Voyage of the Dawn Treader*, readers are told that Eustace's parents—and perhaps Lewis's vague use of "they" here is meant to include Eustace as well—are "very up-to-date and advanced people" (3). But we get the feeling that the Scrubbs' interest in being so up-to-date does not stem from a genuine desire to stay informed about recent learning or cultural progress, but simply so they can belittle others.

The narrator notes that the Scrubbs are also "vegetarians, non-smokers, and teetotalers" (3). Did Lewis have something against these three groups? The answer is a definite no, only against vegetarians, nonsmokers, or teetotalers who were oppressive, contemptuous, or judgmental—people like the Scrubbs who would look down on anyone who did not share their practices and who thought their actions somehow made them better than everyone else. Lewis's negative associations with how "very up-to-date" and "advanced" the Scrubbs are show "the false identification which some people make of refinement with virtue," as noted in *Surprised by Joy* (5).

In a letter dated March 15, 1955, Lewis wrote that he always attempted to concentrate on what he termed "mere" Christianity and to avoid "interdenominational" questions, but he noted that he made one exception:

> I do however strongly object to the tyrannic and unscriptural inso-lence of anything that calls itself a Church and makes tee-totalism

a condition of membership. Apart from the more serious objection (that Our Lord Himself turned water into wine and made wine the medium of the only rite He imposed on all His followers) it is so provincial (what I believe you people call "small town"). Don't they realize that Christianity arose in the Mediterranean world where, then as now, wine was as much part of the normal diet as bread? (*Collected Letters*, Vol. 3, 580)

It can be argued that wine is as much a part of the Narnian diet as it is the Mediterranean. As Paul Ford has observed, "The spirit of revelry is alive in Narnia, and wine is an important part of celebration" (457). Later in chapter one, after Edmund, Lucy, and Eustace are plucked from the sea, the first thing Caspian will do is to order spiced wine to warm them.

What about Lewis's position on vegetarianism? Except for its association here with Eustace's family, vegetarianism is actually portrayed in a positive light in Lewis's fiction. In chapter eleven, readers will meet Coriakin, a higher-order being who appears to be a vegetarian, as he will not share in the omelet and lamb feast he furnishes for Lucy, because he does not eat these things, "only bread" (163).

Similarly, during Jane's first visit with Ransom in *That Hideous Strength*, the third book of Lewis's space trilogy, Jane is given a "more substantial" lunch downstairs, while Lewis has his hero eat only "a roll of bread" (146), a plant-based meal that seems to be typical for him. Ransom's vegetarianism is first described in *Perelandra*. Upon returning to Earth after a visit to the unfallen world of Venus, where meat is not consumed, Ransom states that he is not interested in a breakfast of "bacon or eggs or anything of that kind" but instead requests fruit, bread, or porridge (27).

Lewis was not a vegetarian or a teetotaler himself, but he was a proponent of temperance. In *Mere Christianity*, he notes that this virtue, which now usually means "teetotalism," has changed its meaning. Lewis notes, "When the second Cardinal virtue was christened 'Temperance,' it meant nothing of the sort. Temperance referred not specially to drink, but to all pleasures; and it meant not abstaining, but going the right length and no further" (78). Lewis concludes that individual Christians may decide "to give up all sorts of things for special reasons," but the moment they start claiming these things are bad in themselves and looking down their noses at others who do use them, they have taken a "wrong turning" (79). Clearly Eustace and his parents are the type of people who look down their noses at anyone who does not share their attitudes and practices.

If he were writing the Chronicles today, Lewis, himself a heavy smoker of both cigarettes and a pipe, might not have cast nonsmokers in this somewhat negative light by including Eustace's family among them. In a letter written in 1956, a few years after *The Voyage of the Dawn Treader* was published, Lewis pointed out that Christ would not have made miraculous wine at Cana if he had intended for his followers to be teetotalers. Lewis continues, "Smoking is much harder to justify. I'd like to give it up but I'd find this very hard, i.e., I *can* abstain, but I can't concentrate on anything else while abstaining—not-smoking is a whole time job" (*Letters of C. S. Lewis* 454).

Perhaps because of this concern about smoking, Lewis—unlike Tolkien, who features pipe smoking prominently by nearly all his heroes—has relatively little tobacco use in the Chronicles. In *The Lion, the Witch and the Wardrobe*, readers were told that after the dinner at the Beavers' house, Mr. Beaver got his pipe "lit up and going nicely" (75). In *Prince Caspian*, Trumpkin lit up his pipe after supper. In *The Silver Chair*, Puddleglum will smoke a "very strange, heavy sort of tobacco" in his pipe (70). However, it is significant that no human and certainly none of the children are ever pictured smoking in the Chronicles. The closest we come to a human smoking will be at the end of chapter eight here in *The Voyage of the Dawn Treader*, where Rhince will complain that his "baccy's running a bit low" (129).

## The Scrubbs and Cambridge

Having looked at the fact that Eustace's family are vegetarians, nonsmokers, and teetotalers, should anything be made of the fact that, as we will learn in chapter two, the Scrubbs live in Cambridge? Did Lewis have something against Oxford's sister school, and was this his way of showing it—by having people like the Scrubbs live there? Possibly. In his book *Tolkien and Lewis: The Gift of Friendship*, Colin Duriez has pointed out that during the 1930s, "Lewis increasingly found himself confronting a new approach to criticism, much of it coming out of the Cambridge University English School" (66). Duriez explains:

> The Cambridge School was markedly different from Oxford's, especially after syllabus reform in 1928. Anglo-Saxon was optional, "practical criticism" was introduced, literature before Shakespeare was downplayed, and writers of the modern period were taught. The new approach tended to reevaluate the traditional literary canon, and some of Lewis's favorites, such as Milton and Shelley, were casualties. (66–67)

Lewis was also troubled, as Duriez notes, by a wider tendency coming out of Cambridge "to see poetry as the expression of the poet's personality" (67), a tendency Lewis referred to as "the Personal Heresy."

The fact that the Cambridge English School saw itself, like Eustace's family, as very up-to-date and advanced suggests that Lewis's decision to have the Scrubbs live in Cambridge may not have been purely random. His stance that poetry was more than an expression of the poet's state of mind led to what Duriez has labeled as "a courteous dispute" with the Cambridge scholar E. M. W. Tillyard (67). Lewis wrote an essay titled "The Personal Heresy in Criticism," which then became the first chapter in *The Personal Heresy: A Controversy*, a book he and Tillyard published in 1939. A final piece of evidence for Lewis's intentional decision to put the thoroughly modern Scrubbs in Cambridge may be found in the fact that the initial "E" in Tillyard's first name stood for Eustace.

That said, as Marvin Hinten has pointed out, any contention Lewis may have against Cambridge was "good-natured" (34). As Hinten rightly concludes, "Clearly Lewis harbored no genuine resentment against Cambridge." As confirmation of this, it could be noted that Lewis made Elwin Ransom, the protagonist of *Out of the Silent Planet*, a fellow of Cambridge College. In 1954, two years after *The Voyage of the Dawn Treader* was published, Lewis himself accepted the chair of medieval and Renaissance English at Cambridge, a position he very much enjoyed and held until the summer of 1963.

## He Liked Bossing and Bullying

In addition to the facts about Eustace's family, one of the very first things Lewis's narrator tells us about Eustace Clarence Scrubb is that when it came to friends, "he had none" (3). Eustace's condition of being friendless, self-centered, and dominated by the desire to dominate is a state in which Aslan will not abandon him. Like Edmund's earlier condition in the first book, Eustace's sorry status cries out for mercy and redemption. Lewis, as he did previously with Edmund in *The Lion, the Witch and the Wardrobe*, again wants to remind his readers that the worst sinners—or in Eustace's case, the worst stinkers—can become the greatest saints. After being freed from his self-centered, dragonish nature in this story, Eustace will, in the next book, be an important member of the team Aslan will send to free Caspian's son from his years of captivity in Underland. Then in *The Last Battle*, Eustace and Jill will rescue King Tirian. Given Eustace's future roles, it could be argued that in *The Voyage of the Dawn Treader*, he is saved from a self-centered life so that he can save others.

Here the news that his cousins Edmund and Lucy are coming for a visit makes Eustace quite glad even though he dislikes them. This might at first seem paradoxical, but as we saw before with the White Witch and King Miraz, dominators need someone to dominate. If the only happiness for these bosses and bullies comes from bossing and bullying, then they must first have people around in order to give them a bad time, as Eustace does here.

Evan Gibson offers the following analysis of Eustace's condition at the start of the story:

The proud person looks down upon everyone else and imagines himself to be vastly superior. He seeks the company of others, but it is only in order to lord it over them. Although an attempt to characterize Eustace brings all sorts of vices flocking to the mind—his complaining, rudeness, cowardice, etc.—his constant attempt to degrade everything and everyone in order to enhance his own self-image seems to overshadow and make mild all his other faults. (169)

Like the White Witch and Miraz before him, Eustace is unable to see any flaws in himself. All of Lewis's villains share this same lack of capacity for self-criticism. As Gibson points out, Eustace needs to receive the self-knowledge that only Aslan can give to be able to see how dragonish his attitudes are. Gibson concludes that there is hope for a person only "when he begins to see himself as he actually is" (169). This same lack of capacity for self-criticism will be seen later when the crew of the *Dawn Treader* meets the Dufflepuds, whose flaws are as invisible to them as they themselves are to the crew.

We are given an additional detail about Eustace in this opening paragraph. Readers are told, "He didn't call his Father and Mother 'Father' and 'Mother,' but Harold and Alberta" (3). Certainly in this fact about Eustace that Lewis includes, we are meant to see not just the snobby trendiness already discussed but also Eustace's lack of respect for his elders, his defiance of authority, and his general insolence.

There is another point to be found in Eustace's practice. In his essay "Membership," Lewis points out that when St. Paul claimed we are all members of the same body, he meant "what we should call *organs*, things essentially different from, and complementary to, one another. . . . The grandfather, the parents, the grown-up son, the child, the dog, and the cat are true members (in the organic sense), precisely because they are not members or units of a homogeneous class. They are not interchangeable" (334–35). Lewis concludes, "That is why the modern notion that children should call their parents by their Christian names is so perverse. For this is an effort to ignore the difference in kind which makes for real organic unity" (335).

We find the opposite of bland homogeneity in Narnia. Narnia would not be Narnia if it were inhabited only by badgers.

## Sitting on the Edge of the Bed

Here at the start of *The Voyage of the Dawn Treader*, we learn that Susan has gone on her own adventure, her own journey from the familiar into the unknown. She, of all the children, has been chosen to join her parents on her father's sixteen-week lecture trip to America. In Mrs. Pevensie's belief that Susan "would get far more" out of a trip to America than Edmund and Lucy (5), readers may simply hear the suggestion that since Susan is older, she might better appreciate the new people and new places. But Mrs. Pevensie may also be hoping the trip will aid in Susan's positive growth.

In *Prince Caspian*, Susan began down a negative track, but then toward the end of the story she seemed to have reversed this direction. Here in *The Voyage of the Dawn Treader*, we find hints that Susan has once again taken a negative turn. In this same paragraph, she is described as being "no good at school work" and "very old for her age," two attributes that hint at a lack of a proper focus, something her parents may be hoping the trip to America could help remedy. This somewhat negative description will be the last we hear of Susan for a good while, and it is significant in preparing us for what will come later. The next report of her will come in *The Last Battle*, where Peter will state, "My sister Susan is no longer a friend of Narnia" (154).

As we encounter Edmund and Lucy here in the first chapter, we learn that they have been sent to stay at their cousin Eustace's house while their parents and Susan are gone. With this third adventure to Narnia, we can begin to see a pattern and, through this pattern, what Lewis is trying to say about the start of adventures.

First, Lewis seems to be saying that *adventures can and typically do begin in unlikely places*—in an empty room of an old professor's house, on a deserted train platform, and now while Edmund and Lucy are sitting on the guest bed in their cousin's house.

Second, Lewis's pattern of beginnings also seems to be saying that *negative circumstances—big and small—may be more likely to lead to great adventures and personal growth than positive ones.* In the first book, the bombings from the war had separated the children from their parents. Then one morning they woke to find a dismal rain falling, which meant they were stuck inside at the professor's house. Peter suggested they spend the rainy morning exploring, and as the narrator reported, "That was how the adventures began" (6). At the start of the adventure in *Prince Caspian*, the children were "all rather gloomy" as they waited on a platform for the trains that would take them off to school. Here in *The Voyage of the Dawn Treader*, Edmund and Lucy are even gloomier than they were at the start of the previous adventure. Then they were only going back to school. Now they must endure a lengthy visit at Eustace's house.

Lewis's pattern of negative circumstances serving as the gateway to adventure can be seen in the books that follow as well. In *The Silver Chair*, Jill and Eustace begin their adventure two weeks into their miserable term at Experiment House, with eleven weeks of "hopelessness" still to come (8). In *The Magician's Nephew*, Digory, who used to live in the country where he had "a pony, and a river at the bottom of the garden" (4), is forced to move into his mad uncle's house in London, a setting he refers to as "a beastly hole" (5). After he meets Polly, readers are told, "Their adventures began chiefly because it was one of the wettest and coldest summers there had been for years. That drove them to do indoor things" (7).

Perhaps of all the adventures in the Chronicles, it is Shasta's that begins in the unhappiest of circumstances. When the story of *The Horse and His Boy* opens, Shasta, who in reality is the son of King Lune of Archenland, is living as the adopted son of Arsheesh, a harsh and brutal Calormen who forces him to hard labor and frequently beats him. One day a turbaned Tarkaan from the south arrives and informs Arsheesh he wants to buy the boy. But rather than being a turn for the good, this would be an even worse condition. Bree, the Tarkaan's horse, warns Shasta, "You'd better be lying dead tonight than go to be a human slave in his house tomorrow" (12). And thus begins Shasta and Bree's quest to reach Narnia.

There is something about negative situations like these—more so than positive ones, Lewis suggests—that can lead to new possibilities. At the end of the first book, the professor gave the children this advice about getting back to Narnia: "It'll happen when you're not looking for it" (188). And his statement proves true in a deeper way than readers might realize. We seldom see unpleasant situations as the ones most likely to lead to great adventures—at least at the start. We seldom welcome negative situations as holding the greatest potential for growth. In *The Silver Chair*, when Eustace initially suggests that Puddleglum should stay behind, the Marshwiggle is the only one who can recognize their difficult quest as a chance for growth and wisely replies, "I'm not going to lose an opportunity like this. It will do me good" (75).

## His Cousins the Four Pevensies

Although the name Pevensie was used several times in the first Narnia film, it is not until the third paragraph of the opening page of *The Voyage of the Dawn Treader* that readers first learn this last name of Peter, Susan, Edmund, and Lucy. Since there do not seem to be any direct connections to the name, Lewis may have chosen it simply because he liked the sound.

An alternative theory worthy of consideration has been suggested by Marvin Hinten, who proposes that Lewis took the name from the town of Pevensey, located on the southeast coast of England. Pevensey was the point of entry for the Norman invasion, and Hinten observes, "Similarly, the Pevensie children are in the Chronicles the point of entry from our world into the realm of Narnia" (33). If Lewis borrowed the name from the English town, he changed the spelling slightly.

Assuming that Lewis borrowed the town name, it is possible that he came to know it through Rudyard Kipling's fantasy *Puck of Pook's Hill*. Lewis indicates his familiarity with and enjoyment of the novel in a letter to Arthur Greeves dated December 2, 1918, and also in a diary entry dated July 3, 1924. In Kipling's story, two children perform *A Midsummer Night's Dream* on a fairy ring near Pevensey, an action that allows the real Puck to appear. Further support for Lewis's possibly choosing the name because of its associations with the novel can be found in the fact that in the first chapter, Puck objects to being called a fairy and asks the two children, "How would you like to be called 'mortal' or 'human being' all the time? Or 'son of Adam' or 'daughter of Eve'?" (18). The latter two terms are frequently used to refer to humans in the Chronicles of Narnia.

### "I'll Smash the Rotten Thing"

Besides its new geographic setting, *The Voyage of the Dawn Treader* differs from the earlier two Chronicles in another significant way: it does not lead up to a coronation. With this third story about Narnia, Lewis begins to introduce a more common character. Unlike the Pevensies and Caspian, Eustace never becomes Narnian royalty, and through this shift, Lewis will suggest that the character growth and maturation that come from adventures is something everyone needs—not just kings, queens, and princes. As Doris Myers has observed, "Eustace, who is neither royal nor special, has the same duty to become brave and honorable as 'their majesties'" (140). Myers calls this new path that Lewis establishes with Eustace and then follows with Jill, who is also not destined to be a monarch, "the ordinary path to wholeness."

Three ways that this third Chronicle differs from its predecessors have been mentioned: it features a different lineup of English children, it does not take place in Narnia, and it includes a human not destined to become a monarch. A fourth way in which it may be different has to do with whether or not Eustace comes to Narnia by choice. In *The Lion, the Witch and the Wardrobe*, after entering the professor's old wardrobe as a hiding place, the children suddenly found themselves in the snowy forest near the lamp-post, where they had the choice of either staying or returning the way they had come.

Don King points out in his essay "The Wardrobe as Christian Metaphor" that all who enter Narnia in the first story are called, but "none are compelled to stay" (25). In *Prince Caspian*, although the four children were pulled off the train platform without being asked, it is clear they preferred to be in Narnia rather than on their way to school, particularly since this was Aslan's will. As Lucy stated, "But we want to be here, don't we, if Aslan wants us?" (102).

By contrast, Eustace will not want to be in Narnia. His first words after being pulled on board the *Dawn Treader* will be, "Let me go. Let me go back" (13). But since there will be no way for him to return to England, he must remain. And so the question arises: to what extent is Eustace forced into Narnia, and to what extent does he enter Narnia as a result of his own actions? The case can be made that here in chapter one, Eustace is *mostly* responsible for what happens to him.

After spying at the door, Eustace enters Lucy's bedroom uninvited. He then ignores not one but three suggestions from Edmund to leave. Finally, as the picture of the Narnian ship comes to life, Eustace rushes toward the painting, intending, as he states, to "smash the rotten thing" (10). Edmund cries out a warning, but once again his cousin ignores him. When Eustace tries to pull the picture off the wall, he suddenly finds himself "standing on the frame," where he loses his head and falls into the sea, pulling Edmund and Lucy along with him. In all of these actions, Eustace has exercised his free will. He chose to spy at the door, he chose to enter the room uninvited, he chose to remain in the room unwanted, and he chose to attack the painting despite Edmund's warning. He could have made a different choice at any of these stages.

If Eustace is mostly responsible for being drawn into Narnia here in chapter one, what else may be a factor? The most obvious element is the picture itself, which has somehow come alive at this moment and no other—not before Eustace arrived, nor, presumably, after he would have left. And this coincidental timing creates a sense of providence here.

There is a feeling of providence in other elements as well that combine to allow the children to enter Narnia again. Edmund and Lucy are in the bedroom looking at the painting because their father has been invited to lecture in the States this summer and their parents can afford to take only Susan with them. The professor just happened to have lost the big house that he appeared to comfortably own just two years earlier. He has "somehow become poor" (5) and so has room only for Peter. Even the fact that Aunt Alberta has this picture at all seems to be more than just coincidence. We learn that it had been a wedding present from someone Aunt Alberta "did not want to offend" (6), but we never learn who this giver was, or how this person happened to possess a picture of a Narnian ship, or why he or she chose to give this picture to the newly married Scrubbs, who were sure not to appreciate it.

In *The Lion, the Witch and the Wardrobe*, the four children almost seemed to be guided by an invisible hand as Mrs. Macready showed the visitors around the professor's house: "Whether it was that they lost their heads, or that Mrs. Macready was trying to catch them, or that some magic in the house had come to life and was chasing them into Narnia—they seemed to find themselves being followed everywhere" (53). Finally, when there was no place else to go, they took refuge in the wardrobe room. When Mrs. Macready started to bring the tour into the room, they had to hide inside the wardrobe, for, as Peter declared, "There's nowhere else." Similarly, here in *The Voyage of the Dawn Treader*, we are told that Edmund and Lucy came to stay with Eustace because events coincided in such a way that "it really couldn't be helped" (4).

Besides a sense of providence, Lewis also used prophecies and promises to give his stories a driving force and a sense of destiny. In his essay "On Stories," Lewis describes a kind of story that turns on fulfilled prophecies. He comments, "Such stories produce (at least in me) a feeling of awe, coupled with a certain sort of bewilderment such as one often feels in looking at a complex pattern of lines that pass over and under one another. One sees, yet does not quite see, the regularity" (14–15). Certainly *The Lion, the Witch and the Wardrobe* was this kind of story, with the double prophecies that Aslan would return and that "Adam's flesh and Adam's bone" would one day sit "at Cair Paravel in throne" (81). *Prince Caspian* and *The Voyage of the Dawn Treader* could be said to turn on fulfilled promises rather than prophecies—the promises that the children would one day get back to Narnia.

## "Ca—Ca—Caspian!"

While readers will be told in *The Magician's Nephew* that the wardrobe was made from the tree that sprang from the Narnian apple Digory planted in his back garden, no clue is ever given about the origins of this picture of the Narnian ship in the Scrubbs' house. Stephen Yandell speculates, "The *Dawn Treader* painting was possibly made by Digory, Polly, or one of the Pevensie parents. Its frame might also have been made from the same wood from the fallen tree used for the wardrobe" (499). No matter what its source, the picture serves as yet another conduit between our world and Narnia, one that—like the wardrobe and the train platform earlier—comes alive at a certain time and then cannot be used again. At the end of *The Lion, the Witch and the Wardrobe*, the professor advised the children, "I don't think it will be any good trying to go back through the wardrobe. . . . You won't get into Narnia again by *that* route" (188). The same can be said about the picture that pulls in Edmund, Lucy, and Eustace here at the start of *The Voyage of the Dawn Treader*.

The three children are quickly rescued from the chilly waters and soon find themselves standing on the deck of the *Dawn Treader*, where Edmund and Lucy are reunited with Caspian—now King Caspian—and Reepicheep. Eustace cries, vomits, vomits again, cries again, and insists on being put ashore "at the next station" (15). Worst of all, he insults Reepicheep. Only sneezes from Edmund and Lucy and their need for dry clothes keep the gallant mouse from demanding immediate satisfaction. This conflict between Eustace and Reepicheep, like the one between Nikabrik and Caspian introduced early in the second book, will get worse before finally having a resolution.

Readers may be so caught up in the rush of events at the end of chapter one that they fail to notice the absence of one element that, under the circumstances, might have been expected. Caspian speaks only three lines in this chapter. He asks who Eustace is, he orders spiced wine to warm everyone up, and, referring to Eustace, he comments to Edmund, "This is a merry shipmate you've brought us" (15). What Lewis does *not* have him say is anything like, "Wow! We were just sailing along, when suddenly—plop, plop, plop—you three appeared out of nowhere, splashing into the sea right beside us. How did you get here?"

In *Prince Caspian*, a great deal of attention was put on the unique ability of Susan's horn to summon help. In *The Lion, the Witch and the Wardrobe*, a similar importance was placed on the wardrobe's amazing power to open a passage between the worlds. With the first two stories as a backdrop, here in chapter one of *The Voyage of the Dawn Treader*, the lack of any mention of the actions of the picture of the sailing ship, and the lack of any expression of amazement or wonder by Lucy and Edmund or by the crew who witnessed their astonishing arrival, seems somewhat remarkable.

Perhaps Lewis's point here is that *how* a person gets to Narnia is not nearly as important as *what* he or she does after arriving and *how* the adventure can change that person for the better. Alternatively, perhaps Lewis is giving us a look at how seasoned followers of Aslan react to extraordinary travel between worlds. Edmund, Lucy, Caspian, and Reepicheep have been through this before. Counting each one-way trip, this is Edmund's seventh passage between worlds and Lucy's ninth. They have already seen that Aslan—whether acting through a wardrobe, a magic horn, or a doorway of sticks in the air—can send people back and forth between England and Narnia with no more trouble than it takes to pass in and out of a room. In this respect, Edmund, Lucy, Caspian, and Reepicheep could be said to be displaying the type of wisdom and experience seen in the professor in the first story. In *The Lion, the Witch and the Wardrobe*, when Peter asked, "Do you really mean there could be other worlds—all over the place, just round the corner—like that?" the professor calmly replied, "Nothing is more probable" (50).

Here, if the question was raised, "Do you really mean there could be a picture of a Narnian ship that, at certain times and under certain circumstances, would allow someone to travel from a Cambridge bedroom to the great eastern ocean of Narnia?" Edmund, Lucy, Caspian, and Reepicheep might similarly respond, "Nothing is more probable." And so might we, if we have read the first two Chronicles and become seasoned armchair travelers ourselves.

The chapter ends with Lucy, always one to embrace the adventure that falls to her, looking out of her window at the water rushing past. Rather than questioning how or why they have come to Narnia, she is simply enjoying the experience and feels quite sure they are in for "a lovely time" (18).

## Discussion Questions

Here in chapter one, the adventure begins for Edmund, Lucy, and Eustace. Although we may never travel through a magic picture or sail on uncharted seas, Lewis would suggest that we each have a journey of our own to make.

1. What are your adventures? When are you taken from your familiar, comfortable routines and thrust into less predictable, less controllable, and less comfortable situations?

In *The Silver Chair*, Prince Rilian is tempted to throw caution to the wind and travel to the subterranean world of Bism. Jill will then turn to Eustace in the hope that he will share her concern for returning to the safety and security of Narnia as quickly as possible. But as she looks at Eustace, the narrator will relate, "Her heart sank as she saw that his face was quite changed. He looked much more like the Prince than like the old Scrubb at Experiment

House. For all his adventures, and the days when he had sailed with King Caspian, were coming back to him" (206).

2. How have your adventures changed you? What "treasures" have you brought back? You might consider greater knowledge, a deeper faith, a higher perspective, or other aspects of growth and development.

3. In *The Last Battle*, Reepicheep will invite everyone to "come further up and further in" (203). If your encounter with the Chronicles of Narnia is like an adventure, one that takes you "further up and further in" each time you read, what might you gain from this armchair adventure of reading?

In this chapter, we saw two points that Lewis makes about adventures. First, adventures can and typically do begin in unlikely places. And second, negative circumstances may be more likely to lead to great adventures than positive ones.

4. Can you think of other Narnia adventures that begin in unlikely places or in unlikely ways?

5. What about in your own life? Can you think of difficult circumstances that have led to great adventures and so to times of above-average growth?

6. What might be some reasons that negative times lead to more growth than positive ones?

Lewis noted the false identification that some people make by mistaking refinement for virtue. Eustace could be said to be refined in the sense that he is well educated and very up-to-date.

7. Do people today mistake refinement for virtue? If so, what aspects of refinement might be taken as virtues?

In Eustace's limerick, "Some kids who played games about Narnia / Got gradually balmier and balmier" (7), Lewis lays a foundation he will use later. In *The Last Battle*, it will be Eustace who will describe Susan's dismissal of Narnia. He will report, "Whenever you've tried to get her to come and talk about Narnia or do anything about Narnia, she says, 'What wonderful memories you have! Fancy your still thinking about all those *funny games we used to play when we were children*'" (154, emphasis added). Edmund's earlier flaws helped him become "a grave and quieter man" at the end of *The Lion, the Witch and the Wardrobe*, someone who was "great in council and judgment" (184). Here Lewis will have Eustace's flaw of wanting to appear more grown-up than others make him more perceptive of this trait when it appears in others.

8. Do you agree with Lewis's suggestion that flaws can sometimes be turned into strengths? If so, what other weaknesses, besides those seen in Edmund and Eustace, have the potential to become strengths?

TWO

# On Board
# the *Dawn Treader*

## An Even Higher Hope

Lucy and Edmund change into dry clothes, and with
Eustace in bed with seasickness, they have their first
real talk with Caspian. One of the first things that
becomes apparent is that the special creatures that
made Narnia so unique in the first two stories—the
fauns, dwarfs, centaurs, dryads, naiads, and vast array
of talking animals—have been left behind. Except for
Reepicheep, the entire crew is human. Besides serving
as another way to make this third book in the series
different, what else does this change accomplish?

First, featuring more ordinary characters this time
will emphasize the strangeness and wonder of the
unique beings that the crew will encounter on the
journey. Second, having Reepicheep as the only talking
animal will give him the prominence he will need in a
story where he is a main character. Finally, it could be

argued that Narnia's fauns, centaurs, badgers, and giants simply are not well suited for life on a ship. When Lewis chose to write about a sea voyage, to some extent his choice of characters was made as well.

Next we learn that the year the children have been in England corresponds not to the thirteen hundred years that passed during their first absence, but to only three years in Narnia, long enough for Caspian to grow into a young man. The most significant implication of this time shift is that Edmund is not in the position of Caspian's mentor, as Peter was in the previous book. Caspian, who according to Lewis's notes was thirteen in *Prince Caspian*, is now sixteen. With Edmund—who is now twelve—as more of an equal than a role model, Caspian can take the next step in his development as a leader, doing more and making more decisions than he did in the previous story.

Edmund asks the young king, "All going well?" (19). Caspian, with perhaps a trace of resentment at this suggestion of a lack of responsibility on his part, replies, "You don't suppose I'd have left my kingdom and put to sea unless all was well." He continues, "It couldn't be better. There's no trouble at all between Telmarines, Dwarfs, Talking Beasts, Fauns and the rest" (20). Other rulers might have used this time to take it easy, relax, and enjoy the status quo— not Caspian. In Caspian's desire to set forth on a quest, again we find Lewis's message about the need for greater development—the ongoing need to do more than stay where everything is safe and predictable and rest on one's past accomplishments, to continue further in and further up with ever greater adventures and the growth that comes from them.

Caspian tells Edmund and Lucy that he has sworn an oath to "sail east for a year and a day" (20), a mission that is mirrored in the ship's name, in order to either find the seven friends of his father who were sent away by Miraz or to learn of their deaths, a task that had its roots in the previous story. In chapter five of *Prince Caspian*, Doctor Cornelius told of "the seven noble lords, who alone among all the Telmarines did not fear the sea," who were "persuaded" by Miraz to sail away and look for "new lands beyond the Eastern Ocean" (59–60). Cornelius concludes that, as Miraz intended, "they never came back" (60).

In having Caspian use the phrase "a year and a day" here, Lewis may be seeking to resonate with readers' memories of the Arthurian legends, where this formula appears in a number of places. In one instance found in Malory's *Le Morte d'Arthur*, Sir Gawain swears an oath in words similar to Caspian's, stating, "Therefore I make this vow: to set off in search of the Holy Grail tomorrow and not to return for at least a year and a day" (365).

Readers might wonder why exactly Caspian would need to go looking for these seven lords. If they are dead, he can do nothing to help them. If they are alive, we might expect that at some point they would return with a report—whether they had found new lands or not. In chapter three, Lord Bern will make it clear that the seven knew theirs was no simple mission of exploration, but an unofficial exile. As he will tell Caspian, "There was no purpose in returning to Narnia while your Majesty's uncle held the reins" (47). Thus Caspian's mission is not only to find the missing friends of his father but also to tell them it is now safe to return home.

Next Caspian tells Lucy and Edmund that Reepicheep has "an even higher hope" (21). This second, higher quest is, as the mouse explains, to travel to the very eastern end of the world and reach "Aslan's own country." Lewis indicates the magnitude of this second mission by having Edmund respond in an "awed" voice: "I say, that *is* an idea."

In *Mere Christianity*, we find Lewis's often-quoted statement, "If I find in myself a desire which no experience in this world can satisfy, the most probable explanation is that I was made for another world" (136–37). This longing for another world runs all through the Chronicles. Beginning with their first visit, Narnia has been an object of yearning for the Pevensies. At the end of *The Lion, the Witch and the Wardrobe*, the professor replied to their question about returning: "Yes, of course you'll get back to Narnia again someday" (188). In *Prince Caspian*, the first thing we learned about the young prince was his longing for the old Narnia. Caspian lamented, "I wish—I wish—I wish I could have lived in the Old

Days" (42). After the children were drawn from the train platform into the dense woods, Lucy's first words were, "Oh, Peter! Do you think we can possibly have got back to Narnia?" (5).

In *The Horse and His Boy*, Shasta will state, "I've been longing to go to the North all my life" (14). Bree shares this longing for "the happy land of Narnia" (11). In Edmund and Lucy's first appearance here in *The Voyage of the Dawn Treader*, Lewis showed them gazing at the painting of the ship from Narnia and longing to return. Edmund's very first words in that scene expressed this yearning: "The question is whether it doesn't make things worse, *looking* at a Narnian ship when you can't get there" (7).

Given all this longing for Narnia, the question arises: why would Reepicheep or anyone want to leave? Lewis never fully gives us an answer but implies there is something that Narnia in its current form lacks. In "The Weight of Glory," he describes a longing for "something in the universe from which we now feel cut off, to be on the inside of some door which we have always seen from the outside" (42). In *The Last Battle*, those with this form of longing are able to finally pass through that door.

In the final chapter of *The Voyage of the Dawn Treader*, Caspian's desire for what lies beyond Narnia will become so great that he will try to abdicate in order to go with Reepicheep to the world's end. Aslan will visit the young king in his cabin with instructions that he must return to Narnia. But Caspian never loses his longing for this other world, and in *The Silver Chair*, Glimfeather will tell Eustace and Jill, "He never talks about it, but we all know he has never forgotten that voyage to the world's end. I'm sure in his heart of hearts he wants to go there again" (55–56).

For Lewis himself, this longing for a world just over the horizon began when he was very young. In *Surprised by Joy*, he writes of his boyhood at Little Lea, the family home on the outskirts of Belfast, and describes the vague feelings of desire aroused by the distant line of the Castlereagh Hills, which he and his brother could see from their nursery windows. Lewis comments that though they were not very far off, to him as a child they were "unattainable" and so taught him "longing" (7). Lewis goes on to note that it is difficult to find words strong enough to describe this sensation he went on to feel again at various times and places throughout his life. Exactly what this was a longing for is not clear, as Lewis asks, "It was a sensation, of course, of desire; but desire for what?" (16). Certainly it was more than a boy's longing for the hills on the horizon. Later in life, Lewis would identify this sensation as a longing for heaven.

## To Find All You Seek

Next Reepicheep tells Lucy and Edmund about the verse that was said over him in the cradle:

> Where sky and water meet,
> Where the waves grow sweet,
> Doubt not, Reepicheep,
> To find all you seek,
> There is the utter East. (21)

In the final chapter of the book, readers will learn what the first part—"Where sky and water meet / Where the waves grow sweet"—means. But Lewis will not say much about what the "all you seek" part refers to. Here in chapter two, Reepicheep himself admits, "I do not know what it means. But the spell of it has been on me all my life" (22).

In the chapter on heaven in *The Problem of Pain*, Lewis provides a fuller discussion of this underlying longing, although he still remains somewhat vague. There Lewis describes it as "that something which you were born desiring" (131). He continues, "You have never *had* it. All the things that have ever deeply possessed your soul have been but hints of it—tantalizing glimpses, promises never quite fulfilled, echoes that died away just as they caught your ear."

If Lewis does not say anything more specific about this desire, this is as it must be. In *Surprised by Joy*, Lewis calls this journey toward the object of our deepest longing a journey "into the region of awe" (221). There he describes it as something that refuses to identify itself with "any object of the senses, or anything whereof we have biological or social need, or anything imagined."

Readers are given two further windows into this longing for the land beyond the world's end. In *The Last Battle*, Jewel will reach the borders of this region with the others and will declare: "I have come home at last! This is my real country! I belong here. This is the land I have been looking for all my life, though I never knew it till now. The reason why we loved the old Narnia is that it sometimes looked a little like this" (196). For a second window, we might look to Lucy's words on the next to last page of *The Voyage of the Dawn Treader*. After being told that she and Edmund will never return to Narnia, Lucy will sob, "It isn't Narnia, you know. It's *you*" (247), suggesting that at the root of the children's longing for Narnia—and in Reepicheep's case, for Aslan's country—is a longing for Aslan himself.

It is worth pointing out that here in chapter two, Lewis chooses to associate this special longing with Reepicheep, who in the final chapter of *Prince Caspian* was told by Aslan, "I have sometimes wondered, friend, whether you do not think too much about your honor" (208). Like most of Lewis's protagonists, Reepicheep matures through his experiences. If in the previous book, Reepicheep was a little too focused on his personal honor, here in *The Voyage of the Dawn Treader*, he will be seeking something much different.

In Reepicheep's statement, "When I was in my cradle a wood woman, a Dryad, spoke this verse over me" (21), readers may find one of the small inconsistencies that turn up in the Chronicles from time to time. In *Prince Caspian*, Doctor Cornelius stated that the Telmarines had "silenced the beasts and the trees and the fountains" (51). So where did the dryad who spoke Reepicheep's verse come from? Perhaps not every last one of the tree spirits were silenced, or perhaps one was present at Reepicheep's birth but was later silenced.

### Eustace of Course Would Be Pleased with Nothing

Drinian, the ship's captain, gives Edmund and Lucy a summary of the journey so far, including a brief mention of the daughter of the Duke of Galma—a girl who had eyes for Caspian but whose interest was not returned by the young king. Through this unforced, natural account near the start of the story of a romance that did not work out, Lewis, the consummate craftsman, prepares us for Caspian's relationship with Ramandu's daughter at the end of the book.

Earlier in his report on Eustace, Edmund stated, "I don't think we can do anything for him. It only makes him worse if you try to be nice to him" (19). Here in the middle of chapter two, even after Lucy's cordial heals Eustace of his seasickness, we are given another telling detail about him. Lewis's narrator states, "Eustace of course would be pleased with nothing" (29).

Despite the fact that the *Dawn Treader* is "a beauty of her kind . . . her lines perfect, her colors pure, and every spar and rope and pin lovingly made" (29), Eustace can only keep on "boasting about liners and motorboats and aeroplanes and submarines." Here he may remind some readers of Weston, Lewis's antagonist in *Out of the Silent Planet*, who stood amid the beauty of Meldilorn and declared to the great Oyarsa, "Your tribal life with its stone-age weapons and bee-hive huts . . . has nothing to compare with our civilization—with our science, medicine and law, our armies, our architecture, our commerce, and our transport system" (134).

In most stories for young people, we get to know the positive characters very well and come to understand what makes them who they are. One of Lewis's greatest strengths is that he provides insight into his negative characters as well. This was seen with the early Edmund as readers were shown how step-by-step he rationalized his betrayal in *The Lion, the Witch and the Wardrobe*. Although we never agreed with Edmund's actions early in the first book, we were given a penetrating view of his condition.

The same is true for Eustace. Because of the way his parents have raised him, because of the school he has gone to, and most of all because of the patterns in which he has chosen to think and act until he can no longer break free of them, it has become impossible for anyone to help him or for any good thing to please him. No one can free him from his overly critical way of looking at those around him. Because Eustace has no compassion of his own, any show of kindness toward him is viewed with distrust. In this sense, Eustace has become nearly like the dwarfs found in *The Last Battle.* "Their prison is only in their own minds," Aslan will observe about the dwarfs. "Yet they are in that prison; and so afraid of being taken in that they cannot be taken out" (169).

Eustace is *nearly* like the dwarfs in *The Last Battle.* He is on the path toward becoming beyond Aslan's aid. If left to his own, Lewis suggests, Eustace would arrive at the same endpoint they reach— but he is not there yet. Alan Jacobs comments on this similarity between Eustace and the dwarfs:

> Something like this could very well have happened to Eustace: he could have continued believing that Edmund and Caspian are prigs, the crew incompetent, and everyone preoccupied with plans to make him miserable. The diary that he keeps indicates that he had gone a long way toward constructing a rock-solid narrative of superiority and paranoia—had he not been transformed into a dragon. It was only the good fortune, or good grace, of that dreadful metamorphosis by which Eustace was saved. (134)

At this point early in the story, we are still a long way from Eustace's transformation into a dragon. Nevertheless, we can still say it has been good fortune or good grace that has brought him to Narnia.

In contrast with Eustace, whom nothing will please, Lucy is "almost too happy to speak," with the taste of salt on her lips, the immense crimson sunset, the quiver of the ship, and the thought of "unknown lands on the Eastern rim of the world" (29–30). Lucy's joy here highlights another similarity between Eustace and the dwarfs near the end of *The Last Battle.* While others around them are elated by their surroundings—by life at sea or by the delights found beyond the stable door—Eustace and the dwarfs are blind to the glories that are all around them.

Jonathan Rogers has made the point that the doubts Eustace had back in England about his cousins' stories of Narnia, while expressed in a rude manner, at least were understandable because "even a person of imagination could hardly be expected to believe Edmund and Lucy's tale of Narnia if he has never seen Narnia for himself" (55). But Rogers goes on to observe, "The amazing thing about Eustace is that he can't see anything remarkable in Narnia once he gets there. His sense of wonder is so stunted that even the experience of being flung through a picture frame and into another world neither impresses him very much nor alerts him to the fact that he is in for experiences that his modern assumptions and sensibilities can't account for."

Earlier it was noted that in *Surprised by Joy*, Lewis described his experience of joy as being brought "into the region of awe" (221). One of the many things that could be said about Eustace at this point is that he has lost the capacity for awe. Because of this, he is unable to see the wonders around him.

In the previous chapter, the issue of whether Eustace has been drawn into Narnia against his will was raised. Here in chapter two, Eustace demands to be put ashore so that he can "lodge a disposition" with the British Consul (27). Finally, the others are able to convince Eustace they have "no more power of sending him back to Cambridge—which is where Uncle Harold lived—than of sending him to the moon." Once again Eustace seems compelled to stay in Narnia.

A decade before writing *The Voyage of the Dawn Treader*, Lewis explored a similar problem of free will in *The Screwtape Letters*. There Lewis, through Screwtape, discusses the complex way that God, whom Screwtape calls the Enemy, both will and will not seem to "override" free will (39). Screwtape first states, "The Irresistible and the Indisputable are the two weapons which the very nature of His scheme forbids Him to use. . . . He cannot ravish. He can only woo."

Screwtape concludes that, given the Enemy's insistence on voluntary cooperation, merely overriding a human will would be useless because what God wants are "servants who can finally become sons" (39). It is significant that later in chapter seven, Aslan will not remove Eustace's dragon skin without permission. He will tell Eustace, "You will have to let me undress you" (108).

Despite his talk about God not overriding human will, Screwtape then complicates the issue a bit. He divulges to Wormwood that the Enemy is prepared to do "a little overriding at the beginning" (39–40). While Screwtape's observations here are made specifically about new Christians, they hold relevance for Eustace's situation as well. It could be argued that Eustace both has and has not come to Narnia through his own choices. In this sense, Eustace could be said to resemble Ransom, whose journey to Mars in *Out of the Silent Planet* comes as a result of a mixture of force and his own choices.

If Aslan is doing a little overriding of Eustace's free will here at the beginning, we could say that Eustace is being both a little ravished and a little wooed.

### He Now Started a Diary

The narrator states that what Eustace thought about being on board the *Dawn Treader* had "best be told in his own words" (30). In the characters of the White Witch, the early Edmund, Miraz, and Glozelle, Lewis has shown us the old adage that no one does evil in his (or her) own eyes. Now in chapter two of *The Voyage of the Dawn Treader*, Lewis, in a stroke of genius, allows us to actually see the world through Eustace's eyes by telling the story through the entries in his diary. How can Eustace not see what a "tick" he is? How can he think that Edmund, Lucy, and Caspian are responsible for all his problems? By showing the world as it appears to Eustace, Lewis allows us to conceive, at least partially, how Eustace is able to see himself as blameless and everyone around him as at fault.

Keeping a diary is another similarity that Eustace and his creator share. Lewis kept a diary for nearly five years in his twenties, from 1922 to 1927. Years later, writing in *Surprised by Joy*, Lewis states that one effect of his conversion was that it cured him of the "time-wasting and foolish practice" of keeping his diary (233). One problem, Lewis contended, was that although he put down each day what he saw as important, he was blind to what would be important in "the long run." It is significant that after Eustace's transformation, he too will give up the practice of writing in his diary.

Kath Filmer has rightly observed that Eustace's diary is a hodge-podge of "complaints, self-pity, hypochondria, and petty spite" (45), and that these complaints about the others are "turned against Eustace himself" because they say much more about him than about those he is commenting on. In a perfect illustration of the pot calling the kettle black, Eustace writes that the others have "shut their eyes to Facts" (30). He complains that Caspian "doesn't seem to know anything at all" (31), when, of course, it is Eustace himself who best fits this description.

Lewis makes the point that this is the way wickedness is. In the first story, the White Witch referred to the Narnians who were loyal to Aslan as "traitors" (156), when she was the one guilty of treason. In *Prince Caspian*, Miraz calls Glozelle and Sopespian cowards and "as lily-livered as hares" (183), when he himself did away with his brother in a cowardly, underhanded manner. Perhaps the most blatant illustration of Eustace's lack of self-knowledge will come in chapter five, when he will claim in his diary, "I always try to consider others whether they are nice to me or not" (73).

Eustace's first diary entry amounts to nothing more than a two-page list of one complaint after another. He complains about the waves and that the rest of the crew takes no notice of the rolling sea. He complains about the ship, and his specific criticisms here say much about his shallow, self-focused values. He complains that the *Dawn Treader* has "no proper saloon, no radio, no bathrooms, no deck-chairs" (30). Readers may be confused why Eustace, a tee-totaler, would grumble about the absence of a saloon here. While in American Westerns a saloon is an establishment with a bar that serves alcohol, on a ship it is a large cabin for the common use of the passengers.

Eustace's selfish, shallow, material values mirror those held by Edmund in the first part of *The Lion, the Witch and the Wardrobe*. There, as Edmund trudged through the snow on his way to the witch's castle, he thought of the things he would have after he was made king, of "what sort of palace he would have and how many cars and all about his private cinema and where the principal railways would run" (91).

Evidence of the similarities between the early Eustace and the early Edmund can be found in the following description of Edmund, in which Eustace's name could easily be substituted, with the observations being just as accurate. Evan Gibson writes that Edmund is "a small boy whose tendency to selfishness and bullying needs to be checked before it colors his whole life" and "this is one reason why he has found his way into Narnia" (136). The Eustace we get to know here in the diary entries is, like Edmund was at the start of the first book, just a step or two away from doing something very evil.

Jonathan Rogers has noted that in *The Voyage of the Dawn Treader*, the issue of "the overweening self appears again and again" (52). While Eustace will be the primary vehicle for Lewis to express what he wants to say about this topic, readers will learn in the narrow escape on Deathwater Island that even Edmund and Caspian occasionally have to battle their desire for self-importance. Lucy too, as Rogers notes, will fall "prey to vanity" as she reads through Coriakin's book of spells.

In the preface he wrote to the 1961 edition of *The Screwtape Letters*, Lewis describes hell as a state where everyone is "perpetually concerned about his own dignity and advancement, where everyone has a grievance, and where everyone lives the deadly serious passions of envy, self-importance, and resentment" (ix). Eustace's envy, self-importance, and resentment have become such a way of life that he can conceive of no other way to live. All this will change, but for now Eustace cannot get past thinking about himself.

## Eustace's First "Correction"

Chapter two ends with the story of Eustace's attack on Reepicheep. Eustace comes upon Reepicheep as the mouse is sitting far forward in the *Dawn Treader*, "gazing out at the eastern horizon and singing softly in his little chirruping voice the song the Dryad had made for him" (32–33). It is particularly telling that Eustace interrupts him in this state. Anyone else on board would have been sensitive enough to see that Reepicheep was caught up in deep longing and would have left him alone entirely or perhaps might have gently whispered something like, "Still dreaming of that place where sky and water meet, Reep?"

Within just a few days on ship, Eustace has located the smallest creature around him and, thinking he can torment him, has come up with a plan. We are told that Eustace thought it would be "delightful" to catch hold of Reepicheep's long tail, to swing him around "once or twice upside-down," and then to "run away and laugh" (33). Readers may be reminded of Peter's comment to Edmund near the start of *The Lion, the Witch and the Wardrobe*: "You've always liked being beastly to anyone smaller than yourself" (46).

Eustace's treatment of Reepicheep has been the first action he has taken since arriving in Narnia, and it typifies the story of his whole life. Here we see his central reason for living, the formula for the only version of happiness he knows: to dominate, torment, and intimidate others. This is what he was up to in Lucy's bedroom before he was interrupted by the actions of the sailing ship in the picture. Now he gets back to the business of his life.

In *Mere Christianity*, Lewis observes, "How monotonously alike all the great tyrants and conquerors have been" (226). He could, perhaps, more accurately have written, "How monotonously alike all tyrants and conquerors—*great and small*—have been." In the first three Chronicles, Lewis has given us a major tyrant in the White Witch, a minor tyrant in Miraz, and now in Eustace a miniature tyrant. Despite their different magnitudes, they share many similarities.

During the hundred years of winter she imposed over Narnia, what did the White Witch do all day? Here is an attempt at her daily to-do list: (1) make sure it is still winter, (2) sharpen stone knife, (3) check statues, (4) polish wand, (5) yell at wolves, (6) check statues again, and (7) make sure no one is happy, having fun, or enjoying themselves in any way—if they are, torment or tyrannize them until they are not. In *The Chronicles of Narnia: The Patterning of a Fantastic World*, Colin Manlove has commented on the joyless life of the White Witch, noting, "She is concerned only with maintaining her power over Narnia. She does nothing with it and exists for no other reason than to keep it" (36).

What does Eustace like to do with his time? On the first page readers were told that he likes to kill beetles and pin them on a card. He likes tormenting people as well as insects, but only if he believes they cannot or will not strike back. In addition, we learned that Eustace, although quite bright in school, does not care much "about any subject for its own sake" (30), but only about the marks he can earn in that subject so he can ridicule anyone with a lower score. A tyrant's only version of happiness—whether it be the witch, Miraz, or Eustace—requires that he or she take happiness away from others. Aslan wants the creatures of Narnia to be happy, to have fun, to be free, and to celebrate and enjoy life. His opponents want just the opposite.

Eustace's mistreatment of Reepicheep, his idea of a joke, lasts for only moments as the gallant mouse keeps his head, and although he is swung round and round, he is able to draw his sword and make "two agonizing jabs" in Eustace's hand (34). After being dropped to the deck, Reepicheep gives Eustace the chance to draw his own sword and defend himself, a courtesy not extended when Eustace sneaked up from behind and grabbed his tail. Eustace announces that he does not have a sword and has no intention to fight in a fair fight, so Reepicheep lays into him with "the side of his rapier" (35), an instrument of discipline that proves to be "as supple and effective as a birch rod."

The narrator tells us, "Eustace (of course) was at a school where they didn't have corporal punishment, so the sensation was quite new to him" (35). The real problem is not that Experiment House does not have corporal punishment but that the school has no punishment whatsoever. So while the sensation of a spanking is new to him, even more novel is the sensation of being corrected at all and the implication that he is in need of correction.

Appropriately, at the end of the next Chronicle, *The Silver Chair*, it will be this same form of correction that Aslan will prescribe for Eustace's former colleagues, the bullies at Experiment House. There he will tell Eustace and Caspian, "Sons of Adam, draw your swords. But use only the flat, for it is cowards and children, not warriors, against whom I send you" (240). Then the bullies' faces will suddenly lose their "meanness, conceit, cruelty, and sneakishness" (241), qualities that sum up Eustace's actions here, and will take on "one single expression of terror." In the final pages of *The Silver Chair*, readers learn that "from that day forth things changed for the better" (243).

In mentioning Eustace's school, Lewis is not placing the blame for Eustace's misbehavior on his teachers or the headmaster. Lewis is always careful to preserve each character's free will and accountability for his or her choices. Eustace's experiences at Experiment House help us to understand his misconduct, not excuse it. Evan Gibson has argued that "it would be distorting Lewis's purpose" to place the responsibility for Eustace's faults on his environment (168).

After Eustace's "correction" here, he bursts in on Lucy, Edmund, and Caspian, complaining of Reepicheep's response to his "joke" (35). Reepicheep makes no apology for his disciplinary actions but merely states, "If I had known that he would take refuge here I would have awaited a more reasonable time for his correction" (32). Like some of his colleagues at Experiment House, Eustace too will undergo a change for the better—but it will take a much more dramatic form of correction than what Reepicheep administers.

For the first seven chapters of *The Voyage of the Dawn Treader*, Eustace, like all those dominated by an overweening sense of self-importance, will suffer from a critical case of spiritual blindness. In *Letters to an American Lady*, C. S. Lewis remarks on this blindness: "How difficult it is to avoid having a special standard for oneself!" (58). By way of illustration, Lewis points out that a murderer seldom describes his own act by the word *murder*. And how many thieves call themselves thieves or refer to what they do as stealing? When Eustace tries to steal water in chapter five, he will not admit to his crime, not even to himself in his diary. How many people with double standards—one for themselves and one for everyone else, as with Eustace—describe themselves as hypocrites?

In an essay titled "Miserable Offenders," Lewis observes that "those who do not think about their own sins make up for it by thinking incessantly about the sins of others" (124), a description that fits Eustace perfectly here. He has many shortcomings, but before he can begin to face them, he first must realize they exist. Like all who share his spiritual blindness, the first lesson Eustace has to learn is that he has lessons to learn.

## Discussion Questions

The longing for something just over the horizon is a key element throughout *The Voyage of the Dawn Treader*. Just as Reepicheep explains that the spell of the nursery prophecy has been on him all his life, the longing Lewis experienced as a boy haunted him, to his great delight, all his days. As mentioned earlier, Lewis often gazed out his bedroom window to the Castlereagh Hills, a view that stirred this longing.

1. What has served to kindle longing in your life and has taken you "into the region of awe"? It might be a certain view from a window, as it was for Lewis, or perhaps it is a certain sound—distant church bells, a far-off train, or the wind in the leaves. Longing can also be sparked by certain times of year, kinds of weather, or smells.

In his essay "On Three Ways of Writing for Children," Lewis suggests that fairy tales are another element that can arouse longing in us, that certain stories can stir us and trouble us—to our lifelong enrichment—with a "dim sense" of something beyond our reach (38).

2. Do the Chronicles of Narnia ever function in this way for you? If so, where and how do they give you this dim sense of something just over the horizon?

3. Later in life, Lewis saw behind all these moments of longing what he called a longing for heaven. In what ways have you experienced this in your own life?

Readers find Lewis's insights into evil just as penetrating as his insights into goodness. In Lewis's portrait of Eustace, his goal is not that we will stand off to the side and say, "Thank goodness I am not like that," but rather that through this portrayal of selfishness, we see aspects of ourselves—aspects that we, like Eustace, have been blind to. In *The Screwtape Letters*, Screwtape advises his nephew Wormwood that he should bring the man he is tempting to a state where he can undergo self-examination for an hour "without discovering any of those facts about himself which are perfectly clear to anyone who has ever lived in the same house with him or worked in the same office" (12).

In *Mere Christianity*, Lewis points out, "A moderately bad man knows he is not very good; a thoroughly bad man thinks he is all right" (93). Eustace, of course, epitomizes the latter. He sees nothing at all wrong with his behavior.

4. What aspects of Eustace seem realistic?

5. What aspects of Eustace can you see in yourself? To what extent are we blind to our faults like Eustace is?

6. What are some other aspects of yourself—positive or negative—that reading the Narnia books has helped you to see?

## THREE

# The Lone Islands

## Land in Sight

With the conflict between Eustace and Reepicheep temporarily on hold, the crew of the *Dawn Treader* arrives at the Lone Islands, the site of their first adventure. As Paul Ford notes, when Lewis wrote *The Voyage of the Dawn Treader*, he had not yet "invented the history of how the Lone Islands came to be Narnian" (290). And so here in chapter three, Lewis inserts the following statement from the narrator: "I have never yet heard how these remote islands became attached to the crown of Narnia" (38). This declaration is followed by the promise, "If I ever do, and if the story is at all interesting, I may put it in some other book."

The Lone Islands were in the back of Lewis's mind even in the first story. They were first mentioned in chapter six of *The Lion, the Witch and the Wardrobe*, when the four children arrived at Mr. Tumnus's ransacked cave and found a statement from Maugrim, the White Witch's wolf, accusing the faun of treason "against her Imperial Majesty, Jadis, Queen of Narnia, Chatelaine of Cair Paravel, Empress of the Lone Islands, etc." (58). The witch's dwarf used this title again seven chapters later when he announced that "the Queen of Narnia and Empress of the Lone Islands" desired safe conduct in order to speak with Aslan (140).

The next mention of the Lone Islands occurred early in *Prince Caspian*. In the scene where the children searched among the items in the treasure chamber beneath the ruins of Cair Paravel, one of them commented, "I say, isn't that the armor you wore in the great tournament in the Lone Islands?" (26). Later as the children sailed from Cair Paravel to the mainland, Lucy was reminded of the voyage "to Terebinthia—and Galma—and Seven Isles—and the Lone Islands" (113). Still later, Peter declared his title of "Emperor of the Lone Islands" in the challenge letter to Miraz (177), a title Aslan then promised to Prince Caspian in the story's final chapter.

Despite these references in the first two stories, the Lone Islands remained—like Susan's bow and to some extent her horn—an element waiting to be used in a later book. It will not be until *The Last Battle* that Lewis will keep his narrator's promise to tell us more about this location. There Jewel will recount the story of King Gale, the ruler ninth in descent after King Frank. Jewel will explain to Jill how early in Narnia's history, Gale delivered the Lone Islanders from a dragon and in return was given the Lone Islands "to be part of the royal lands of Narnia forever" (100).

Here in chapter three, Lucy recalls the "nice kind of loneliness" on Felimath (38), the nearest of the Lone Islands, how it was "all grass and clover," and wishes she could walk there again. Caspian joins in her desire and asks, "Why shouldn't we go ashore in the boat and send it back, and then we could walk across Felimath and let the *Dawn Treader* pick us up on the other side?" No one thinks to mention that Lucy's recollections are from a time 1,300 years before. No one thinks to ask whether the formerly uninhabited Felimath might have become more dangerous in the thirteen centuries since Edmund and Lucy were last there.

The narrator jumps in to comment, "If Caspian had been as experienced then as he became later on in this voyage he would not have made this suggestion" (38). Once again Lewis turns to the role of adventure in the maturation process. There is a saying, "It's the sea that makes the sailor." We could say that Caspian's quest will be the making of him, just as Peter's adventures helped make him who he was, and just as our own ordeals help to grow and mature us.

If we were to complain that these adventures are often associated with hardship, Lewis would not disagree. In his essay "Answers to Questions on Christianity," he suggests, "If you think of this world as a place intended simply for our happiness, you find it quite intolerable: think of it as a place of training and correction and it's not so bad" (52). The fact that Caspian learns to be more cautious from this experience will be made clear at the next unknown destination they reach. When the *Dawn Treader* arrives at Dragon Island, Eustace will record in his diary that "Caspian wouldn't let us go ashore because it was getting dark and he was afraid of savages and wild beasts" (75).

### It Was Delightful to Be Ashore Again

In the passage from "The Weight of Glory" that was cited earlier, we find Lewis's claim, "You and I have need of the strongest spell that can be found to wake us from the evil enchantment of worldliness which has been laid upon us for nearly a hundred years" (31). How exactly does Lewis go about breaking this enchantment? In *The Narnian*, Alan Jacobs argues that Lewis begins his disenchanting spell in a surprising way: "by calling us back to our pleasures, to the things in life that we enjoy, and not the things that we think we ought to like . . . but to what really and truly delights us" (189).

Here on Felimath, Lewis shows us this kind of pleasure. Readers are told, "Lucy was of course barefoot, having kicked off her shoes while swimming, but that is no hardship if one is going to walk on downy turf. It was delightful to be ashore again and to smell the earth and grass. . . . It was much warmer here than it had been on board and Lucy found the sand pleasant to her feet as they crossed it. There was a lark singing" (39).

In *Celebration of Discipline*, Richard Foster points out "the lust for affluence" that is prevalent everywhere in our contemporary society (80), a lust that mirrors the spell of worldliness Lewis described. Part of Foster's cure for this condition is the development of "a deeper appreciation for the creation" and points to the need we have to learn how "to enjoy things without owning them" (93). By way of specific ideas of how we might do this, Foster urges, "Get close to the earth. Walk whenever you can. Listen to the birds. Enjoy the texture of grass and leaves."

Lucy's delight here as she walks barefoot over the sand and turf mirrors Foster's suggestion perfectly. Her deep contentment stands in stark contrast to the worldliness and the discontent that Deathwater Island will elicit in Edmund and Caspian in chapter eight, where each lusts after more money and more authority—elements that neither character needs or even enjoys.

Lewis will title chapter fifteen "The Wonders of the Last Sea." In that chapter the crew of the *Dawn Treader* will find that they need less sleep, do not want to eat very much, and will not want to talk except in low voices—the awe they experience is too great. There the sun will shine with otherworldly brightness, and the water will be perfectly clear and sweet to drink. Here in chapter three, Lucy experiences a more ordinary kind of wonder on Felimath, a more everyday "nice kind of loneliness" (38).

## A Kidnapper and a Slaver

Not long after Edmund, Lucy, Caspian, Eustace, and Reepicheep are put ashore, they meet up with the danger the narrator's comment has prepared us for as they are captured by a band of lawless ruffians. Pug, one of Lewis's minor villains, is, as Caspian correctly labels him, "a kidnapper and slaver" (42). Like the other villains Lewis has depicted, Pug does not see anything wrong with his behavior. As he asserts, "I've got my living to make same as anyone else" (42). Lewis will use what seems to be a coincidental meeting as the first step in the escape from these villains.

Early in *Prince Caspian*, there was a chance meeting that in retrospect seemed too coincidental and too critical to be mere chance. There in chapter three, just as Peter, Susan, Edmund, and Lucy reached the channel between the island and the mainland, the two soldiers just happened to arrive, bringing Trumpkin there to be drowned. If the children had turned up a few minutes later or if Trumpkin and his captors had arrived a few minutes earlier, the valiant dwarf would have been executed and the children would never have known where they were supposed to meet Caspian and his forces.

Here in chapter three of *The Voyage of the Dawn Treader*, we find a similar chance meeting with a powerful feeling of providence behind it. Just as Pug is about to set sail with his five new prisoners for the slave market in Narrowhaven, "at that moment" a fine-looking bearded man—who we later learn is Lord Bern—happens to come out of an inn and see them (44). Because Lord Bern comes out of the inn at that moment, he ends up purchasing Caspian's freedom. Because he frees Caspian, they are able to come up with a plan for freeing the others.

The fact that these events line up so perfectly may lead readers to conclude, as Shasta will later in *The Horse and His Boy*, that Aslan is "at the back" of what may seem to be coincidences (208). Shasta comes to his conclusion after he learns that, in a scene reminiscent of the one here involving Lord Bern's arrival, the boat he was in just happened to come to the right place at the right time for him to be rescued. In *The Silver Chair*, one of the important lessons Jill and Eustace will learn is, as Puddleglum states, "There are no accidents" (154).

In an essay aptly titled "'Caught Up into the Larger Pattern': Images and Narrative Structures in C. S. Lewis's Fiction," Colin Manlove argues that Lewis saw accident and design as "more closely entwined than we suppose" (268). Lewis's point can be found in the hermit's words to Aravis in *The Horse and His Boy*: "Daughter, I have now lived a hundred and nine winters in this world and have never yet met any such thing as Luck" (148). Later Shasta will at first consider it lucky that he was able to find the mountain pass in the night, but then he will conclude, "It wasn't luck at all really, it was *Him*" (168). The same could be said about Bern's appearance at just the right moment to free Caspian.

Beginning here in chapter three, the issue of freedom and enslavement will run throughout *The Voyage of the Dawn Treader*, although later Lewis will be more concerned with spiritual freedom and enslavement than with its physical form seen here. As Jonathan Rogers has pointed out, "True freedom in *The Voyage of the Dawn Treader* is freedom from the self, freedom to turn one's attention outward, toward the things that give purpose and meaning to the self" (52). In later chapters, Eustace will be set free from his self-centeredness, while the Dufflepuds, as Rogers notes, will "stay trapped in a prison of their own making" (53). Even Lucy, as we will see in chapter ten, must struggle with her own forms of enslavement. There it will be made clear that she is to some extent bound by what her friends say about her and by her jealousy of Susan.

### "Don't Separate Us, Whatever You Do"

Seeing that Caspian is about to be sold, Lucy begs Lord Bern, "Oh, please, please. Don't separate us, whatever you do" (44). Lord Bern regretfully explains that he has only enough money to purchase Caspian and can do no more than warn Pug to treat the others well. In this scene, Lewis embeds a great lesson for his readers. Here Lucy thinks the worst thing that could happen to the five captives is to be split up. When what she perceives as "the dreadful moment" of separation comes (45), she bursts into tears. But in fact, Lord Bern's purchase of Caspian and the subsequent splitting up of the captives is a fortunate happening. Without Caspian's departure, there would have been no opportunity for rescue.

Readers found a similar lesson in *Prince Caspian*. When the four children went to retrieve the gifts in the ancient treasure chamber, they perceived Susan's missing horn as "a shattering loss" (27). But in reality, Susan's earlier misplacing of the horn was, as the children later came to see, an amazing stroke of good fortune, for it allowed Prince Caspian to use it to call them back to Narnia.

Lewis explored this concept of our sometimes being mistaken about what is best for us in all three books of his space trilogy. In *Out of the Silent Planet*, the narrator explains, "The last thing Ransom wanted was an adventure" (13). In *Perelandra*, the thing the Lewis character most dreads is to be "drawn in" (10), something that he, in his limited knowledge, refers to as "sheer bad luck." In *That Hideous Strength*, Jane finds herself thinking similar thoughts: "Take care. Don't get drawn in. . . . You've got your own life to live" (112). In all three characters, after what they believe to be the worst possible thing happens, it becomes clear that it was the best possible thing.

In these portrayals of characters who mistakenly think they know what is best for them, Lewis is mirroring his own reluctant conversion, an event he resisted and tried fervently to avoid. In *Surprised by Joy*, Lewis writes that he came to faith like a prodigal who is brought in to the fold "kicking, struggling, resentful, and darting his eyes in every direction for a chance of escape" (229).

In *The Last Battle*, Lewis will revisit the idea of our limited perception about what would be best for us. There Jill and the others will be upset that Narnia has passed away. As Jill will lament, "I *did* hope that it might go on forever" (182). But without the death of the old Narnia, the new Narnia, "where every chapter is better than the one before" (211), could never have come about.

## "Not by My Counsel"

Lord Bern waits to talk until he and Caspian are in an open place beyond the village, presumably so no one will hear him. Then he explains that he purchased Caspian because of his resemblance to the previous King Caspian, who had been Bern's sovereign before Miraz took power. Caspian announces that the resemblance is not accidental and that he himself is the son of Bern's former monarch. Bern, who has been taught by experience not to simply accept wild assertions, asks for proof of the former slave's amazing claim. Using his wits, Caspian declares, "First by my face. Secondly because I know within six guesses who you are" (46).

The fact that Caspian keeps his head here shows that he has matured in the three years since his "tongue-tied" days in the previous story (175). But for the second time, Caspian cannot remember the names of all seven lost lords, which is Lewis's way of reminding us that the young king still has some growing to do—growth that will be aided by his mentoring here from Lord Bern.

One of Lewis's most central points throughout his writings is that life is for learning and growing. Through example after example in the Chronicles, Lewis suggests that this learning and growing comes through a mixture of experience, successes and failures, and mentoring at key times. Early in *The Lion, the Witch and the Wardrobe*, Peter and Susan went to the professor for advice about Lucy. Later Peter was given guidance from Aslan.

While Caspian has been parentless for most of his life, Lewis has not left him without guidance. In the second adventure, Caspian had a number of mentors, including Doctor Cornelius, High King Peter, and Aslan. In *The Voyage of the Dawn Treader*, Caspian will receive counsel from Drinian, Lord Bern, Lord Rhoop, Reepicheep, and the former star Ramandu.

In *The Way into Narnia*, Peter Schakel writes this about Caspian's development: "Although he learned a great deal through his flight to the wilderness and his military service with the old Narnians, he was left at the end of *Prince Caspian* a new king with a great deal more to learn about himself and the world" (63). Here in chapter three, Lord Bern helps balance the young king's naïveté with a more mature understanding of the sometimes harsh realities in the world. Bern introduces Caspian to the finely nuanced intricacies of the political situation in the Lone Islands, where Gumpas is governor and Caspian, in theory, is king and emperor. "All is done in the king's name," he explains, but notes that Gumpas would not be pleased to find that "a real, live King of Narnia" had arrived (47).

Bern concludes, "If your Majesty came before him alone and unarmed—well he would not deny his allegiance, but he would pretend to disbelieve you. Your Grace's life would be in danger" (47). Thus the young Caspian is reminded that in defeating Miraz, he did not defeat treachery, and he must continue to be on guard against wicked men and their deceits. Given his decision to stroll on the island before making sure it was safe, it is clear he needs this reminder.

Since the *Dawn Treader* has only "thirty swords if it came to fighting" (48), Lord Bern advises Caspian, "It must not come to plain battle." He explains, "Your Majesty must work by a show of more power than you really have." This is the second time Caspian has faced superior forces. When the old Narnians were outnumbered in *Prince Caspian*, they too were forced to use unconventional means. It was then that Peter put forward the strategy of challenging Miraz to single combat. Having learned from this earlier situation, Caspian will play a somewhat greater role in the plan this time. He calls the *Dawn Treader* into shore, and Bern explains their plan of running up signals to "all the other ships we haven't got but which it might be well that Gumpas thinks we have" (49). The chapter ends with Bern, still more in charge than Caspian, sending a messenger to the island of Doorn to order preparations for their arrival the following day.

## Discussion Questions

In this chapter, the narrator commented, "If Caspian had been as experienced then as he became later on this voyage he would not have made this suggestion" (38). Lewis's point once again is that it is adventures and their difficulties, rather than easy times, that bring about growth and maturity. In *The Problem of Pain*, Lewis examines the struggles and pain we all encounter in life. Toward the end of the work, borrowing a phrase from the English poet John

Keats, Lewis concludes that if the world is a "vale of soul-making," (97), it seems "on the whole to be doing its work."

1. Do you agree with the saying "It's the sea that makes the sailor"—that the challenges and difficulties of life make us who we are—and that in this sense the world can be seen as "a vale of soul-making"? If so, how has this been true in your own life?

Here in chapter three, we found a coincidence with a powerful feeling of providence behind it—as Pug was about to set sail to Narrowhaven with his prisoners, Lord Bern just happened to come out and see them. Back in chapter one, the fact that the picture of the Narnian ship just happened to be in the bedroom and just happened to come alive while Eustace was there also seemed more than mere coincidence.

2. Can you think of other seeming coincidences in the Narnia stories? What do you think Lewis's point is in these?

3. Have you had coincidences in your life that seemed to be more than mere chance? How would you explain them?

It was suggested that one of Lewis's messages is that learning and growth come not only through experience but also by special mentoring at certain key times. Mentors appear throughout the Chronicles—characters like the professor, Mr. Beaver, Doctor Cornelius, Lord Bern, Puddleglum, the hermit, and Aslan himself—and provide advice and guidance for younger, inexperienced characters. Lewis assigns mentors their greatest role in *The Great Divorce*. There as each of the riders on the bus is greeted by a specially chosen guide at the outskirts of heaven, the fictional Lewis meets up with his own great mentor, the writer George Macdonald.

In the title of his book *C. S. Lewis: Writer, Dreamer and Mentor*, Lionel Adey suggests that one role Lewis assumes for his readers is that of a teacher or guide.

4. Who have been mentors in your life—in person or through their writings?

5. If you include C. S. Lewis among your guides or unofficial teachers, what are some of the most important lessons you have learned from his writings?

# FOUR

# What Caspian Did There

## "Open for the King of Narnia"

In *The World According to Narnia*, Jonathan Rogers correctly observes:

> Like so many other stories of great journeys, *The Voyage of the Dawn Treader* is episodic in its structure. The *Dawn Treader* carries its passengers from adventure to adventure across a world of astonishing variety. That variety, which makes *The Voyage of the Dawn Treader* such a pleasure to read, makes it difficult to write about. The different episodes vary not only in setting and character, but also in theme. (53)

Rather than having a typical narrative structure with opening exposition, a rising conflict, a climax, and a resolution—as the first two books did—the events in Lewis's third Chronicle are structured more like separate beads on a string. Many times it seems that the only connection between the various episodes is that the boat happens to go there.

Having noted this, it could also be argued that the conflicts and antagonists that the crew of the *Dawn Treader* must face are to some extent organized from weaker to stronger. In this sense the story may be said to mirror most people's lives as they go from youth to maturity. This progression from weaker to more powerful opponents, and to needing less and less outside help, makes sense in a story in which the protagonists gradually will grow in courage, strength, and wisdom. Certainly in this first episode, the encounter with Gumpas and Pug, the children face their weakest opponents and receive the most help—in this case from Lord Bern and some of his people.

Following Bern's suggestions, the next day Caspian orders his men "into full armor" with everything "trim and scoured" to give the impression of more strength than they actually have (51). With Caspian, Bern, and Drinian, the crew members of the *Dawn Treader* make their way through the town of Narrowhaven and into Gumpas's castle with no difficulty. Here Caspian shows for the first time that, when needed, he can be both cunning and commanding. Finding the governor's guards in a slovenly state of disarray and hoping to avoid a fight with them if he can, the young king tells their captain, "Command a cask of wine to be opened that your men may drink our health. But at noon tomorrow I wish to see them here in this courtyard looking like men-at-arms and not like vagabonds" (55).

Inside the hall, they find Gumpas, the consummate bureaucrat, busy at work. Readers are told, "He glanced up as the strangers entered and then looked down at his papers saying automatically, 'No interviews without appointments except between nine and ten p.m. on second Saturdays'" (56). Again taking the lead, Caspian nods to Bern, who, with the help of Drinian, physically removes Gumpas from his chair. Caspian then sits down in it, telling the pencil-pushing functionary, "My Lord, you have not given us quite the welcome we expected" (57).

Gumpas's response to the presence of the king of Narnia here is similar to the response Eustace had upon first entering Narnia: complete denial. Since there was no official announcement of Caspian's arrival "in the correspondence" and no mention of it "in the minutes" (57), Gumpas claims that, despite what he can see with his eyes, it cannot possibly be happening.

It could be argued that Gumpas here presents one possible future outcome for Eustace should he not change the path he is on. And while Gumpas may seem to be nothing more than an officious administrator with an overinflated view of himself, underneath lies something much more sinister, something much more Miraz-like. The narrator points out, "Had he known that Caspian had only one ship and one ship's company with him, he would have spoken soft words for the moment, and hoped to have them all surrounded and killed during the night" (58). Like Miraz, Gumpas is a man with no virtues besides initiative, no principles besides expediency, no goals beyond self-aggrandizement. If the slave trade will produce a "burst of prosperity" (58), as Gumpas asserts, then slavery is fine. If murder is needed to get this interfering boy king out of the way, then from Gumpas's way of seeing things, murder is acceptable as well.

### "Have You No Idea of Progress?"

Caspian addresses Gumpas and demands, "I want to know why you have permitted this abominable and unnatural traffic in slaves to grow up here, contrary to the ancient custom and usage of our dominions" (58). The young king then orders that the practice must be stopped. The governor gasps, "But that would be putting the clock back. Have you no idea of progress, of development?" (59).

This is not the only place where Lewis explores this practice of justifying immoral practices or beliefs in the name of progress. In *The Screwtape Letters*, Screwtape urges Wormwood to encourage this type of rationalization with his patient. "Don't waste time trying to make him think that materialism is *true!*" the senior devil admonishes (1–2). "Make him think it is strong, or stark, or courageous—that it is the philosophy of the future." Here Gumpas's focus is not on whether slavery is morally right or good, but on whether it represents progress and development—or, as Screwtape would say, whether it represents the philosophy of the future.

Several chapters into *Mere Christianity*, Lewis pauses and directly addresses his readers, using words that almost seemed designed to be an answer to Gumpas's charge of "putting the clock back." Lewis comments, "Would you think I was joking if I said that you can put a clock back, and that if the clock is wrong it is often a very sensible thing to do? . . . We all want progress. But progress means getting nearer to the place where you want to be. . . . If you are on the wrong road, progress means doing an about-turn and walking back to the right road" (28). Here in *The Voyage of the Dawn Treader*, clearly it is Caspian—in seeking to return to "the ancient custom and usage of our dominions" (58), back to a condition where slavery is forbidden—who is the progressive, not Gumpas.

Using typical bureaucratic language—"I can take no responsibility for any such measure" (59)—Gumpas refuses to accept Caspian's command to stop the slave trade. Following this refusal, Caspian relieves Gumpas of his office and appoints Lord Bern as the new duke. In removing a wicked autocrat, putting a halt to his immoral policies, and establishing a new ruler who will govern properly, Caspian retraces the actions of the previous book. The Lone Islands, in this sense, can be seen as a smaller version of the Narnia we saw at the start of *Prince Caspian*—a land that has been taken off track by an evil tyrant, a land in need of restoration to its earlier condition.

Up to this point, the restoration of justice in the Lone Islands has been bloodless. But when one of Gumpas's secretaries interrupts to say, "Suppose all you gentlemen stop play-acting and we do a little business" (60), the newly appointed duke shows that, if needed, he is willing and able to use force. Bern responds, "The question is whether you and the rest of the rabble will leave without a flogging or with one. You may choose which you prefer."

One final step is needed—shutting down the slave market and freeing the slaves, among them Edmund, Lucy, Eustace, and Reepicheep. Again showing more mature thinking, Caspian orders horses from the castle stables to enhance their show of power. Once they reach the market, Pug is quickly stopped, those who had purchased slaves are given their money back, and the friends are reunited, though not without a negative comment from Eustace.

The mere existence of a supposedly imaginary land should have provided the first blow to Eustace's smug worldview and the notion that he knew everything. The correction Eustace received from the flat of Reepicheep's rapier was a second call for change. Here in chapter four, Eustace is given a third indication that he is not quite the gem he thinks he is. While Edmund, Lucy, and Reepicheep were sold quickly, Eustace, or "Sulky" as Pug calls him here, could not even be given away for free. The narrator comments, "Though no one would want to be sold as a slave, it is perhaps even more galling to be a sort of utility slave whom no one will buy" (63). To be a slave no one wanted would be galling for most boys, but not for Eustace. He ignores this third indication that he is not the person he thinks he is and merely tells Caspian, "I see. As usual. Been enjoying yourself somewhere while the rest of us were prisoners" (63).

Each indicator to Eustace of his true condition has grown more severe and harder for him to ignore. The fourth, his transformation to a dragon, will be impossible to disregard.

Given Eustace's negative response to any act of kindness, as seen here and elsewhere, readers may wonder what the point is in Caspian or the others continuing to be nice to him. In chapter six, Lewis will remind readers that kind deeds are never done in vain. After Eustace is transformed into a dragon, he will look back on everything that has happened and will realize "that Caspian would never have sailed away and left him" (93).

Despite being on an otherworldly mission that will take them to the utter east and beyond, our heroes, it should be pointed out, are also very concerned with the here and now. In *Mere Christianity*,

Lewis notes that while Christians are to continually look forward to the eternal world, this does not mean that they are to leave the present world "as it is" (134). He goes on to observe that throughout history the Christians who did the most for the present world were precisely those "who thought most of the next," and Lewis included among them the English evangelicals who worked to abolish the slave trade. In arguing that the Lone Islands had no need of slaves, Caspian was repeating the arguments of believers like William Wilberforce who fought to end the slave trade in England. In restoring justice and proper rule to the Lone Islands, Caspian went beyond his stated intent to find the seven lost lords and sail to the eastern end of the world.

### More on Gumpas, Pug, Aslan, and the Calormen Merchants

It was noted earlier that despite the book's episodic structure, the various encounters in *The Voyage of the Dawn Treader* are ordered so the easier ones occur earlier. It could also be said that the antagonists are ordered with the more ordinary ones earlier. Here in chapter four, our heroes faced Pug and Gumpas—a common thug and a minor autocrat. In later chapters, as they journey further and further away from the known world, the crew of the *Dawn Treader* will encounter greater wonders and will come up against stranger antagonists.

Readers are never told what happens to Gumpas and Pug after their correction here, whether they caused trouble after Caspian left or if they willingly abided by the changes that had been introduced. At one point Caspian threatened Gumpas by reminding him of the law that states, "If the tribute is not delivered the whole debt has to be paid by the Governor of the Lone Islands out of his private purse" (57). But after ousting the governor and installing Bern as duke, Caspian seems content to let this point pass. Pug complains that being forced to return the money he collected that day will "beggar" him (62), but readers may feel that he and Gumpas have gotten off rather easy.

Lewis and Tolkien at times could be quite merciful with their villains and perhaps too ready to give them a second chance. Except for Gumpas being removed from office and Pug being stopped from selling slaves, neither of these two offenders is punished for their offenses—neither is jailed, fined, flogged, or exiled. Like Saruman, after Treebeard took pity on him and released him from Orthanc in *The Return of the King*, the ex-governor and ex-slaver both seem to have potential to create further problems. But Lewis implies there is no one who is beyond redemption. Perhaps, like the many Telmarines who chose to stay in Narnia at the end of *Prince Caspian*, the two will be able to change their ways.

Before we leave the encounter with Pug and Gumpas, two further points should be made. First, except for the providential arrival of Bern, all seems to have been accomplished here in the first adventure without the direct aid of Aslan. We will later discover that although the crew members may not realize it, Aslan is watching over the *Dawn Treader*—an invisible presence ready to intervene when needed and perhaps intervening in unseen ways.

Earlier the great lion gave his general blessing to Caspian's quest. Paul Ford explains, "The voyage is undertaken only because Caspian sought and received Aslan's approval to swear a solemn oath to search for the seven noble lords. Aslan's image in beaten gold is hung above the door of Caspian's cabin, a sign that this quest is made under the Lion's patronage" (67). But Aslan will do more than give his general blessing. As Ford points out, "How Aslan takes care of all of Narnian history and the lives of each person and animal is one of the major themes of the Chronicles" (356). In chapter ten, after Lucy recites the spell to make hidden things visible, the first thing Lucy will see is Aslan himself. When she says how kind it was for him to come, he will answer, "I have been here all the time" (159), a response that could mean either he has been in the magician's house all the time or he has been watching over the crew of the *Dawn Treader* all the time. The latter interpretation is supported by his other appearances on Dragon Island, on Deathwater Island, off the coast of the Dark Island, in Caspian's cabin, and on the final shore.

Second, in this chapter, Lewis introduces the Chronicles' first characters from Calormen. When two "merchants of Calormen" want Pug to return their money (62), readers are provided with this description: "The Calormen have dark faces and long beards. They wear flowing robes and orange-colored turbans, and they are a wise, wealthy, courteous, cruel and ancient people."

While this is the first appearance of Calormen citizens, the country of Calormen was first mentioned in chapter two of *Prince Caspian*, when Peter asked the others, "Don't you remember—it was the very day before the ambassadors came from the King of Calormen—don't you remember planting the orchard outside the north gate of Cair Paravel?" (21). Three chapters later, Trufflehunter referred to the country again in talking about Narnia's non-talking animals to Nikabrik: "You know very well that the beasts in Narnia nowadays are different and are no more than the poor dumb, witless creatures you'd find in Calormen or Telmar" (71). These two earlier comments about Calormen went by without further explanation, until here in *The Voyage of the Dawn Treader*, where readers are told a bit more.

Following this short encounter with the Calormen merchants, the country of Calormen will come up again four more times in *The Voyage of the Dawn Treader*, and each instance will be brief and have negative associations. At the end of this chapter, Bern will express concern about "war with Calormen" (65), a concern that does not seem to materialize since it is not mentioned in the account of the *Dawn Treader*'s return home on the story's final page. In chapter six, after discovering the dragon's hoard, Eustace will declare, "With some of this stuff I could have quite a decent time here—perhaps in Calormen. It sounds the least phony of these countries" (87). In chapter ten, when Lucy is tempted to say the beautification spell, she will have a vision of herself "throned on high at a great tournament in Calormen" where "all the Kings of the world fought because of her beauty" (153–54). And in chapter fourteen, Pittencream, the only crew member who does not go on to the world's end, winds up living in Calormen, where we learn "he told wonderful stories" made up about "his adventures at the End of the World" (216). Having provided these glimpses, Lewis will wait until *The Horse and His Boy*, which is set mostly in Calormen, to more fully describe this land and its inhabitants.

## "Tomorrow for the Beginning of Our Real Adventures!"

In both *The Lion, the Witch and the Wardrobe* and *Prince Caspian*, great victories were always followed by great feasts. Here after the double victories of deposing Gumpas and ending Pug's slave business, readers are told, "That night they had a great feast in the castle of Narrowhaven" (63). The next day "the fullest preparations" are undertaken as the crew will "leave all known lands and seas behind them," and with this venture into the unknown, they will, as Reepicheep declares, begin their "real adventures."

In preparation for this departure into a region where repairs may be difficult or impossible, the *Dawn Treader* is hauled ashore, where "every bit of her was gone over by the most skilled shipwrights" (63). While the ship is being repaired and "victualed and watered as full as she could hold," Caspian makes good use of the time by questioning "all the oldest sea captains" he can find to "learn if they had any knowledge or even any rumors of land further to the east" (64). None of the men Caspian talks to has any helpful information. Either they can tell of no lands beyond the Lone Islands, or they have only "wild stories" of headless men, floating islands, waterspouts, and a fire that burns on the water. One man was told by his father that beyond everything lies "Aslan's country" (65), but he can offer nothing further than this.

Bern tells Caspian that after his six companions sailed away, nothing was ever heard of them again. He concludes, "I've wondered about my friends and wondered what there really is behind that horizon. Nothing, most likely, yet I am always half ashamed that I stayed behind" (65). In a simpler kind of story, the author might have used this chance to allow Lord Bern to join the crew of the *Dawn Treader* and to undo his earlier decision. But for an author like Lewis, who has a more serious purpose, things are not this simple. Earlier Bern told Caspian that he had fallen in love with "a girl of the islands" and they had married (47). In addition, Bern has just taken on the responsibility of ruling as the new duke. Given these responsibilities, it is not realistic for Bern to suggest he join the quest, no matter how much he might have liked to.

Here Caspian is given a reminder that a ruler has responsibilities to those he has been put in charge of and cannot simply do what he wants. In chapter sixteen, when Caspian attempts to abdicate so he can go with Reepicheep to see the world's end, he will seem to ignore or to have forgotten Lord Bern's example here.

### Discussion Questions

In this chapter, Gumpas gave voice to the "Have you no idea of progress?" argument. Certainly many practices were condoned simply in the name of progress during the 1940s and 1950s, when Lewis was writing. In *Surprised by Joy*, Lewis uses the term *chronological snobbery* to refer to this suggestion that anything modern must be superior to anything from the past. There he describes this way of thinking as the belief that anything that has gone out of date is "on that account discredited" (207).

Gumpas's pattern of automatically giving value to any idea or practice that is new goes hand in hand with devaluing any idea or practice from the past. In *The Screwtape Letters*, Screwtape tells Wormwood that his patient must regard the notion of anything from the past being a "possible source of knowledge" as "unutterably simple-minded" (151).

1. How is progress still held up as something to be desired, despite whether or not the specific element in question is good or bad?

2. Can you name some so-called progressive aspects in our world that are not really progress at all?

Both Gumpas and Eustace seem to value progress and development, and therefore it seems they have at least some value that goes beyond mere selfishness. But Lewis gives the impression that both characters are hiding self-interest behind their proclaimed interest in progress. In his essay "Christianity and Culture," Lewis makes the point that "real beliefs may differ from the professed," and "our real standards of value . . . may differ from our professed standards" (28–29). In the scene in *The Magician's Nephew* where Jadis arrives in London, the narrator will point out that witches "are not interested in things or people unless they can use them" (79). And the same can be said for all of Lewis's villains, despite what they may claim to stand for.

3. What suggests that despite his seeming interest in "progress and development," Gumpas is really interested only in his personal gain?

4. Gumpas hides his self-centeredness behind a veil of concern for progress. What other kinds of veils do people use to hide their selfishness, both in Narnia and in our own world?

FIVE

# The Storm and What Came of It

## The Next Few Days Were Delightful

For a brief moment near the middle of *The Last Battle*, there will be nothing particularly spectacular going on. "Oh, this *is* nice!" Jill will say to Jewel. "Just walking along like this. I wish there could be more of *this* sort of adventure. It's a pity there's always so much happening in Narnia" (99). Jewel will then tell Jill that in between the adventures recorded in the Chronicles, there were hundreds and thousands of years when "notable dances and feasts, or at most tournaments" were the only important events (100). These times of peace and plenty, these "good, ordinary times," as Jill will call them, do not make for particularly memorable tales, which is why Lewis sticks to writing mostly about times of conflict. But *mostly* is a key word, for in each Chronicle, along with the great adventures, Lewis will also include a few brief scenes of good, ordinary times as a reminder that we are not to despise but rather to cherish the everyday. This reminder can be found here at the start of chapter five.

As this chapter opens, readers are told, "The next few days were delightful. Lucy thought she was the most fortunate girl in the world" (66–67). What amazing thing is it that causes Lucy to feel so fortunate here? As we read on, we are told that she wakes each morning "to see the reflections of the sunlit water dancing on the ceiling of her cabin," and that she takes delight in the nice but ordinary things she had picked up in the Lone Islands— "seaboots and buskins and cloaks and jerkins and scarves." Upon going out on deck each day, she visits the forecastle to "take a look at a sea which was a brighter blue each morning and drink in an air that was a little warmer day by day." And finally we read, "after that came breakfast" and also "a good deal of time sitting on the little bench in the stern playing chess with Reepicheep."

Lewis presented a similar message about cherishing everyday things at the end of *Prince Caspian*. After the four children returned to the railway station, readers were told it seemed "a little flat and dreary," but only "for a moment" (223). Then readers were told that everything—the familiar railway smell, the English sky, the summer term before them—became "nice in its own way." And in these three commonplace elements—the railway smell, the English sky, and the school term—Lewis depicts what might be labeled a "sacramental ordinary"—a deeply rooted sense of enjoyment of and appreciation for the commonplace, a gratitude that was an essential part of his view of the world.

Lewis's enjoyment of the commonplace began when he was young. In *Surprised by Joy*, Lewis writes about the appreciation for the "Homely," which his friend Arthur Greeves helped to nurture (157). Later in chapter sixteen, the crew of the *Dawn Treader* will encounter a beauty so extraordinary that they will not want to eat or sleep but simply gaze on it. Yet here at the start of chapter five, it is beauty of the everyday type that makes Lucy feel most fortunate.

## The Storm Struck

Two paragraphs after readers are told of Lucy thinking she was the most fortunate girl in the world, the narrator shifts gears to announce, "But this pleasant time did not last" (67). Then we find the kind of short but powerful description typical of Lewis. A "great rack of clouds" builds in the west, the air grows cold, and the sea takes on an ominous "drab or yellowish color like dirty canvas" (68). In a vivid pair of sentences, Lewis heightens the tension, stating, "The ship seemed to move uneasily as if she felt danger behind her. The sail would be flat and limp one minute and wildly full the next."

Drinian calls for Lucy to get below, and Lewis, in one of his more gender-neutral statements, comments that Lucy, "knowing that landsmen—and landswomen—are a nuisance to the crew, began to obey" (69). With difficulty, Lucy is finally able to get inside the cabin and to shut out the sight of the ship rushing into the dark. But she cannot shut out the noises, the "horrible confusion of creakings, groanings, snappings, clatterings, roarings and boomings," which sound even more alarming below than they previously had on deck.

Readers may wonder how an Oxford don writing from his second-floor study in the landlocked suburb of Headington Quarry—a middle-aged scholar who was very much a homebody—was able to provide his readers with such a lifelike description of a storm at sea. One answer is that from the time he could first read, Lewis had read and reread tales of sea voyages—works such as *The Odyssey*, *The Aeneid*, *The Tempest*, and *Gulliver's Travels*—which would have given him imaginative exposure to the dramatic conditions the ocean can produce.

A second answer is that as a youth, Lewis made many journeys on literal seas as well as imaginative ones. In *Surprised by Joy*, he notes that from the time he was first sent to school in England at the age of nine, through the time he was a student at Oxford, he sailed across the Irish Sea six times a year on visits to Little Lea, the family home in Belfast. These numerous crossings produced vivid images of the sea that were always with him. He writes that if he closed his eyes, he could always see the "phosphorescence of a ship's wash" and the "long salmon-colored rifts of dawn or sunset on the horizon of cold gray-green water" (149).

Lucy's love for the sea reflects Lewis's own passion. In a letter written near the time he was writing *The Voyage of the Dawn Treader*, Lewis confessed, "I *do* like salt water in all its forms; from a walk on the beach in winter when there is not a soul in sight, or seen washing past (rather like beaten copper) from the deck of a ship, or knocking one head over heels in great green, ginger-beer colored waves" (*Letters of C. S. Lewis* 393).

On Lewis's very first trip across the Irish Sea, he encountered a storm, though it was not as severe as the one he depicts here in *The Voyage of the Dawn Treader*. In *Surprised by Joy*, he writes of that first sea voyage taken with his brother, Warnie, on a September evening in 1908: "It is a rough night and my brother is seasick. I absurdly envy him this accomplishment" (23). Lewis confesses that throughout his life, he was "an obstinately good sailor" (24). If Lucy mirrors Lewis's own love for the sea and his ability to tolerate rough waters without getting ill, perhaps the realistic depiction of Eustace's seasickness comes from Warnie's predisposition.

## "I Have Had a Ghastly Time"

Next we find a second—and, as it turns out, the final—series of diary entries from Eustace. Here once again he complains of life on board ship, though this time his complaints are intensified by the discomforts caused by the storm. In his typically self-absorbed manner, Eustace writes, "I have had a ghastly time, up and down enormous waves hour after hour, usually wet to the skin, and not even an *attempt* at giving us proper meals" (70).

Earlier it was argued that we can see a bit of the young Lewis in Eustace, in his priggishness and self-centeredness. Lewis, who was always quite honest about his shortcomings, actually might have argued that there was something of himself in all of his villains.

In the preface to the 1961 edition of *The Screwtape Letters*, Lewis explains where he got the ideas for his evil main character: "Some have paid me an undeserved compliment by supposing that my *Letters* were the ripe fruit of many years' study in moral and ascetic theology. They forget that there is an equally reliable, though less creditable, way of learning how temptation works. 'My heart'—I need no other's—'showeth me the wickedness of the ungodly'" (xiii). The reference here to Psalm 36:1 suggests that the source for the wickedness Lewis depicts in his antagonists was himself primarily and others only secondarily.

Of course, Lewis was not as bad as Eustace—at least not as consistently bad. By way of comparison, we can take Eustace's complaining in the diary entry cited above and contrast it with the much less strident complaining about conditions at sea that can be found in Lewis's own diary, *All My Road Before Me*. In the entry for October 11, 1923, Lewis writes, "I crossed last night from Ireland after nearly three weeks at Little Lea. . . . I had a single berth room on the boat deck. It had been so rough that, though I am never sea sick, I was woken up by the rolling and kept awake most of the night" (271).

In another entry, this one from January 9, 1927, Lewis records a mild complaint about the stifling conditions he and his brother had to endure on another crossing: "Called at quarter to seven on the Fleetwood boat, by which Warnie and I crossed last night from Ireland. We had single berth rooms each on deck, but terribly stuffy because the steward had insisted on screwing up the windows in anticipation of a storm which never happened" (426).

In this second set of diary entries from Eustace, we again find that the two most prominent elements are his self-centeredness and his total blindness to it. Thus we find him making statements such as "Caspian and Edmund are simply brutal to me" (71), "very short rations for dinner and I got less than anyone" (72), and "I always try to consider others whether they are nice to me or not" (73). Perhaps the most ironic comment occurs near the end of the entry for September 6, where Eustace characterizes Caspian as an "odious stuck-up prig" (74).

As is revealed in his diary, Eustace, at least on the surface, does not have a totally different morality from the others—for example, he does not put forward brutality or a lack of consideration for others as virtues. We see this fact in his complaint "Caspian and Edmund are simply brutal to me," and in his bragging that he "thought it would be selfish" to wake the others to ask for a drink and so he "took great care not to disturb Caspian and Edmund" (73). What differs is Eustace's unfairness in applying these standards to others and not himself. As Lewis writes in *Mere Christianity*, when people violate one of their own standards, they nearly always assert that their actions do not really go against the standard or that there is "some special excuse" (3). This is exactly the pattern Eustace follows in rationalizing his theft of water during the night, claiming, "I never *dreamed* that this water-rationing would apply to a sick man" (73).

## What Awaited Them on the Island

It is interesting that Lewis titles this chapter "The Storm and What Came of It." What exactly comes from the storm? Because of the damage the storm causes, the crew must land at Dragon Island. Because they land at Dragon Island, Eustace undergoes his dramatic transformation. Thus once again we find that what seems to be a bad thing—the storm and the damage to the ship—is actually a good thing, because it and nothing else, it seems, leads to Eustace's deliverance. Lewis indicates that this second part of the chapter title refers to Eustace by having his narrator tell us, "What awaited them on this island was going to concern Eustace more than anyone else" (75).

Just as it could be argued that earlier Eustace entered Narnia through his own volition when he decided to attack the picture in the bedroom, here, after the crew of the *Dawn Treader* lands on the island, we could again argue that Eustace's transformation into a dragon occurs as a result of a series of decisions he makes—the first of which is his decision to slip away and avoid the work needing to be done. Readers are told that "a delightful idea" occurred to him (78): "Why shouldn't he simply slip away? . . . He at once put his plan into action."

We are a bit surprised when Eustace, who is not known for his perseverance, is both able and willing to keep plugging away steadily at the steep and slippery climb that leads from the shore and the labor being done there. Lewis explains, "This showed, by the way, that his new life, little as he suspected it, had already done him some good; the old Eustace, Harold and Alberta's Eustace, would have given up the climb after about ten minutes" (79). This remark provides a reminder that there has been a purpose for all of Eustace's adventures in Narnia. This purpose has been, and continues to be, to do some good for him.

Having said this, the fact that Eustace, with no pang of conscience, can leave behind the crew—described here as "lean, pale, red-eyed from lack of sleep, and dressed in rags" (78)—to do all the work while he himself has a day of loafing shows that while his new life in Narnia has done him *some* good, there remains much more to be done for him and to him.

Eustace's plan is to stroll inland, to find "a cool, airy place up in the mountains" (78), and then to sleep all day while his shipmates toil. After reaching the ridge, Eustace finds himself not with the spectacular view he had anticipated but wrapped in a fog Lewis describes as "thick but not cold" (79). In some readers this oddly warm fog may conjure up a feeling of the underworld and hints of the death and rebirth to come. This fog also has a feeling of providence, since without it Eustace would never have gotten lost and so presumably would never have stumbled on the dragon's lair.

Wrapped in the clouds, Eustace lies down and attempts to find "the most comfortable position to enjoy himself" (79). However, we are told he "didn't enjoy himself, or not for very long," and here we see the seeds of his inner transformation already beginning to take hold. We learn that Eustace "began, almost for the first time in his life, to feel lonely." Readers may remember a similar moment in Edmund's conversion in *The Lion, the Witch and the Wardrobe*. When the White Witch turned a group of merrymakers into stone, the narrator commented, "Edmund for the first time in this story felt sorry for someone besides himself" (117).

A few points can be made about these two passages. It should be noted that Lewis qualifies both assertions, and in doing so he makes his antagonists more realistic. Here Eustace begins *almost* for the first time in his life to feel lonely—he is not inhuman; he has felt lonely before, just not very often. Similarly, though Edmund felt sorry for the party in the woods, he had felt compassion before—simply not in *The Lion, the Witch and the Wardrobe*.

Lewis will depict a similar turning point for Aravis in *The Horse and His Boy* and will use similar phrasing. Readers will be told that Aravis "was so tired of Lasaraleen's silliness by now that, for the first time, she began to think that traveling with Shasta was really rather more fun than fashionable life in Tashbaan" (103). In this passage and the one describing Eustace, the key word is *began*. Lewis will always depict radical inner change as being something that takes place gradually, not overnight.

So at this point, Eustace worries, "Perhaps the others had gone. Perhaps they had let him wander away on purpose simply in order to leave him behind!" (79). In his essay from *The Chronicles of Narnia and Philosophy*, Kevin Kinghorn points out, "When we observe other people's actions, it is only natural for us to assume that their reasons for acting are the same as ours would be if we were acting as they are" (23). Therefore, Kinghorn argues, "Eustace believes that the others might leave him because, frankly, this is the kind of thing he would do." In *The Magician's Nephew*, Lewis will make much the same point, as the narrator states, "What you see and hear depends a good deal on where you are standing: it also depends on what sort of person you are" (136). Eustace imagines the crew deserting him here because he is the sort of person who would desert others. Thus his response says more about him than it does about the crew.

Readers found a similar moment in *Prince Caspian*, when Nikabrik insisted they kill Caspian because, according to Nikabrik, the young prince was sure "to go back to its own kind and betray us all" (67). Nikabrik, like Eustace, was arguing from his own set of values, and his accusations, like Eustace's suspicions, revealed a great deal about him. Going back to his own kind and betraying those different from him was exactly what Nikabrik, one of Lewis's most racist characters, would do himself. Here in *The Voyage of the Dawn Treader*, the narrator will make the statement that if Eustace "had understood Caspian and the Pevensies at all he would have known, of course, that there was not the least chance of their doing any such thing" (80–81). But unfortunately, Eustace does not understand Caspian and the Pevensies, any more than Nikabrik understood Caspian.

In *The Two Towers*, Tolkien explores this same issue in a scene where Gandalf is talking to Aragorn, Gimli, and Legolas about what Sauron knows and about what he cannot understand. Gandalf explains:

> The Enemy, of course, has long known that the Ring is abroad, and that it is borne by a hobbit. He knows now the number of our Company that set out from Rivendell, and the kind of each of us. But he does not yet perceive our purpose clearly. He supposes that we were all going to Minas Tirith; for that is what he would himself have done in our place. And according to his wisdom it would have been a heavy stroke against his power. . . . That we should wish to cast him down and have *no* one in his place is not a thought that occurs to his mind. (485–86)

In John 1:5 this topic of the limited ability of the wicked to understand the motivations of the good is put this way: "The light shines in the darkness, but the darkness has not understood it." In *The Screwtape Letters*, Lewis has Screwtape complain about this lack of understanding as he writes to his nephew, "Once more, the inexplicable meets us. . . . If only we could find out what He is really up to!" (175).

Similarly, Eustace is unable to comprehend that the others would never leave him. He leaps up "in a panic" to make the descent back down (79), but because of the fog that has now closed in, he cannot see the bay or the ship. He gets lost and ends up in an unknown valley with the sea nowhere in sight. In the next chapter, readers will learn that this is not just any random valley but the valley where he will find the dragon's hoard. We will also be told there that despite the thick fog, Eustace "apparently" and "by amazing luck" has found "the only possible way" down into this valley (83).

But in Narnia there is no such thing as luck. Providence has brought Eustace to Narnia and to this specific place for a specific purpose.

## Discussion Questions

Near the start of chapter five, we were told Lucy thought she was the most fortunate girl in the world, not due to anything spectacular, but simply because of the good, ordinary times she experiences on board the *Dawn Treader*.

1. Where else in the Chronicles do we find Lewis depicting good, ordinary times as worthy of esteem?

2. What are the good, ordinary elements in your own life that cause you, like Lucy, to feel fortunate?

In this chapter's title, "The Storm and What Came of It," we see that once again what seems to be a bad thing—the storm and the damage it causes—will actually be a good thing since it will lead to Eustace's deliverance. We saw this same limited perception during the slavery episode in chapter three, when Lucy begged for the group not to be separated.

3. Where else in the Chronicles do we find similar examples of limited perception, where something seems to be a negative at the time, but turns out later to be a positive?

4. Where in your own life has a negative become a positive?

In this chapter, we read that Eustace's new life has already done him some good. As noted earlier, in *The Silver Chair*, Lewis will have Puddleglum declare to Jill and Eustace, "I'm coming, sure and certain. I'm not going to lose an opportunity like this. It will do me good" (75). In *Surprised by Joy*, Lewis lists a number of books he read as a young person and declares that *The Amulet* by Nesbit was the book that did the most for him.

5. What experiences, books, or people—positive or negative— have done you some good?

6. Were there times when you, like Eustace, did not suspect the good that was being done? If so, how did you finally come to see it?

Near the close of the chapter, readers were told that if Eustace had understood Caspian and the Pevensies at all, he would have known there was no chance of them leaving him behind.

7. Where else in the Chronicles or in life can we find examples of the wicked not being able to understand the good?

## SIX

# The Adventures of Eustace

## Down in the Unknown Valley

Chapter six opens with a structure that may remind readers of a scene from another Chronicle. After a tiring journey, our heroes sit down and enjoy a wonderful meal only to find near the end that one of them has gone missing. In *The Lion, the Witch and the Wardrobe*, after a long walk and a delicious supper with Mr. and Mrs. Beaver, Lucy suddenly asked, "I say—where's Edmund?" (82). Here in *The Voyage of the Dawn Treader*, after everyone has washed up and had a "merry meal" (82), Edmund exclaims, "Where's that blighter Eustace?" By having Eustace continue to mirror Edmund's earlier situation as the black sheep in the bunch and to make a similar disappearance, Lewis sets the stage for the encounter that Eustace will have with Aslan, a meeting that parallels the one Edmund had.

After Eustace's difficult descent in the fog, a hot sun comes out, and Eustace decides he "better have a good drink" from the pool in the valley before attempting to return (83). Hearing a noise, Eustace turns to see an ancient, decrepit dragon crawl out of its den and expire right in front of him. Moments later while Eustace is getting his drink, there is a "peal of thunder," and "big drops of rain" begin to fall (86), causing him to take refuge in the dragon's lair.

Here at the start of chapter six, we again find a *seeming* coincidence of perfect timing in the rapid change in conditions. Dry weather allows Eustace to hike off. Foggy weather causes him to lose his way back. Then hot and sunny weather makes him want to go down to the valley floor for a drink. Finally, rainy weather forces him to take shelter in the dragon's lair.

Paul Ford has noted that "only in *The Last Battle* is Aslan less on scene than in *The Voyage of the Dawn Treader*" (66). If Aslan is "on scene" for so little time in this third Chronicle, it could also be argued that Aslan has been very present behind the scenes in the providential timing of events we have witnessed: in the Narnian picture coming to life at just the right moment, in Lord Bern's opportune arrival to free Caspian, and here in the weather conditions that bring Eustace to the dragon's lair.

This providential timing—of the weather or other occurrences—can be found at other times in the Chronicles. In the first chapter of *The Lion, the Witch and the Wardrobe*, the children woke to find a rain "so thick that when you looked out of the window you could see neither the mountains nor the woods nor even the stream in the garden" (5). By preventing outdoor activities, the rain led to Lucy entering the wardrobe and Narnia. Later in chapter five, the providential appearance of Mrs. Macready and the group of visitors forced the children to take shelter in the wardrobe. As Peter flung open the wardrobe, he exclaimed, "Quick! There's nowhere else" (53).

Here in *The Voyage of the Dawn Treader*, readers can find interesting parallels to the scene with Mrs. Macready. "In less than a minute," Eustace becomes "wet to the skin and half blinded with such rain as one never sees in Europe" (86–87). Then we are told, "He bolted for the only shelter in sight—the dragon's cave" (87).

In unlikely coincidences such as these, David Mills has suggested we find "either a study in Providence or a horribly contrived plot" (23). Most readers of the Chronicles see providence in the timing of incidents like these, not poor writing. Several pages later, Eustace will complain about the showers, referring to them as "this infernal rain" (88), but we might see a very different source behind the downpour that has driven him into the dead dragon's cave. In *The Magician's Nephew*, Lewis will again make use of seemingly coincidental rain showers. Readers will meet a boy named Digory and a girl named Polly whose adventures begin "chiefly because it was one of the wettest and coldest summers there had been for years" (7).

Seemingly insignificant weather that in retrospect had a great impact was an element also used by Tolkien in *The Fellowship of the Ring*. We read that Sam "had a good deal to think about. For one thing, there was a lot to do up in the Bag End garden, and he would have a busy day tomorrow, if the weather cleared" (44). As David Mills has noted, "Because the weather is good, Sam can work in the garden, and because he can work in the garden, he can sneak under the window and listen to Gandalf and Frodo's discussion of the Ring. Because he listens to it, he gets caught doing so, and because he gets caught doing so, he is ordered to go with Frodo" (24). According to Mills, because of the providential weather that morning, Sam goes on the quest and helps Frodo "in ways that no one else could have," and the Ring "is destroyed against all odds."

Here in *The Voyage of the Dawn Treader*, Lewis has the weather play a similar role in the outcome of events.

## Inside the Dragon's Cave: "To Find All You Seek"

Earlier it was noted that *The Voyage of the Dawn Treader*, far more than the other Chronicles, is largely episodic, with events taking place primarily based on where the ship goes and the circumstances the crew encounters. However, starting with chapter six, we can begin to see evidence of what could be seen as an overall unifying structure. Earlier Reepicheep's verse promised, "Doubt not, Reepicheep, / To find all you seek" (21). Events in the coming chapters will allow the other four main characters—Eustace, Caspian, Edmund, and Lucy—to find and be tempted by something they each have been seeking.

Here in chapter six, Eustace, through his dragon form and the pile of treasure, will find avenues to power and self-indulgence—two ends he has been seeking. When the crew puts in at Deathwater Island in chapter eight, Caspian and Edmund will be tempted with the power of command, a temptation Caspian must wrestle with in the final chapter as well. In chapter ten, Lucy will find a way to become more beautiful than Susan as well as a way to know what her friends say about her. The fact that Eustace, Edmund, Caspian, and Lucy find these various temptations so hard to resist suggests that these are things they have been seeking after, at least subconsciously.

Here inside the dead dragon's cave, Eustace discovers a treasure hoard of "crowns, coins, rings, bracelets, ingots, cups, plates and gems" (87)—objects that epitomize greed since the dragon has no possible use for them, only the desire that *he* have them rather than someone else. As Jonathan Rogers has noted, "A dragon's life is devoted to guarding that which cannot do him any good. No hope of happiness from his hoard, and yet a mortal fear of losing the least trinket of it" (61).

After sleeping far into the night, Eustace, in one of Lewis's most dramatic passages, comes out to the pool in the moonlight and very gradually discovers not that another dragon has appeared but that "he had turned into a dragon while he was asleep" (91). How exactly did this happen? Lewis's narrator does not offer a very full explanation. Readers are simply told, "Sleeping on a dragon's hoard with greedy, dragonish thoughts in his heart, he had become a dragon himself."

In his depiction of the dragon hoard and its power to enchant, Lewis had a number of sources to draw on—among them a story by his friend J. R. R. Tolkien. In *The Hobbit*, when Bilbo sneaks down into Smaug's lair, he finds a similar trove with "countless piles of precious things, gold wrought and unwrought, gems and jewels" (184).

*The Hobbit* also has an evil spell associated with the dragon's treasure, similar to the one that affects Eustace. Readers are told that gold "upon which a dragon has long brooded" acquires a mysterious power (223). Thorin, the leader of the dwarfs, is particularly susceptible to its spell. As Tolkien's narrator further explains, "Long hours in the past days Thorin had spent in the treasury, and the lust of it was heavy on him." Several pages later, Thorin will have fallen even further under the spell of the dragon's gold, and Tolkien comments, "Strong was the bewilderment of the treasure upon him" (234).

In the summary found near the end of *The Hobbit*, the narrator refers to this evil enchantment as "dragon-sickness" as he recounts, "The old Master had come to a bad end. Bard had given him much gold for the help of the Lake-people, but being of the kind that easily catches such disease he fell under the dragon-sickness, and took most of the gold and fled with it, and died of starvation in the Waste, deserted by his companions" (255).

Here in chapter six of *The Voyage of the Dawn Treader*, Eustace has fallen under a similar spell of dragon-sickness. And unless he can resist it, he will suffer the same fate as the old dragon whose mound he sleeps on: to die alone next to his pile of useless treasure.

At the start of the story, readers were told that "deep down inside," Eustace liked "bossing and bullying" and giving people "a bad time" (4). In becoming a dragon, he has found what he has been seeking. His first thought is that now "he could get even with Caspian and Edmund" (92). As we will discover, this is just his first thought, and it will not last for long.

### "As a Man Thinks in His Heart, So He Is": Eustace's Mythical Predecessors

Eustace's transformation into a dragon and his later return to human form have several mythical antecedents that Lewis, a keen student of myth, would have been familiar with. One of these is the story *Beauty and the Beast*. In some versions of the myth, it is suggested that the Beast—who at some time prior to the story had been a handsome prince—was transformed into a monster as the consequence of his beastly inner condition. His alteration, like that of Eustace, echoes the claim from Proverbs 23:7 that as a man thinks in his heart, so he is. Both transformations are intended to be redemptive and not merely punitive.

Forced by his external alteration to confront his monstrous internal condition, the Beast must undergo an inner transformation in order to reverse the physical change: he must move from a condition of concern only for self to a concern for others, and in doing so win Beauty's love, as demonstrated by her agreeing to marry him. The moment she does this, he is changed back to his princely form.

In both *Beauty and the Beast* and *The Voyage of the Dawn Treader*, there is a two-step outer change: from human form to monster and then back again. However, the real and more significant transformation is the one that takes place in the heart.

A second mythic antecedent can be found in Carlo Collodi's story *Pinocchio*, published in Italian in 1883, translated into English in 1892, and popularized by Disney in 1940. While the puppet longs to become a real boy, he desires even more to travel to the carefree Land of the Boobies. Candlewick, described as "the laziest and the naughtiest boy in the school" (164), persuades Pinocchio to go with him to a country where there are "no schools, no masters, and no books" (165), where every day is spent "in play and amusement from morning till night" (166). After several months in this land of endless self-gratification, living more like an animal than a boy, the puppet wakes to find that he has grown the ears he has earned, and before the day is out he has been completely transformed into a donkey.

Lewis's use of the dragon's pool here in chapter six calls to mind a third mythic predecessor—the myth of Narcissus. Like Eustace, Narcissus is self-absorbed and insensitive to the needs of others. After spurning those around him, Narcissus falls in love with a reflection of himself that he sees in a clear pool of water. Unable to break away from the image, Narcissus pines away and eventually dies. In his place is the white narcissus flower, a plant typically found bending over water. For Narcissus, there is no redemption: he can never leave the pool of self.

Unless he can undergo a change within, Eustace, like Narcissus, will be trapped in his new form. But unlike Narcissus, Eustace now sees himself for what he really is and detests the sight of his own reflection.

## He Began to See

In a well-known passage from *The Problem of Pain*, Lewis describes the way that God uses affliction—the type that Eustace, the Beast, and Pinocchio are faced with—as an instrument in our salvation. Lewis observes that we will not surrender our self-will as long as all seems to be well, and that the deeper "error and sin" are, "the less their victim suspects their existence" (82). Lewis continues:

> But pain insists upon being attended to. God whispers to us in our pleasures, speaks in our conscience, but shouts in our pain: it is His megaphone to rouse a deaf world. . . . Now God, who has made us, knows what we are and that our happiness lies in Him. Yet we will not seek it in Him as long as He leaves us any other resort where it can even plausibly be looked for. While what we call "our own life" remains agreeable we will not surrender it to Him. What then can God do in our interests but make "our own life" less agreeable to us? (83–85)

As Lewis has shown, error and sin are so deeply a part of Eustace that up until now he has been completely unaware of their existence within him.

Lewis writes that the very moment Eustace understands he can now get even with Caspian and Edmund, he has several other important realizations:

He *realized* that he didn't want to. He wanted to be friends. . . . He *realized* that he was a monster cut off from the whole human race. . . . He *began to see* that the others had not really been fiends at all. He *began to wonder* if he himself had been such a nice person as he had always supposed. . . . He *realized* now that Caspian would never have sailed away and left him. (92–93, emphasis added)

Eustace's pain—the pain from the gold arm ring and, even more, the pain of seeing his own hideous reflection—has become Aslan's megaphone, his tool to rouse someone who has been deaf to all other attempts to get his attention and blind to the reality of his inner condition.

Lewis is careful to point out that Eustace's increase in self-awareness, like his change into a less selfish person, does not take place all at once. In addition to the greater understanding that *begins* to take place here in chapter six, Lewis will add this description in the next chapter: "Eustace realized *more and more* that since the first day he came on board he had been an unmitigated nuisance and that he was now a greater nuisance still" (104, emphasis added).

Eustace begins to see what a beast he has been to the others. And they themselves—though initially dismayed by the news Caspian brings late in the night that "a dragon has just flown over the tree-tops and lighted on the beach" (95)—must now come to see that the great beast standing between them and the ship is not a malice-filled dragon intent on doing them harm, but is Eustace.

At first light, the crew members of the *Dawn Treader*, "all with swords drawn, . . . a solid mass with Lucy in the middle," march down to the beach to face the giant lizard (96). Whether we are meant to include Lucy among all those with drawn swords is left unexplained, but certainly there is no talk of leaving her out of the anticipated battle. This would suggest that Lewis's position on females taking part in fighting is more complicated than the statement made by Father Christmas in *The Lion, the Witch and the Wardrobe*, where Susan and Lucy were told they were "not to be in the battle" (109). This scene will be reprised in chapter nine, where Caspian will lead the landing party to their encounter with the invisible voices with the command, "Arrow on the string, Lucy—swords out, everyone else" (137).

As the company draws near, we are told that "instead of rising up and blowing fire and smoke, the dragon retreated" (96). They quickly see that it does not intend to attack them and seems to want to communicate. Finally Reepicheep calls out, "If you will swear friendship with us raise your left foreleg above your head" (97). At once everyone can see that the dragon's leg is "sore and swollen" beneath the golden bracelet Eustace had put on before going to sleep. Overcome by compassion and forgetting her fear, Lucy the Valiant does not hesitate but runs forward to try to ease the dragon's suffering. Her cordial reduces the swelling and eases the pain a little but cannot dissolve the gold—a detail that will become significant later in the next chapter.

## Discussion Questions

In his essay "Aslan Is On the Move: Images of Providence in The Chronicles of Narnia," Russell Dalton argues that *The Voyage of the Dawn Treader* "closely follows the mythic pattern of the heroes' quest" and that in these tales, "the role of providence is present" but is "often a mysterious force that remains deep in the background" (134). Here in chapter six, even the death of the old dragon happens at just the right time—and not a couple hours or a few days later—to allow for Eustace's transformation.

1. Where can you see the role of providence so far in *The Voyage of the Dawn Treader*?

2. Does Lewis's portrait of providence correspond to your own experiences? In what ways?

In *Letters to an American Lady*, Lewis asks, "How many people in the whole world believe themselves to be snobs, prigs, bores, bullies, or tale-bearers?" (59). Now, and only now, Eustace finally comes to see how bad he has been.

3. Why was Eustace unable to see his egregious flaws before?

4. Why is it that Eustace now is able to see himself as he really is?

One of Lewis's most important messages—to his young readers especially, but also to his older ones—is that the self-centered life is not fun, exciting, satisfying, or even very interesting. We saw this previously in the depictions of the White Witch and Miraz, who were never shown as laughing, hanging out with friends, or having a good time. In this chapter, Lewis presents this truth about the selfish life once again in the form of the decrepit dragon, who, despite having everything it wants, in the end dies alone, "an old, sad creature" (85).

5. What other things might Lewis be saying about the self-centered life through his depiction of the old dragon?

6. Why do you think Lewis chose to give his readers this message about the wages of self-centeredness so often?

## SEVEN

# How the
# Adventure Ended

**"You're Not—Not Eustace by Any Chance?"**

Chapter seven continues the action from the previous chapter without a break. Seeing the device stamped on the bracelet the dragon bears, Caspian instantly recognizes it as belonging to Lord Octesian. While it will never be clear whether Octesian was killed by the old dragon or if he died of other causes, Edmund concludes, "I think it's a safe guess that Octesian got no further than this island" (99).

Although the recognition goes by rather quickly, identifying the bracelet as having belonged to Octesian is critical to the quest to find all seven lords—alive or dead. It also adds a further layer of meaning to the title of chapter five, "The Storm and What Came of It." Now the storm can be seen as necessary not only for Eustace's redemption but also for successful completion of the *Dawn Treader*'s mission. Without the storm, the ship would not have needed to come ashore for repairs, and the whereabouts of Octesian might never have been discovered.

Identifying the bracelet is also critical for the realistic identification of the dragon as Eustace. When asked—because of the bracelet—if he has "devoured a Narnian lord" (99), the dragon that is Eustace shakes his head. Next Lucy asks—again because of the presence of the bracelet—if perhaps he is Octesian under an enchantment. The dragon again shakes his head, but does so "sadly" this time. This curious response leads Lucy to ask, "Are you someone enchanted—someone human, I mean?" At this point, the dragon nods violently. Given the fact that Eustace has been missing since the day before and the fact that they now know that the dragon is a human under a spell, it now seems very logical when someone—we are not told who—asks, "You're not—not Eustace by any chance?" (100).

After learning the truth of the dragon's identity, the crew of the *Dawn Treader* is quick to offer their consolations. Readers are told, "Nearly everyone said 'Hard luck' and several assured Eustace that they would all stand by him" (100). Lucy, again showing her courage and compassion, goes beyond just words and kisses the scaly face.

In the previous chapter, it was clear that Eustace's attitudes changed for the better almost immediately following his external change into dragon form. The very moment he realized he could get even with Caspian and Edmund, he also realized that "he didn't want to" but instead "wanted to be friends" (92). The others are quick to see this change. We are told that it is clear to everyone that Eustace's character has been "rather improved by becoming a dragon" and that now he is "anxious to help" (101). In this second detail, Lewis creates a stark contrast to the last action of the old Eustace trying to get out of work, showing just how different he now is.

Eustace, as a dragon, is more than happy to provide food for provisioning the ship's empty stores. One day, he returns from a distant valley, "flying slowly and wearily but in great triumph" (101), with a great pine tree to replace the broken mast. In *The Problem of Pain*, Lewis argues that the more virtuous people become, the more they enjoy virtuous actions (89). This was seen after Edmund's transformation in *The Lion, the Witch and the Wardrobe*, where one of his first actions was to selflessly fight his way "through three ogres" and smash the witch's wand in the Battle of Beruna (178). Here too, Eustace enjoys being "a comfort to everyone" on chilly evenings as "the whole party would come and sit with their backs against his hot sides" (101–2).

Despite his newfound pleasure "of being liked and, still more, of liking other people" (102), we are told that Eustace shudders at his hideous reflection and is "almost afraid to be alone with himself," but at the same time he is also "ashamed to be with the others." So on evenings when his heat is not needed, he slinks off by himself. At these times, to Eustace's surprise, it is his former adversary Reepicheep who becomes his friend, telling him stories of other turns of "Fortune's wheel" that had affected "emperors, kings, dukes," and others (103). Here, as Doris Myers notes, Lewis, through Reepicheep, is giving voice to "the medieval-renaissance tradition of Boethian philosophy," a set of beliefs that had an impact on Lewis's own thinking (146).

In 1962, when asked by *The Christian Century* for a list of the books that did the most to shape his vocational attitude and philosophy of life, Lewis listed ten works, among them *Phantastes* by George MacDonald, *The Everlasting Man* by G. K. Chesterton, and *Descent into Hell* by fellow Inkling Charles Williams. Also appearing on this list was *The Consolation of Philosophy* by the Roman philosopher and theologian Boethius, who lived from AD 480 to 524. In Book II of *The Consolation of Philosophy*, we find this passage about the fickleness of Fortune, which Reepicheep's words echo: "When Fortune turns her wheel with her proud right hand, she is as unpredictable as the flooding Euripus; at one moment she fiercely tears down mighty kings, at the next the hypocrite exalts the humbled captive" (18–19). As Marvin Hinten has observed, "Appropriately, considering the title of Boethius's work, Reepicheep is using this same concept to console Eustace with philosophy" (37).

Despite the importance he gave the book, in the end Lewis may have had some doubts about the power of philosophy to console, since the narrator offers the following comment about Reepicheep's words: "It did not, perhaps, seem so very comforting at the time, but it was kindly meant and Eustace never forgot it" (103). Alternatively, perhaps Lewis is suggesting that one has to be at a certain maturity level to be consoled by philosophy and that Eustace is not there yet.

## Never Having Read the Right Books

In the days that follow, Eustace tries "more than once" to write out in the sand the story of what happened (100). But, as we are told, "Eustace (never having read the right books) had no idea how to tell a story straight." This makes the fifth time in *The Voyage of the Dawn Treader* where Lewis has raised the need for young people to read—not just books, but the right books. All told, the value of reading will be mentioned by Lewis seven times in *The Voyage of the Dawn Treader*, and the frequency with which he returns to this topic reveals the importance it had for him.

Back in chapter one, readers were told that Eustace liked books "if they were books of information and had pictures of grain elevators or of fat foreign children doing exercise in model schools" (3), clearly not the kind of books Lewis would have recommended as essential for young people. In one of his diary entries in chapter five, Eustace recorded how he needed Edmund to explain what Caspian meant when he declared that anyone stealing water would "get two dozen" (74). In a condescending aside, Eustace explained how Edmund happened to know what the phrase meant: "It comes in the sort of books those Pevensies read."

In chapter six, as the old dragon came out of its cave, the narrator commented, "Edmund or Lucy or you would have recognized it at once, but Eustace had read none of the right books" (84). Lewis's narrator revisited this point several pages later, stating, "Most of us know what we should expect to find in a dragon's lair, but, as

I said before, Eustace had read only the wrong books. They had a lot to say about exports and imports and governments and drains, but they were weak on dragons" (87).

The benefits of reading the right kind of stories will be highlighted again in chapter eight, when Edmund, "the only one of the party who had read several detective stories" (124), will be the first to realize that the remains of Lord Restimar could not have come from a fight. Lewis will mention the importance of reading a final time in chapter thirteen, when Eustace will volunteer to stay overnight at Aslan's table. This, readers will be told, "was very brave of him because never having read of such things or even heard of them till he joined the *Dawn Treader* made it worse for him than for the others" (197).

In *The Magician's Nephew*, Digory—who, like Edmund, has a greater awareness from having read the right books—will be able to quickly recognize his malicious uncle for what he is, telling him, "You're simply a wicked, cruel magician like the ones in the stories" (27). Because of his reading, Digory will also be able to accurately predict, "Well, I've never read a story in which people of that sort weren't paid out in the end" (27–28). Finally, readers may remember that in *The Lion, the Witch and the Wardrobe*, reading the right books allowed Peter to be able to correctly identify the robin as being on their side, as he told Edmund, "They're good birds in all the stories I've ever read" (61).

So what exactly is Eustace—or anyone else—missing by not having read the right books? One of Eustace's most fundamental flaws is a narrow viewpoint, one that is bounded and surrounded by self. As Lewis notes in *An Experiment in Criticism*, "Each of us by nature sees the whole world from one point of view with a perspective and selectiveness peculiar to himself" (137). Lewis maintains that reading great books provides an antidote for this natural narrowness: "One of the things we feel after reading a great work is 'I have got out'" (138).

In a diary entry made on July 4, 1926, Lewis noted that he was rereading *The Well at the World's End* by William Morris. He observed that "what are now quite big things in one's mental outfit" can often be traced to books read when one is young (*All My Road* 421). Lewis thought it plausible that his adult feelings for nature had at least partially come out of "the brief, convincing little descriptions of mountains and woods" that he had read in Morris's book as a youth.

In *Surprised by Joy*, Lewis begins, "I am a product of . . ." and then provides a list of elements that had played a foundational role in his life (10). He mentions items such as long corridors, empty sunlit rooms, attics explored in solitude, and "the noise of wind under the tiles." He concludes the list with the statement that he is also the product of "endless books," acknowledging the vital part that books had played in making him who he was.

### The Undragoning of Eustace: Beginning

After six days on what they now call Dragon Island, Edmund wakes to find "a dark figure moving on the seaward side of the wood" (104). It is Eustace, now transformed back into a boy, but so changed that at first Edmund "thought it was Caspian." This may seem a small detail, but the fact that the new Eustace may be mistaken for the young king says a great deal about him. The encounter goes like this:

> The stranger said in a low voice, "Is that you, Edmund?"
> "Yes. Who are you?" said he.
> "Don't you know me?" said the other. "It's me—Eustace."
> "By jove," said Edmund, "so it is." (105)

Edmund's failure to recognize Eustace is understandable, and the exchange is full with meaning. Eustace is not the boy he was but instead the boy he was meant to be, and so is only now truly Eustace. Gradually he shares with Edmund the details surrounding his return to his original form, or as he says, the story of how he stopped being a dragon.

Eustace tells of his meeting with Aslan and their journey to a garden on the top of a mountain. Are they high in Aslan's country, as Eustace and Jill will be at the start of *The Silver Chair*, or just somewhere deep within the island? The information Lewis provides makes it impossible to say for sure one way or the other. Paul Ford argues that we can find some similarities—Eustace is de-dragoned by Aslan in a mountaintop garden, and the garden in *The Magician's Nephew* and *The Last Battle* is located at the top of a steep green hill—but because of other differences, "it is not clear whether Lewis intended the garden in *The Voyage of the Dawn Treader* to be the same as the garden in *The Magician's Nephew* and *The Last Battle*" (221). Earlier we were told that Eustace flew "over the whole island and found that it was all mountainous" (101), but he never mentions seeing a garden or a well anywhere. Here he explains to Edmund that the lion, at this point still unnamed, led him "a long way into the mountains" until, as Eustace states, "we came to the top of a mountain I'd never seen before" (107). In the end, the most we can do is to reach the same conclusion as Paul Ford, who simply calls this location a "mysterious mountaintop" (67).

Aslan shows Eustace a well and—in a way that does not use words—tells him that he must undress before bathing in the healing waters. As a dragon who is not wearing clothes, Eustace understands this to mean that he must remove his scaly skin, like a snake. And so he peels off a layer of his dragon hide and starts to go down into the well only to find that there is another layer of dragon skin beneath the one he has removed.

Eustace tells Edmund what happens next, and this passage merits careful reading if we are to understand what Lewis is saying through it. Eustace continues:

> "Oh, that's all right, said I, it only means I had another smaller suit on underneath the first one, and I'll have to get out of it too. So I scratched and tore again and this under-skin peeled off beautifully and out I stepped and left it lying beside the other one and went down to the well for my bathe.
>
> "Well, exactly the same thing happened again. And I thought to myself, oh dear, how ever many skins have I got to take off? For I was longing to bathe my leg. So I scratched away for the third time and got off a third skin, just like the two others, and stepped

out of it. But as soon as I looked at myself in the water I knew it had been no good.

"Then the lion said—but I don't know if it spoke—'You will have to let me undress you.'" (108)

First, it should be noted that on his own, Eustace is, in some measure, successful in ridding himself of several layers of his dragonish nature. He is partially able to "undress" himself—but only partially. He frees himself of one dragon skin, then a second, and then a third. Thus Lewis seems to suggest that humans, after they have seen the error of their ways, may be able to improve somewhat on their own, but not to the full degree needed. Lewis shows that Eustace can shed the surface layers of his dragon nature somewhat easily, without much pain and without Aslan's help. The deeper layers will be just the opposite.

A number of Lewis scholars see this point differently. In *The Way into Narnia*, Peter Schakel claims, "Three times Eustace peels off his dragon skin, and three times it grows right back" (64), as though Eustace accomplishes absolutely nothing on his own. Similarly, Jonathan Rogers asserts that "the dragon hide grows back before he can get into the baptismal pool" (64). Both readings differ slightly from Eustace's own interpretation that he finds he has "another smaller suit on underneath the first one" (108).

Evan Gibson offers this comment on the scene: "The process of 'undragoning' Eustace expresses a truth which most adult readers probably recognize immediately. Man's unassisted efforts to change himself always result in failure" (170). Lewis's point actually seems to be somewhat more nuanced than this, and may be better stated as: man's unassisted efforts to change himself may result in a limited success, but not one that goes to the heart of the problem. Paul Ford makes this distinction, noting that Eustace "tries three times and fails to really remove his dragonishness" (67).

In *The Letters of C. S. Lewis to Arthur Greeves*, we find a moving account of Lewis's own spiritual transformation, one that mirrors Eustace's attempt here to remove layer after layer of dragon skin. Lewis writes about his battle with his "besetting sin" of pride and observes, "I have found out ludicrous and terrible things about my own character. . . . There seems to be no end to it. Depth under depth of self love and self admiration" (339).

Marvin Hinten has explained Eustace's efforts this way: "Despite several sheddings of skin . . . he is unable to change himself, thereby making one of Lewis's favorite theological points from his adult nonfiction, that Christianity is not simply a matter of self-improvement but of becoming something entirely different" (38).

In *Mere Christianity*, Lewis describes the process of transformation and notes that in one sense, the road back to God is a "road of moral effort" that consists of "trying harder and harder" (146). But Lewis points out that this trying is not ever going to bring us home; instead, it leads up to a vital moment when the sinner turns to God and says, "You must do this. I can not." Lewis further explains, "Handing everything over to Christ does not, of course, mean that you stop trying. To trust Him means, of course, trying to do all that He says" (147). This idea will be expressed in the next chapter, where readers will be told that Eustace "had really been trying very hard to behave well" (117).

Thus we see that while Eustace can make some surface changes, ultimately he needs Aslan to change him completely. It is also significant that Eustace definitely has a choice of whether to remain as he is or be transformed. Aslan will not act without his consent, as he tells Eustace, "You will have to let me undress you" (108). And Eustace tells Edmund, "I just lay flat down on my back to let him do it" (109). In *The Screwtape Letters*, Lewis makes this same point about God's way of intervening, mentioned earlier in chapter two—that God cannot ravish but can only woo.

Lewis, through his own experience, knew that the convert always has a choice. In *Surprised by Joy*, he uses the images of a lobster and a suit of armor, which can perhaps be seen as Lewis's own versions of Eustace's dragon shell, and concludes, "I could open the door or keep it shut" (224).

In the transformation of Eustace into a dragon and back into a boy, we are given a moving account of salvation. Lewis makes it clear that Eustace has a choice of whether to accept or to reject the redemption Aslan extends. He can say no to Aslan's offer to undress him and can retain his dragon nature; if so, he can expect the same fate as the old dragon he replaced—to live as his own little god, to follow no laws beyond his own desires, and to die alone and miserable.

Permission is also a critical element for the transformation of the ghosts in *The Great Divorce*. In one of the most memorable encounters in the book, a man with a red lizard on his shoulder, which represents lust, must give his bright angel permission to kill it. To emphasize this point, Lewis has the angel ask not once but nine times if the man wants the lizard killed. When the man asks why the angel does not simply kill the creature without asking, the angel replies, "I cannot kill it against your will. It is impossible. Have I your permission?" (99). Finally the man gives his consent to the painful process, and Lewis as narrator tells us, "Next moment the Ghost gave a scream of agony such as I never heard on Earth."

Eustace's ordeal is equally painful. He tells Edmund, "The very first tear he made was so deep that I thought it had gone right into my heart" (109). After this initial painful tear, there comes a second, more horrible pain—that of "pulling the skin off"—which Eustace describes as hurting "worse than anything I've ever felt." Once the skin is off, there will come yet a third pain of being thrown into the water, an action Eustace claims "smarted like anything."

## The Undragoning of Eustace: Middle

How can anyone endure the terrible pain that dying to old ways brings about? Eustace confesses, "The only thing that made me able to bear it was just the pleasure of feeling the stuff peel off" (109). He then expands this point of how the pain of shedding his dragon skin was compensated by the joy of being relieved of it. He compares the process to picking at an old sore and tells Edmund, "It hurts like billy-oh, but it *is* such fun to see it coming away" (109). Here Edmund interrupts Eustace's story for the first time in three pages to declare, "I know exactly what you mean." We are reminded that Edmund *does* know about the pain of sin and, even more, about the pleasure of repentance. During his own death to old ways in *The Lion, the Witch and the Wardrobe*, Edmund experienced his own version of the process Eustace describes here.

There is a good reason why Lewis has Eustace meet Edmund first, even though Lucy and Reepicheep have been closer to him. Eustace says he will tell the others how he became a dragon, but to Edmund alone he says, "I want to tell you how I stopped being one" (106). The distinction is significant. In *The Lion, the Witch and the Wardrobe*, no one was ever told any of the details of Edmund's meeting with Aslan. As Paul Ford has noted, "Respect for the privacy of 'one's own story' is important in Narnia" (351). Here Lewis may be suggesting an expansion of Aslan's statement to Aravis in *The Horse and His Boy* that "no one is told any story but their own" (202). In this meeting between Edmund and Eustace, Lewis may be saying it can be helpful for sinners with similar histories of transgression and redemption to share their stories with each other. As if to underscore this point, after Eustace is reunited with the rest of the crew, Lewis says that then everyone heard "the earlier part of his story" (111), the story of how Eustace became a dragon—not the second part, which Eustace told only to Edmund.

Though readers know that Edmund is the right choice for Eustace to tell his story to here, Eustace would not have known about Edmund's transformative encounter with Aslan. Perhaps Eustace had simply observed the change that had previously taken place in his cousin and knew Edmund would understand better than the others.

After Edmund's brief interruption, Eustace continues telling his story. The dragon skin is now lying on the grass, but "ever so much thicker, and darker, and knobbly-looking" than the other layers had been (109), suggesting Aslan has removed something that went deeper and was more appalling than what Eustace had been able to shed on his own. Given what we have seen of Eustace, the thick, dark skin might represent the deep-seated pride, selfishness, cruelty, and arrogance that permeated him through and through. Eustace calls it "beastly stuff."

Next to this skin is Eustace himself—although in what form Eustace does not exactly say. He merely states: "And there was I as smooth and soft as a peeled switch and smaller than I had been" (109). Eustace may not have actually been in the form of a boy at that point, for he tells Edmund that he notices he has "turned into a boy again" only after Aslan throws him into the water. So was Eustace supposed to be a disembodied soul? Lewis never makes it clear.

Readers who are tempted to see Aslan's well on the mountaintop as the Narnian form of Christian baptism should remember that unlike baptism in our world, which is for all followers of Christ, this scene is unique in the Chronicles. Eustace is the only one who is taken there and the only one who undergoes a transformation in this way. The flowing water is better seen simply as a universal image of renewal. Similarly, in *The Silver Chair*, a thirsty Jill will be revived by water flowing from a stream, and later Caspian will be returned to life from this same stream. Evan Gibson rightly observes, "We must remind ourselves to resist the temptation to see allegory where Lewis meant only examples and illustrations. These are adventures in another world which convey truth in their own terms. The illustrations may at times run parallel to earthly parables but must not be taken as mirror images of them" (170).

Eustace tells Edmund that although initially the water is painful, it quickly becomes "perfectly delicious" (109). Then he notices that all the pain from his arm, a relatively minor woe, is also gone. "And then I saw why. I'd turned into a boy again," Eustace states.

In a comment that goes by rather quickly, we are given further evidence that the inner transformation Eustace has undergone is genuine. He tells Edmund, "You'd think me simply phony if I told you how I felt about my own arms. *I know they've no muscle and are pretty mouldy compared with Caspian's*, but I was so glad to see them" (109–10, emphasis added). The old Eustace—like the White Witch and Miraz—never saw any flaws in himself and never acknowledged that someone else might be superior to him in any way.

## The Undragoning of Eustace: End

The lion takes Eustace out of the water and dresses him in "new clothes" (110). While on a symbolic level these clothes signify Eustace's new life, they seem on the literal level to be ordinary Narnian clothes since no one else comments on them.

Anyone still unconvinced of the change in the former record stinker should take note of how he concludes the account of his adventure. Lewis has Eustace finish his story by saying to Edmund, "I'd like to apologize. I'm afraid I've been pretty beastly" (110). Eustace offered Reepicheep an apology back in chapter two, but it was forced and made "sulkily" (35). This time there is no doubt that Eustace's regret is truly felt.

Apologies—the real kind with no excuses—play a key role all through the Chronicles, particularly after meetings with Aslan. In *The Lion, the Witch and the Wardrobe*, Edmund's very first action after his encounter with Aslan was to apologize. Readers were told, "Edmund shook hands with each of the others and said to each of them in turn, 'I'm sorry,' and everyone said, 'That's all right'" (139).

At the end of *The Silver Chair* when Jill meets with Aslan, she will have a similar response. There we will be told that Jill will remember only "how she had made Eustace fall over the cliff, and how she had helped to muff nearly all the signs, and about all the snappings and quarrelings," and she will want to say "I'm sorry" (236). After Aravis has her meeting with the great lion at the end of *The Horse and His Boy*, the first thing she will tell Cor is, "There's something I've got to say at once. I'm sorry I've been such a pig" (204).

With an echo of the Pinocchio story, Edmund tells Eustace, "Between ourselves, you haven't been as bad as I was on my first trip to Narnia. You were only an ass, but I was a traitor" (110).

Pinocchio's redemption mirrors Eustace's in its emphasis on a tough outer skin and a change through a water immersion. After being changed into a donkey, Pinocchio is purchased by a man who, seeing his tough hide, plans to skin Pinocchio to make a drum for the band of his village. The man casts Pinocchio into the sea, intending to drown him, but a short time later when hauling in the rope, he finds not a donkey but a puppet. Pinocchio, like Eustace, has received supernatural help in his change back, as he explains, "The good Fairy, as soon as she saw that I was in danger of drowning, sent immediately an immense shoal of fish, who believing me really to be a little dead donkey, began to eat me" (200). After his tough outer layer has been removed, Pinocchio finds himself back in his original form.

Of course, there is one further transformation for Pinocchio. When the puppet begins thinking in his heart with human compassion, particularly for Geppetto, he turns into a real boy. Pinocchio's second change is both complete and permanent. The novel ends with the boy Pinocchio speaking these words: "How ridiculous I was when I was a puppet! And how glad I am that I have become a well-behaved little boy" (223). The implication is that once changed, Pinocchio never returns to his old ways. The same could be said of the Beast—as we are told that he and Beauty live happily ever after. The change Eustace makes is less absolute and thus more realistic.

Any look at Eustace's outer and inner transformations would be incomplete without a brief look at his life afterward. In the very next chapter, Eustace will be the first to take action as the *Dawn Treader* is encircled by the great sea serpent. Instead of worrying about himself, he will begin to hack away at the monster's coils. Lewis will note, "It is true that he accomplished nothing beyond breaking Caspian's second-best sword into bits, but it was a fine thing for a beginner to have done" (117).

Eustace has undergone a symbolic death to his old self and a rebirth to a new life, but Lewis describes this redemption as taking place gradually over time. Here in chapter seven, we are told, "It would be nice, and fairly nearly true, to say that 'from that time forth Eustace was a different boy.' To be strictly accurate, he began to be a different boy. He had relapses. There were still many days when he could be very tiresome. But most of those I shall not notice. The cure had begun" (112).

And this is Lewis's point. Eustace has *begun* traveling down the right road. He still has further to go—growth is a gradual process and will take time. This is true not only for Eustace but for all of Lewis's characters, and for us as well. In *The Screwtape Letters*, Screwtape discusses the ongoing nature of this kind of change, explaining, "The Enemy will be working from the center outwards, gradually bringing more and more of the patient's conduct under the new standard" (11).

On June 13, 1951—a little more than a year after finishing *The Voyage of the Dawn Treader*—Lewis wrote a letter of encouragement with a number of parallels to Eustace's story, including an echo of his statement "the cure had begun." Lewis reminded his correspondent, "Of course God does not consider you hopeless. If He did He would not be moving you to seek Him (and He obviously is). What is going on in you at present is simply the beginning of the *treatment*" (*Letters of C. S. Lewis* 412).

In *The Problem of Pain*, Lewis sums up his point about the difficult process of transformation with these words: "Pain hurts. That is what the word means. I am only trying to show that the old Christian doctrine of being made 'perfect through suffering' is not incredible" (94). Eustace, through the pain of being transformed into a dragon, is prodded and pushed to see the only path that will lead out of his spiritual misery.

### "Well—He Knows Me"

One minor question is answered in this chapter. After Aslan's sacrifice in *The Lion, the Witch and the Wardrobe*, Lucy and Susan debated whether they should tell Edmund "what the arrangement with the Witch really was" (180). Susan was against this, Lucy for it. Paul Ford has observed, "It is possible that Lucy won her argument with Susan and told Edmund what Aslan did for him, for he grows up to be a graver and quieter man than Peter" (162). Here in *The Voyage of the Dawn Treader*, Edmund explains to Eustace who Aslan is, telling him, "He is the great Lion, the son of the Emperor-beyond-the-Sea, who saved me and saved Narnia" (110–11). Clearly by this point in time—in some way that is not disclosed—he has learned about the arrangement Aslan made to die in his place.

In Edmund's words, we find a few other items worth noting. First, in answer to Eustace's question about whether Edmund knows Aslan, Edmund replies, "Well—he knows me" (110), a statement that says two things. One, it suggests that Edmund does *not* "know" Aslan; at least, he does not *fully* know him, and this was an important lesson the Pevensies learned on their last adventure. In *Prince Caspian*, they came to understand that Aslan is not a tame lion and will do things that they do not expect or even understand—such as appearing to only one of them and not acting in the same way every time. Two, while Edmund may not know Aslan fully, Aslan does know him. What exactly did Aslan say to Edmund during their private conversation in *The Lion, the Witch and the Wardrobe*? Readers never find out. But Edmund's comment here suggests it was something convincing him that Aslan really knew him—in the same way it could be said that Aslan really knows Eustace.

Second, if Lucy was too gracious to tell her siblings, "I told you so," after seeing Aslan not once but twice in *Prince Caspian*, here Edmund sets the record straight. When he explains to his cousin, "We've all seen him," he makes it a point to add that "Lucy sees him most often" (111). Edmund could have stopped after the first statement. The second piece of information about Lucy is not needed, but Edmund feels a reason to add it. By having Edmund say this, Lewis provides a satisfying look back at the events in the previous book and sets up the vision of Aslan that only Lucy will have as the albatross circles the ship in chapter twelve.

Chapter seven ends with Eustace not wanting Octesian's arm ring and offering it to Caspian, who then offers it to Lucy. When

Lucy does not care to have it, Caspian tosses it up in the air for anyone to "catch as catch can" (112). In an odd coincidence, it gets stuck on "a little projection on the rock" as neatly as if it were "a well-thrown quoit" (113), a rubber ring thrown at a peg in a game like darts. We are told, "No one could climb up to get it from below and no one could climb down to get it from above" (113).

While Lewis may have intended this incident simply as a satisfying end to the chapter, he may also be using it to say something about Eustace. If Octesian's arm ring represents one particular sin of Eustace—his greed—then we can say that although Eustace's "disagreeable self" will reappear a bit in the next chapter (115), and although at the end of *The Last Battle*, he will still have "the bad habit of interrupting stories" (163), Eustace will never again be seen to be greedy as he was here on Dragon Island, where he pushed Octesian's golden ring high up on his arm and filled his pockets with diamonds. In this final incident, perhaps Lewis is saying that Eustace is able to completely leave this one aspect of his dragonish nature—his greed—behind him forever.

## Discussion Questions

Eustace's transformation into a dragon and then back into a boy is one of the most well-known episodes in all the Chronicles and also one of the most moving and unforgettable. Donald Glover notes, "How Lewis hit on the transformation of Eustace, the metamorphosis into a dragon, as the first incident in this part of the journey, we can only wonder, but there is no question of its absolute appropriateness" (152).

1. Why do you think this incident is so well known, so effective, and so well liked?

2. What do you think Lewis is saying about the human heart and the process of change through Eustace's transformation into a dragon and then back again?

Throughout his writings, Lewis makes use of a number of comparisons to capture the process of dying to one's former self. Here in *The Voyage of the Dawn Treader*, he suggests that dying to self is like having an old skin torn off and being dressed in new clothes. In *Surprised by Joy*, as was noted, he compares his transformation to removing a suit of armor. Later in that same work, he says the process was like a snowman "at long last beginning to melt" (225). Christ also used a number of images for this process, including that of a seed falling to the ground and dying.

3. Which of these images resonates with your own experience of dying to self? What other images can you think of?

In Eustace's conversion, we find the Chronicles' most detailed account of transformation. At least in this one instance, Lewis suggests that great pain—pain that must be taken seriously—is a part of the process. In *The Problem of Pain*, as noted earlier, Lewis calls pain God's "megaphone to rouse a deaf world" (83). In his essay "Miserable Offenders," Lewis compares the pain of "a serious attempt to repent and really to know one's own sins" to the "great pain" of going to the dentist and having a tooth removed (124), but adds that this pain gets "less and less every moment when you have had the tooth out."

4. How accurate do you think Lewis is in his inclusion of great pain as a part of some—and perhaps even of all—great changes?

The joy and relief Eustace has after his transformation should not be overlooked. When Edmund asks him if his arm is all right, we are told that Eustace laughs with "a different laugh from any Edmund had heard him give before" (106). This laugh as much as anything else makes it clear that Eustace has undergone an inner transformation as great as his external one.

5. What does Eustace's laughter here show about who he has become?

In *Beyond the Shadowlands*, Wayne Martindale, building on an idea from an unpublished paper by Michael Ward, points to the fact that the *Dawn Treader* is a "dragon ship" and maintains that "the undragoning of Eustace is a microcosm of the whole novel" (108).

6. Do you see any connection between the undragoning of Eustace and the fact that Lewis chose to give the ship that the entire crew lives on a prow "shaped like the head of a dragon with wide-open mouth" (6)? If so, how might these be connected?

# EIGHT

# Two Narrow Escapes

## Narrow Escape One: The Sea Serpent

Not every stop on the voyage turns into an adventure. A day out from Dragon Island and under fair winds, the *Dawn Treader* puts ashore briefly so the crew can have a look at "a low green island inhabited by nothing but rabbits and a few goats" (114). A further search turns up only bones, broken weapons, ruins of stone huts, and "blackened places where fires had been," prompting them to name the place Burnt Island. Were any of these fires made by the exiled Narnian lords? Lewis never says. The crew also finds a small coracle, or skin boat, which Reepicheep decides to keep since "it was just the right size for him" (115). Perhaps the valiant mouse is simply tired of being too small for many of the man-sized objects on the ship. Perhaps he has a premonition that he will need the coracle later.

Despite their heroic nature, Lewis makes it clear that, like us, the protagonists in the Chronicles also have their more ordinary, petty sides. Very shortly after their return to Narnia in *Prince Caspian*, the hungry children got into an argument about whether they should have eaten their sandwiches so soon. Readers were told, "One or two tempers very nearly got lost at this stage" (11). They got into another tiff after a long hike when they were unexpectedly stopped by the deep gorge the Rush had carved. Lucy scolded Susan, "Don't nag at Peter like that," and Edmund scolded back, "And don't you snap at Su like that either" (124). Two chapters later, the entire party was annoyed with Lucy's report of seeing Aslan again, primarily because of the irritation of being woken up in the middle of the night.

Here in *The Voyage of the Dawn Treader*, it takes just one day of ordinary raining and two lost games of chess for Eustace to get "like his old disagreeable self" and for Edmund to wish that he and Lucy "could have gone to America with Susan" (115). Through these events Lewis suggests that it is often the small irritations—not the big sacrifices—that lead to most of the bickering and conflict. Lewis makes a similar point in *The Screwtape Letters*, where Screwtape advises Wormwood about the vital importance of the "daily pinpricks" between Wormwood's patient and his mother (11), minor annoyances such as "tones of voice" and "expressions of face" (13).

Finally the rain stops, and off to the ship's stern there appears something like "smooth rounded rocks, a whole line of them with intervals of about forty feet in between" (115). This will be the silly but dangerous sea serpent that will almost sink the *Dawn Treader*, but neither we nor the crew know this yet. Lewis, as storyteller, nearly always will want his readers to walk—or in this case, to sail—*with* his main characters, not out in front of them, and will typically let us know only what they know.

In *The Lion, the Witch and the Wardrobe*, when Mr. Beaver told the children that Aslan was on the move, the narrator was able to jump in to tell readers, "None of the children knew who Aslan was any more than you do" (67). In *Prince Caspian*, when the four children found themselves whisked off the train platform to a deserted island, we were given no more clue that it was Narnia than they were. Here in *The Voyage of the Dawn Treader*, we share the crew's dread and hold our breath with them as they are "pursued by an unknown something" (116). Through this practice of having us know only what the characters know, Lewis allows us to feel what the characters feel and, presumably, to learn what they learn.

The first narrow escape referred to in the chapter's title comes as the great sea serpent reaches the *Dawn Treader* and begins to wrap its coils around the ship. Eustace is the first to act. He draws his sword—Caspian's second best, which has been loaned to him—and begins hacking at the serpent's body with such great force that he breaks the blade "into bits" (117). Eustace has indeed come a long way since chapter two where he hid behind a claim of pacifism to avoid a duel with Reepicheep. Now the former pacifist and former coward leads the charge against the great foe. Readers are told that even though Eustace's efforts are ineffective against the iron-plated hide, nevertheless "it was a fine thing for a beginner to have done."

If we contrast the new, selfless Eustace we find here with the old, selfish one, we can see a fundamental difference. Kath Filmer describes the old Eustace in this way:

> Eustace is concerned only for himself; that is clear from his willingness to take more than his ration of water and so deprive others on the voyage. He seeks to protect himself from reproof or punishment by lying, despite being caught with the cup in his hand, and he protests at the unfairness of the others when they accept a (true) version of the episode from Reepicheep the mouse. At every stage of the event and its consequences, Eustace is seen to be self-serving and greedy. (46)

If right after his transformation back to a boy, Eustace was mistaken for Caspian, now, in drawing his sword and pitting himself against the great sea serpent, he resembles Reepicheep as he appeared in *Prince Caspian*—ready to attack anything no matter what the size.

As mentioned earlier, the Reepicheep we find in *The Voyage of the Dawn Treader* has matured, as all of Lewis's heroes do. In a demonstration of this growth, Reepicheep now calls out, "Don't fight! Push!" Earlier, the valiant mouse would have seen not fighting as a mark on his honor. Here he is concerned with doing what is needed to save the *Dawn Treader*, not what will bring him the greatest glory. If this means simply pushing on the sea serpent's coils, which in effect is pushing the ship forward so it can slip through, then this is the action he will take.

Reepicheep's strategy works, and soon they are safely "running before a fresh breeze" (120), leaving the sea serpent searching the water for the remains of the ship. A cheer is raised for Eustace and Reepicheep, the heroes of the day. Actually, the entire crew, including Lucy—who went for the axe Caspian had requested to chop off the carved stern—has played a role in the adventure. One character who might have played a part but chose not to is Aslan, and his absence is significant. When Susan used her horn to call for help in *The Lion, the Witch and the Wardrobe*, Aslan made it clear that it was important for Peter to face the wolf on his own and in doing so to "win his spurs" (130). Here in the adventure with the sea serpent, Aslan could easily have saved the *Dawn Treader*—directly, through battle as he did with the White Witch, or indirectly, through a puff of wind that would have pushed the ship out of reach. But as seen at other times in the Chronicles, Aslan will not do for our heroes what they need to do for themselves. In this way he allows them to win their spurs, to grow into something more than they were before.

## Narrow Escape Two: Deathwater Island

A few days after the encounter with the sea serpent, weather again plays a providential role in the quest. Earlier the storm forced the *Dawn Treader* to put in for repairs at Dragon Island, where Lord Octesian's arm band was found and Eustace was transformed. Now dangerous winds cause Drinian to suggest they take refuge in a nearby harbor. After "a long row against the gale" (120), they reach safety and anchor offshore at the island where the remains of Lord Restimar will be found. Who can say if our heroes would have come here without the violent winds and rough seas? We can say that once again the weather has brought them to the exact spot they need to be in order to find the next missing lord. Without the rough weather, they might have sailed right by.

The next morning the small boat is sent to shore with several water casks to fill. Two streams empty into the bay, and Drinian initially steers toward the closer one. Suddenly rain begins to pelt down, leading Edmund to suggest they aim for the other stream. Though it is further, he explains, "There are trees there and we'll have some shelter" (121). Drinian reluctantly changes direction for the more distant stream, and Lewis includes this comment about his decision: "He had had an anxious day yesterday, and he didn't like advice from landsmen. But he altered course; and it turned out afterward that it was a good thing he did" (121). The narrator's concluding remark refers to the fact that—as we later discover—the stream they were first headed toward would have turned anything it touched to gold. Had the rain not come up just then, certainly it would have meant the death of one or more of the crew, and so again the weather takes on a special role.

After the casks are filled, Reepicheep, Caspian, Eustace, Edmund, and Lucy decide to climb a nearby hill to "see what could be seen" and then follow Lucy's suggestion to "go along a bit and come down by the other stream, the one Drinian wanted to go to" (122). After fifteen minutes the group arrives at the source of the second stream, "a more interesting place than they had expected," with a small but deep mountain lake surrounded by cliffs except for a channel that flows down to the sea. As they sit down for a rest, they discover the remains of a sword, a mail shirt, a helmet, and a dagger, as well as a few Narnian coins—"all that's left of one of our seven lords," Edmund concludes (123).

As they wonder how he may have died, Edmund, the only one of the group who has read "detective stories" (124), declares that since there are no bones, the missing lord "can't have been killed in a fight," for what enemy would have carried away the body but not the armor? When Lucy suggests that a wild animal might have done exactly that, Edmund—in typical detective fashion—points out that an animal would not have been able to get the mail shirt off.

Lucy, perhaps speaking for them all, suggests that they get away from the place where this unexplained death has occurred. Soon they come to "the little opening where the stream came out of the lake" (124), and here for the third time in as many pages, the weather again plays a key role in the outcome. The narrator states, "If it had been a hot day, no doubt some would have been tempted to bathe and everyone would have had a drink." But it is not hot—earlier, readers were told it was "too cold to stay long on the ridge for the wind still blew freshly from the north" (122). If Aslan is behind the weather here at Deathwater Island—in the way Shasta claims in *The Horse and His Boy* that he "seems to be at the back of all the stories" (208)—it may be through his agency that the rough winds caused the crew to seek shelter in the harbor, the rain caused them to choose the safe stream because of its tree overhang, and the coolness led to no one being tempted to go swimming.

Eustace is the only one interested in a drink. He bends down to scoop up some water in his hands, but just as he is about to touch the surface, Lucy and Reepicheep cry out. On the bottom of the lake is "a life-sized figure of a man, made apparently of gold" (125). After the tip of Caspian's spear and the toes of Edmund's boots are turned to gold by the water, the group realizes that the figure in the pool is not a golden statue but a man who has been turned to gold.

Lucy, feeling compassion for the poor victim's condition, states, "What a horrible thing" (127). Suddenly comprehending the implications of what they have seen, Edmund states, "What a narrow shave *we've* had."

"Narrow indeed," Reepicheep concurs (127). In this repetition of Edmund's conclusion, Lewis reminds readers that had the day been hotter, one or more of the group might have been turned to gold before they realized their danger.

Caspian decides to further test the water's power by dipping a spray of heather into the pool. He draws out "a perfect model of heather made of the purest gold, heavy and soft as lead" (127).

Immediately the gold begins to cast an evil spell. Talking slowly as though speaking aloud his inner thoughts, Caspian says, "The King who owned this island would soon be the richest of all Kings of the world" (127–28). He commands that the others tell no one about the magical water and threatens to kill anyone who disobeys him.

"Who are you talking to? I'm no subject of yours," Edmunds snaps back. "If anything it's the other way round" (128). Caspian puts his hand to his sword, and despite Lucy's request that they stop, things are about to get out of hand when Aslan appears, this time as "the hugest lion that human eyes have ever seen."

Aslan is described as "shining as if he were in bright sunlight though the sun had in fact gone in" (128), and oddly no one can agree on exactly how big he is. Moments later the great lion is gone, and with him all memory of the incident. Some time afterward, Lucy—whose memory of the incident has been magically restored either by intention or through Lewis's mistake—cannot say whether Aslan was "the size of an elephant" or "the size of a cart-horse." In either case, the narrator comments, "It was not the size that mattered."

So what does matter here? Why include the discrepancy about Aslan's size? What are we to make of the fact that he seems to be in bright sunlight?

Aslan's appearance here is more otherworldly than in the previous two stories, and in these details Lewis seems to be preparing us to revise our image of exactly who or what Aslan is. In *Prince Caspian*, the great lion made the famous statement to Lucy, "Every year you grow, you will find me bigger" (141). This promise seems to be holding. Here in *The Voyage of the Dawn Treader*, Aslan will be not merely bigger in size but bigger in substance. In chapter twelve, he will appear as an albatross and in the final chapter as a lamb.

Toward the end of *The Horse and His Boy*, Lewis will continue his hints at Aslan's true nature. Aslan will first appear to Shasta as a lion surrounded by a golden light—somewhat as he does here on Deathwater Island. Then just for a moment before he disappears, the lion's form will change. Readers will be told, "Then instantly the pale brightness of the mist and the fiery brightness of the Lion rolled themselves together into a swirling glory and gathered themselves up and disappeared" (166). What exactly this "swirling glory" is, Lewis leaves unexplained, but the implication is that Aslan is both a lion and something more.

The conflict in this scene, the second of the two narrow escapes, lasts for only four short paragraphs, but Lewis may be saying a number of important things in this brief clash of wills. Back in *Prince Caspian*, when the young prince told his uncle about the kings and queens from Narnia's Golden Age, Miraz ridiculed his nephew's belief in "all those silly stories" (44) and mockingly asked, "How could there be two Kings at the same time?" When kingship is seen merely as a vehicle to advance one's own will and self-interests—which is the way Miraz viewed the title—it would be impossible to have two kings. We see proof of this here in the clash between Edmund and Caspian, and—it could be noted—in the conflict between Peter and Caspian that Andrew Adamson created for the second film.

This conflict also serves as a catalyst for an appearance by Aslan. This is only the second time readers have seen him in *The Voyage of the Dawn Treader*, and this time he is present for only one paragraph. What can be said about his role so far?

First, as has been noted already, Aslan has intervened to do only those things our heroes cannot do for themselves. Eustace could not fully undragon himself, and here, it would seem, the curse of Deathwater Island is too great for Edmund, Caspian, and Lucy to break free from on their own.

Second, so far in this story Aslan has seemed inclined to work behind the scenes. When he appeared to Eustace, he did so in a dreamlike way. Here in chapter eight, one moment everyone saw the great lion and "knew it was Aslan" (128), and the next moment no one can remember what happened, leaving the group looking at each other "like people waking from sleep" (129).

Certainly, had he wanted to, Aslan could have appeared and *not* erased the memory of his intervention. But for some reason,

Aslan wants to continue to remain offstage—perhaps in this case so that there will be no memory at all of the magical water to tempt our heroes in the future. In *Prince Caspian*, after appearing only to Lucy, Aslan told her, "Things never happen the same way twice" (143). In *The Voyage of the Dawn Treader*, Aslan is continuing to do things differently—here much less directly—than he did previously.

Lewis never answers the question of *why* he has Aslan work more behind the scenes than directly in them, but readers find a similar pattern in the final scene from *The Screwtape Letters*. Wormwood's patient is killed by a bomb, and at the moment of death—and only at that moment—he sees the angels who, unknown to him, have been there all along helping him. Screwtape comments, "He realized what part each one of them had played at many an hour in his life when he had supposed himself alone, so that now he could say to them, one by one . . . 'So it was *you* all the time'" (173–74).

Finally, it should be noted that the temptation on Deathwater Island is greed, but not greed for gold. What Caspian, Edmund, and Lucy fall prey to here could be better classified as a greed for superiority.

Caspian is not concerned primarily with how much gold he would have, but only that he would have more than other rulers, that he would be "the richest of all Kings" (128). In this way, Caspian succumbs to the sin of pride as described in *Mere Christianity*. There Lewis notes that pride does not get pleasure merely from having something, but from having more of this something than someone else. Lewis explains, "We say that people are proud of being rich, or clever, or good-looking, but they are not. They are proud of being richer, or cleverer, or better-looking than others. If everyone else became equally rich, or clever, or good-looking there would be nothing to be proud about. It is the comparison that makes you proud; the pleasure of being above the rest" (122).

This pleasure of being above the rest—particularly of being above Caspian—is at the heart of Edmund's declaration, "I am one of the four ancient sovereigns of Narnia and you are under allegiance to the

High King my brother" (128). This same greed for superiority can be seen in Lucy's disparaging comment, "That's the worst of doing anything with boys. You're all such swaggering, bullying idiots."

Whether we call this sin a greed for superiority or simply pride, it was present in a huge measure in Eustace before his meeting with Aslan. And in this fact we can find a unifying element in Aslan's two appearances so far. After appearing in chapter seven to free Eustace from this sin, Aslan now appears to fulfill this same role for Caspian, Edmund, and Lucy.

If we look at Aslan's future appearances, once again we find this same element. Lucy will be about to give in to this same temptation for superiority in chapter ten by saying the spell that will make her more beautiful than Susan. There again, presumably because she is unable to resist the spell on her own, Aslan will appear just long enough to free her. In the book's final chapter, Caspian will have a second bout with his need for superiority and will need a second intervention by Aslan. In words that echo the conflict here, Caspian will tell the others, "I had thought you were all my subjects here, not my school masters" (239). Of the three heroes, Edmund will be the only one not to give in to the temptation of superiority again later in the story, perhaps because this was already his second meeting with Aslan; his initial one occurred on the children's first adventure.

Caspian vaguely remembers that he has been "making an ass" of himself (129), and Reepicheep recalls just enough to know "this is a place with a curse on it" and to suggest that it be named Death-water. The group also remembers they had come across the body of one of the missing lords. With the finding of Lord Bern, the arm band of Lord Octesian, and the golden body of Lord Restimar—whose name will be learned later—three lords have been found and four more still remain to be discovered.

## Discussion Questions

In this chapter, we learned that one or two tempers very nearly got lost over nothing more serious than a boring day of rain.

1. Do you find that small, petty annoyances often cause more dissension and conflict than more heroic challenges? If so, why?

As noted, here in *The Voyage of the Dawn Treader*, we find several weather-related incidents with suggestions of a behind-the-scenes role by Aslan. Lewis never indicates one way or another if the weather here is just luck, although in *The Horse and His Boy*, he will have the hermit state, "I have now lived a hundred and nine winters in this world and have never yet met any such thing as Luck" (148).

2. Should we make anything of the lucky accidents the weather creates not once but three times in this chapter? If so, what?

3. What, if anything, might Lewis be saying about "luck" in our world?

In this third story, Lewis has Aslan work more behind the scenes than directly in them. One possible reason for this might be that he saw divinity working that way in our own world, particularly as believers grow and develop.

4. In what ways do you see providence at work behind the scenes in our world?

Here in chapter eight, Aslan appeared for a second time. In this visit and the previous one on Dragon Island, he intervened to bring freedom from a greed for superiority, or pride. In *Mere Christianity*, Lewis maintains that pride is the one vice that no one in the world is free of (121). In Caspian's desire to be the richest king, Edmund's need to be seen as having more authority than Caspian, and Lucy's implication that she is superior to them both, we see that our heroes are no exception to this claim.

5. What might Lewis be saying by the need for Aslan's intervention here on Deathwater Island?

# NINE

# The Island of the Voices

## Invisible Enemies

With favorable winds—possibly yet another, though less dramatic, weather-related act of providence—the *Dawn Treader* sets out from Deathwater Island on its quest to find the remaining four lords. As the ship sails further and further east, the crew enters a region that becomes gradually more and more removed from the ordinary world. While there were strange elements on Dragon Island and Deathwater Island, at least the geography of both places was what would have been expected.

Here in chapter nine, for the first time some of the crew think the sun looks "larger than it looked from Narnia" (131). We are also told that this island where they stop to replenish their dwindling supplies is "a very different country from any they had yet seen." Previously when they landed, the crew found a rough, natural landscape. Now, as Paul Ford notes, they find "park-like grounds" and a "Georgian-style manor house" (281)—more like what might be found in England than in Narnia.

Although the others will have parts to play, the adventure on the Island of the Voices will largely be Lucy's. To bring her out from the rest, Lewis has her drop back to remove "a little stone in her shoe" and then has her become further delayed because her shoelace "had got into a knot" (131). After the encounters with a treacherous slaver, a dangerous storm, a great dragon, and a deadly stream, what effect do these little annoyances have? Why include something as commonplace as a stone in a shoe and a knotted lace?

In spite of the magical trappings he includes, in this adventure Lewis will have Lucy battle elements every child meets. Lucy will face feelings of being inferior to her sister, will worry about what her friends think of her, and will have to confront her fears of the unknown. Her first "real fright" in the magician's house will be nothing more than a funny mirror with "hair on the top of it and a beard hanging down from it" (148). By having Lucy combat such ordinary difficulties, Lewis allows his readers, particularly younger ones, to identify with her. To set the stage for these encounters, Lewis—through the stone in her shoe and the difficult lace—must first remind us that Lucy is, after all, still a little girl.

Of course, Lewis has another narrative constraint here. He needs someone to separate from the group, become concealed and so overhear the plans of the invisible warriors, and then report them to the rest. Having our heroes learn that there is a band of invisible enemies before actually encountering them is a technique Lewis uses to heighten the suspense in this chapter.

Lucy falls so far behind she can no longer hear the rest. Then "almost at once" she hears a strange "thumping," as if "dozens of strong workmen were hitting the ground as hard as they could with great wood mallets" (131–32). As she crouches in hiding against a tree, she overhears the leader tell the others, "Mates, now's our chance" (133). As Lucy listens in secret, this chief orders his troops down to the shore to get between the landing party and the *Dawn Treader* in order, as he explains, to "catch 'em when they try to put to sea."

After the mysterious warriors thump off, Lucy catches up with the landing party at the great house. After some discussion about what to do, Reepicheep argues, "It is folly to think of avoiding an invisible enemy," and concludes, "I'd sooner meet them face to face than be caught by the tail" (136). Caspian concurs and tells the rest, "Well, let's get on with it. We must go and face them. Shake hands all around—arrow on the string, Lucy—swords out, everyone else—and now for it" (137).

Lewis has shown readers this kind of courage before, where being brave is not an absence of fear but is doing what needs to be done in spite of being afraid. In Peter's first battle in *The Lion, the Witch and the Wardrobe*, Lewis made a point of telling us that as he faced the wolf, "Peter did not feel very brave; indeed, he felt he was going to be sick. But that made no difference to what he had to do" (131).

## "We Want Something That Little Girl Can Do for Us"

Upon reaching the shore, the landing party sees the boat still where they left it and the smooth sand "with no one to be seen on it" (137). Then the narrator comments that "more than one doubted whether Lucy had not merely imagined all she had told them," an observation that serves as a reminder of the conflict in *Prince Caspian*, where Lucy's story of seeing Aslan was doubted, largely because of her age. The narrator's observation highlights the fact that Lucy is much younger than the rest of the crew, further setting the stage for her task at the magician's house.

The doubts about Lucy's story are short-lived. Almost immediately the group is confronted by a voice that commands, "No further now. We've got to talk with you first" (137). This chief voice announces, "We want something that little girl can do for us" (138).

Over the course of what the chief refers to as "a long story" (138), he reveals that the island is the property of a great magician and that the invisible people are or were his servants. The chief claims this magician "told us to do something we didn't like" and that they subsequently rebelled and were punished. This long story of the chief is also a familiar story to readers of the Bible: the old story of authority, disobedience, and correction.

Readers will find two versions of this conflict. Here we get the Dufflepuds' version, and as might be expected, it differs significantly from the magician's. Two chapters later, Coriakin will explain to Lucy that the Dufflepuds' work was "to mind the garden" to raise food for themselves (164), a task that for some readers will parallel the story of Adam and Eve, who were to tend the Garden of Eden. The magician will tell Lucy that the Dufflepuds would not take their water from the stream that came right past the garden, but insisted on "trudging up to the spring with their buckets two or three times a day and tiring themselves out besides spilling half of it on the way back" (165).

What seems perfectly reasonable to readers seemed a terrible imposition to the Dufflepuds. They refused to obey the magician's order—a command that was in their best interest—and were subsequently punished with "an uglifying spell" (139).

The chief then tells of how, resentful of being ugly, they sneaked upstairs where his daughter, Clipsie, read the spell of invisibility from the magician's book. Now, "mortal tired of being invisible" (140), the Dufflepuds want Lucy to "go upstairs and go to the magic book and find the spell that takes off the invisibleness, and say it" (141). Refusal will result in instant death to Lucy and her comrades. Despite Edmund's protests, Lucy agrees to meet their demands, telling the others, "I don't want to be cut to bits with invisible swords any more than anyone else" (143).

George Sayer records that Tolkien disapproved of Lewis's Narnia books on a number of counts, one charge being that they were "carelessly" written (313). Earlier it was noted that Lewis may have made a minor slip by having one of the supposedly silenced dryads speak Reepicheep's prophecy. Here some readers may find further support for Tolkien's charge in the way Lewis fails to establish the necessity for Lucy's ordeal in the magician's house.

One problem some readers may have is that Lewis never gives any reason exactly why it must be a little girl who reads the spell. The chief simply says it must be a little girl or the magician himself, or "it won't work" (140). Why won't it work? "Because nothing happens," the chief says. In some medieval tales, such as the story of the taming of the unicorn, virgins were assumed to have magical powers. Perhaps in having two young girls—Clipsie and Lucy—read the spells, Lewis is echoing this tradition. Alternatively, perhaps Lewis is simply saying that this is the way enchantments sometimes work. The requirements of a magic spell—whether they may seem arbitrary or not—are what they are.

A second more serious problem is that readers are never given any reason why Lucy must go *alone* to read the spell. This oversight is made more prominent by the fact that it is clear that Clipsie did not go upstairs alone but was accompanied by the other Dufflepuds. The chief explains, "We waited till we thought this same magician would be asleep in the afternoon and we creep upstairs and go to this magic book, as bold as brass, to see if we can do anything about this uglification" (139). Throughout the Narnia tales we find numerous instances where a character must face a trial or test on his or her own, and this is as it should be. But Lewis typically will provide a more convincing context for why the character must face the challenge single-handedly. Here, for example, he could have simply made it a requirement that the spell be said not only by a young girl but also by one who is acting on her own.

Whether readers see the need for Lucy to go alone as a problem or not, Lewis goes on to make good use of the incident to further allow for Lucy's growth. When Edmund objects to Lucy's going, Reepicheep defends her decision, stating, "The service they ask of her is in no way contrary to her Majesty's honor, but a noble and heroical act. If the Queen's heart moves her to risk the magician, I will not speak against it" (143). Up until now, we have mostly seen Lucy's compassion. Now through her adventure in the magician's house, we will also see her valor—the courage and daring that during her reign in *The Lion, the Witch and the Wardrobe* caused her to be known as Queen Lucy the Valiant.

While a small element, Reepicheep's statement here—like his command, "Don't fight! Push!" during the sea serpent episode—is a further indicator of the noble mouse's growth in maturity. The old Reepicheep in *Prince Caspian* who was overly concerned about his own honor would never have let a lady go into danger while he stood idly by.

In assigning this quest to Lucy here in *The Voyage of the Dawn Treader*, one that only she can accomplish, Lewis reminds us that great deeds are not only for the mighty. By having Lucy assume the primary role in undoing the spell from the magician's book, Lewis was mirroring Tolkien's decision in *The Lord of the Rings* to have the four small hobbits play key roles in the quest to destroy Sauron and the Ring. In *The Fellowship of the Ring*, Elrond tells the council that "neither strength nor wisdom" will be factors in the war against Sauron and that the quest may be attempted by "the weak with as much hope as the strong" (262). Though there are plenty of great warriors among the elves, wizards, dwarfs, and men, Frodo, Sam, Merry, and Pippin each have a unique task in the battle for Middle-earth. And it is Éowyn, a young woman, who with Merry defeats the great Lord of the Nazgûl.

When Lucy's decision is announced here, the attitude of the invisible people completely changes. Loud cheering breaks out, and the chief, "warmly supported by all the others," invites the Narnians "to come to supper and spend the night" (144). These two actions—the cheering and the invitation—along with their silly responses are our first indications that the Dufflepuds may not be as sinister as they first seemed.

## Discussion Questions

Here in chapter nine, the crew of the *Dawn Treader* comes up against adversaries who are different from any they have faced before—ones who cannot be seen. The Dufflepuds and the magician are invisible, but in the end neither turns out to be as bad as imagined. When Eustace is fearful of accepting the Dufflepuds' offer of supper, Lucy maintains, "I'm sure they're not treacherous. They're not like that at all" (144). Similarly, when Caspian raises the issue of the magician, Lucy responds, "But he mayn't be as bad as they make out. Don't you get the idea that these people are not very brave?" (143). In Lucy's two responses here, Lewis may be saying something about the invisible foes readers often face in their own lives.

1. At this point in the story, readers are beginning to feel along with Lucy that the invisible speakers may not be as threatening as they first seemed. Would you say most unknown threats in life turn out to be less than our fears have made them to be? If so, how has this been true in your own life?

Early in the adventure, Eustace observes it is no use trying to hide from foes they cannot see, and the landing party decides to face their invisible enemies instead of fleeing from them. As Reepicheep declares, "I'd sooner meet them face to face than be caught by the tail" (136).

2. What might Lewis be saying here about the best way to deal with fears, both real and imagined?

In this chapter, we find that Lucy—who is the youngest and, except for Reepicheep, the smallest member of the crew—is the only one who can accomplish what needs to be done.

3. Can you think of other stories where the key figures would not be considered mighty or powerful? What might these stories be saying about the roles that we ourselves may play?

# TEN

# The Magician's Book

## The Evening before Lucy's Big Adventure

The Dufflepuds have been gradually making the shift from serious adversaries to comic associates. At the dinner scene here in chapter ten, they complete this change. As the invisible people serve up the feast for their guests, the narrator comments, "It was very funny to see the plates and dishes coming to the table and not to see anyone carrying them" (145). The Dufflepuds' banquet is indeed amusing, although some readers might see an inconsistency between this scene and one that occurred a few pages earlier.

In chapter nine, the Dufflepuds threatened to cut the throats of the landing party, and Reepicheep raised doubts about their weapons. "Are they invisible too?" he asked (142). Then readers were told, "The words were scarcely out of his mouth before they heard a whizzing sound and next moment a spear had struck, quivering, in one of the trees behind them." Lewis seemed to be implying that anything that touches the invisible

Dufflepuds—their clothes, their weapons, and so on—also becomes invisible. Here in the banquet scene, Lewis appears to be violating his earlier principle as the landing party is able to see the plates and dishes the Dufflepuds are holding.

During the feast, Eustace and Edmund speculate on what the invisible servers might look like. As Eustace observes the bouncing dishes, he wonders, "Do you think they're human at all? More like huge grasshoppers or giant frogs, I should say" (145). In his essay "On Three Ways of Writing for Children," Lewis touched on the topic of the "night-fears" that often plague young people and confessed, "Giant insects were my specialty" (39). Thus Lewis is inserting an autobiographical element into Lucy's character here as Edmund tells Eustace, "Don't put the idea of the grasshoppers into Lucy's head. She's not too keen on insects; especially big ones."

The narrator notes that the banquet would have been more enjoyable had it not been "so exceedingly messy" and if the conversation had not "consisted entirely of agreements" (146). These agreements will take three forms. First, the Dufflepuds make statements impossible to disagree with, such as, "What I always say is, when a chap's hungry, he likes some victuals," or, "Getting dark now; always does at night." Second, as we have seen, the Dufflepuds always take the same opinion as their leader. And finally, in the following chapter, they will agree with everything both the chief and Lucy say, even when, as Lucy will point out, they are saying "just the opposite" (171).

Through the Dufflepuds' silly propensity for agreement, Lewis creates amusing and memorable characters, but he may have two more serious purposes here.

In chapter eleven, the magician will note that, yes, the Dufflepuds do agree with every word the chief says, but maintains, "It's better for them to admire him than to admire nobody" (164). In that same chapter, Aslan will ask the magician if he is weary of ruling "such foolish subjects" (161). Lewis's point is that growth from foolishness to wisdom occurs in stages, never all at once, and one of the first steps is to go from admiring only your own self to admiring a leader—even if this leader is not all that admirable. In *The Last*

*Battle*, the attitude of the dwarfs, who are kin to the Dufflepuds, will be "the Dwarfs are for the Dwarfs!" (83). Here in *The Voyage of the Dawn Treader*, Lewis suggests that the Dufflepuds' position of blindly following one of their own is one step better than the position of "I am for me."

The Dufflepuds will come to admire Lucy as well, and this will be another positive step for them. When she and the chief disagree, the Dufflepuds will agree with Lucy's opinion that they are not ugly even as they also agree with the chief's opinion that they are. In the Dufflepuds' acceptance of thoroughly different claims, Lewis may be critiquing modern man's lack of logical consistency, as he did in the opening chapter of *The Screwtape Letters*. There Screwtape tells Wormwood, "Your man has been accustomed, ever since he was a boy, to have a dozen incompatible philosophies dancing about together inside his head" (1).

Whether by the presence of reason—as seen in *The Lion, the Witch and the Wardrobe* in the professor's statement, "Logic! Why don't they teach logic at these schools?" (48)—or by its absence seen here in the Dufflepuds, Lewis makes clear the essential role reason has in personal growth. In the same letter from Screwtape, the senior devil warns his pupil of the dangers of awakening his patient's reason, for "once it is awake, who can foresee the result?" (2).

## The Journey Upstairs

Morning soon comes. At breakfast, even though Lucy tries "to talk and eat ordinarily" (146), she is clearly apprehensive about what she may face upstairs in the magician's house. Earlier Lucy deliberately faced danger—in chapter six, when she and the others walked down to the beach to meet the dragon, and then again in chapter nine, when she and the other members of the landing party chose to confront the invisible inhabitants of the island. Both of these times Lucy faced danger with the others. Now she must go alone.

After climbing up the stairs, Lucy must walk past "room after room" and dreads that "in any room there might be the magician—asleep, or awake, or invisible, or even dead" (147). Lucy soon sees "strange signs painted in scarlet on the doors," and strange masks, the kind it was easy to imagine "were doing things as soon as your back was turned" (148). Then at the sixth door, Lucy has what the narrator refers to as "her first real fright" when "a wicked little bearded face" seems to pop out of the wall (148).

In making Lucy the kind of character who is frightened from time to time, Lewis gives us someone we can all identify with. In a letter written the year after *The Voyage of the Dawn Treader* was published, Lewis offered a correspondent these words of encouragement: "You needn't worry about not feeling brave. Our Lord didn't—see the scene in Gethsemane. How thankful I am that when God became Man He did not choose to become a man of iron nerves: that would not have helped weaklings like you and me nearly so much" (*Letters of C. S. Lewis* 431).

Paul Ford observes that in the description of Lucy's walk through the house of the magician, Lewis teaches children about "how to get a job done despite fear" (210). Readers may be reminded of a similar scene in *The Hobbit* where Bilbo has to go by himself down the long tunnel in the mountain. While Lucy has to face the unknown dangers of the magician, Bilbo must face the unknown dangers of the dragon Smaug. Tolkien writes, "Warned by the echoes to take more than hobbit's care to make no sound, he crept noiselessly down, down, down into the dark" (183). At one point Bilbo, like Lucy, receives a fright, and then readers are told, "Going on from there was the bravest thing he ever did. The tremendous things that happened afterwards were as nothing compared to it. He fought the real battle in the tunnel alone" (184).

In *The Horse and His Boy*, Shasta will have a similar moment of truth before his first battle and will tell himself, "If you funk this, you'll funk every battle all your life. Now or never" (186). Lucy, Bilbo, and Shasta all pass their tests of courage. Despite their fears, each of them continues ahead and does what must be done.

Up until now, not much has happened in the two pages since Lucy left the others. Evan Gibson has argued that Lewis shows a mastery of the art of storytelling through his handling of this "technique of delay" in Lucy's ordeal (177). Gibson points out, "It takes Lewis almost six hundred words to propel her up the stairs and down the hall to the room where the book of magic sits on its reading stand." The key to the effectiveness of this delay, Gibson argues, is that we experience each step of the journey with Lucy. He notes, "As the tick-tock of the grandfather clock fades away and she hears nothing but the beating of her own heart, we travel with her and participate in the atmosphere of peril which Lucy's fears project."

The scary face turns out to be nothing more than a little mirror with "hair on the top of it and a beard hanging down from it" (148). With the bearded glass, as it is called, Lewis reminds his readers—young and old—that many of our fears exist only in our minds. Earlier it turned out the Dufflepuds were not as menacing as they first seemed. Here the magician's mirror is no threat at all; in fact, it is actually comical. Lewis will repeat the lesson a few pages later when Lucy finally meets the magician she has been fearing the entire time, only to find an ally and a friend.

Lewis leaves it to the reader to speculate why the little mirror with the hair and beard is hanging in the hallway. Perhaps Lewis includes it just to reinforce the lesson about needless fears and to insert a comic break in the suspense Lucy is facing. However, as we learn later, the magician is doing penance for some sort of error he committed. Perhaps he became too prideful and now has hung the mirror as a reminder not to take himself so seriously.

It takes Lucy a long time to reach the door she has been looking for, this "last door on the left" (147), so long that she begins to wonder "whether the corridor had grown longer since she began her journey and whether this was part of the magic of the house" (149–50). When she finally arrives, she finds the door open and the room "lined from floor to ceiling with books" (150).

From the beginning of *The Lion, the Witch and the Wardrobe*, where readers were shown both the professor's and Mr. Tumnus's libraries, books have been associated with positive characters. The importance of reading the right books, as the Pevensies have—and avoiding the wrong ones, the kind Eustace has read—has already come up a number of times in *The Voyage of the Dawn Treader*. Here the library's presence with "more books than Lucy had ever seen before, . . . all bound in leather and smelling old and learned and magical" (150), is a hint that the magician may not be the evil tyrant the Dufflepuds have made him out to be.

Lewis's study was also filled with books, though not nearly as many as the magician's. For serious research, he would go to Oxford's Bodleian Library, a place he truly loved. In 1928 Lewis wrote his father that if only smoking were permitted and the chairs a bit softer, the Bodleian would be "one of the most delightful places in the world" (*Letters of C. S. Lewis* 252).

## The Magician's Book and the Beautifying Spell

Lucy unclasps the magician's book, and in the narrator's exclamation—"And what a book it was!" (151)—we can hear Lewis's own love not just for books but for the very act of writing as well. Readers are told, "It was written, not printed; written in a clear even hand, with thick downstrokes and thin upstrokes, very large, easier than print, and so beautiful that Lucy stared at it for a whole minute and forgot about reading it. The paper was crisp and smooth and a nice smell came from it."

In *Surprised by Joy*, Lewis explains how he learned to love not only reading but, with help from his friend Arthur Greeves, the physical books themselves. He recalls, "The set up of the page, the feel and smell of the paper, the differing sounds that different papers make as you turn the leaves, became sensuous delights" (164).

In *Imagination and the Arts in C. S. Lewis*, Peter Schakel observes that through scenes such as this one in the magician's library, Lewis encourages young people to become "lifelong readers and lovers of books for whom reading is a holistic experience and who might come to experience at least some of the pleasure reading and books gave to Lewis throughout his life" (39).

As Lucy turns the pages, she finds an amazing assortment of spells. There are cures for warts, toothaches, and cramps. There are spells for "taking a swarm of bees" (151), as well as for finding, remembering, or forgetting things. There are spells on "how to call up (or prevent) wind, fog, snow, sleet or rain" (152). There are spells for producing enchanted sleeps and for giving someone an "ass's head" as was done to Bottom in *A Midsummer Night's Dream*.

Each time magic occurs in the Narnia stories, there will be a certain number of readers—or parents of readers—who will become concerned because of the negative associations magic is sometimes given. Leland Ryken and Marjorie Lamp Mead have made a helpful "distinction in purpose" between the use of magic by someone like Lucy, who "is not seeking her own interests," and the use of magic by someone like the White Witch, whose only goal is her own interests (90).

Tolkien makes a similar distinction in *The Fellowship of the Ring*, raising the question of why our language only has one word—*magic*—for two actions with radically opposite goals. After Sam tells Frodo, "I'd dearly love to see some Elf-magic" (352), Galadriel offers the hobbits the chance to look into her mirror, a water-filled basin that shows "things that were, and things that are, and things that yet may be." Turning to Sam, Galadriel says, "This is what your folk would call magic, I believe; though I do not understand clearly what they mean; and they seem to use the same word of the deceits of the Enemy" (353).

Lucy continues turning the pages of the magic book and comes to a passage for "an infallible spell to make beautiful her that uttereth it beyond the lot of mortals" (153), a spell that perfectly illustrates this distinction of purpose. As Ryken and Mead note, while Lucy's quest to read the spell to make hidden things visible is "a brave deed to help others" (90), her intentions in saying the beautifying spell disregard the needs of others.

As Lucy looks at the drawings accompanying the spell, she sees a second Lucy who recites it. She then sees a picture of herself on a high throne at a great tournament in Calormen where "all the Kings of the world" compete because of her beauty (154). The scene changes, and now instead of tournaments, Lucy's suitors are fighting real wars in which "all Narnia and Archenland, Telmar and Calormen, Galma and Terebinthia were laid waste." The scene changes once more, and now Lucy sees herself back in England, where Susan is "plainer" and jealous of Lucy's "dazzling beauty," but this does not matter because "no one cared anything about Susan now."

Lucy is about to recite the spell when suddenly Aslan appears in the pictures—his first appearance since he intervened to keep Edmund and Caspian from coming to blows on Deathwater Island. With Aslan's intervention, Lucy is able to avoid a temptation that we are meant to think she would otherwise have succumbed to.

Besides being a clear illustration of the distinction in purpose for the uses of magic, Lucy's episode with the beautifying spell is also another clear illustration of Lewis's conception of the power of pride. In the passage from *Mere Christianity* that was cited earlier in conjunction with Edmund and Caspian's conflict, Lewis observes, "We say that people are proud of being rich, or clever, or good-looking, but they are not. They are proud of being richer, or cleverer, or better-looking than others" (122). In his intervention here and on Deathwater Island, Aslan steps in because the temptations of pride prove too strong for our young heroes to resist.

In Lucy's temptation to be beautiful "beyond the lot of mortals" and become a woman that "all the Kings of the world" fight for (153–54), some readers may see parallels to Helen of Troy, whose beauty launched a thousand ships to the Trojan War. They may also see parallels to Galadriel's temptation in *The Fellowship of the Ring*. After Frodo offers to give her the Ring, Galadriel tells him, "You will give me the Ring freely! In place of the Dark Lord you will set up a Queen. And I shall not be dark, but beautiful and terrible as the Morning and the Night! . . . All shall love me and despair" (356).

Unlike Lucy, Galadriel is able to resist the temptation without any outside assistance—at least without any that readers are aware of. In words that suggest she has been able to overcome her pride, Galadriel concludes, "I pass the test. I will diminish, and go into the West, and remain Galadriel" (357).

## The Spell for Eavesdropping

A decade before *The Voyage of the Dawn Treader* was published, Lewis made temptation a central focus of two entire books—*The Screwtape Letters* (1942) and *Perelandra* (1943). He brings the insight he developed earlier to the nuanced depictions of the temptations Lucy undergoes here.

While Aslan intervened in Lucy's first temptation—the spell for beautification—he now does not intervene but allows her to succumb to a second spell that promises to "let you know what your friends thought about you" (155). Why does Aslan intercede sometimes but not others? One answer to this question is that there may be no answer. Beginning with *The Lion, the Witch and the Wardrobe*, Lewis has made it clear that Aslan "is not a tame lion" (182). Lewis will have the magician reiterate this point in the next chapter, as Coriakin will tell Lucy, "It's always like that, you can't keep him: it's not as if he were a *tame* lion" (162). Aslan's comings and goings, his decisions of when to intervene and when not to, are his own and not subject to his followers' preferences or to the reader's understanding.

Why did Aslan deliver Narnia from the White Witch after a hundred years of winter rather than after fifty or even ten? Why did Aslan return to Narnia in time to save Caspian but not Caspian's father? Lewis suggests that questions like these are ones that will not or perhaps cannot be explained. For some readers, these questions about Aslan may evoke similar questions raised about why Jesus heals some people but not others, and why he sometimes intervenes today but other times does not.

If Lewis wants us to see a reason behind Aslan's differing actions in Lucy's temptations here—and he may not—the difference may lie in the kind of outcomes each spell holds. As Jonathan Rogers has pointed out, the spell for eavesdropping will affect only Lucy, while the spell for beautification threatens to cause "geopolitical upheaval" (66).

The Lucy we got to know in the first two books never seemed particularly worried about her friends' opinions of her. So why does she give in now to the temptation to recite the second spell? First, Lucy is older—she was eight in the first book and nine in the second. Now she is ten, and as she gets older, friends and their opinions become more important. Second—and here Lewis shows a keen insight into the nature of temptation—the fact that Lucy had wanted to recite the first spell but did not plays a role in the second. She gives in to the second temptation partly to make up for the first. The fact that Lucy knows this is not a valid justification is shown by the speed with which she does it. Readers are told:

> A little later she came to a spell which would let you know what your friends thought about you. Now Lucy had wanted very badly to try the other spell, the one that made you beautiful beyond the lot of mortals. So she felt that to make up for not having said it, she really would say this one. And all in a hurry, for fear her mind would change, she said the words. (155)

Earlier it was suggested that perhaps Aslan allows Lucy to recite the second spell but not the first because the second spell will affect only her. Additionally, it could be argued that the effects of this second spell, while painful, will ultimately be good for Lucy. After she recites the spell, she hears her friend Marjorie Preston deny that she was "all taken up" with her the previous term (155). This leads Lucy to ask, "I wonder are all my friends the same?" (156).

An important part of growing up is to learn that, when pressured, friends may say hurtful things they do not mean. After he appears, Aslan will explain to Lucy, "You have misjudged your friend. She is weak, but she loves you" (159). Lucy will say to Aslan, "Oh dear. Have I spoiled everything?" and her response may shed further light on the positive effect of this temptation. In writing about the spell for beautification, Donald Glover maintains that Lucy "is nearing the crisis of adolescence which Susan has passed into" (153). Here Lucy worries that she might have spoiled everything with Marjorie Preston by reciting the second spell. Later in life, Lucy will surely again be faced with adolescent temptations, and when she does, she may remember the negative results of giving in to temptation here.

Back in chapter one, readers were told that just before bursting into the bedroom, Eustace "had been listening outside the door" (7). Is it just coincidence that Lewis has Lucy fall prey to the same transgression Eustace committed in our first view of him? Perhaps—lest anyone get too smug—Lewis is reminding us that we should be cautious about judging others. As he comments in *A Grief Observed*, "I'd better keep my breath to cool my own porridge" (74).

When Lucy says to Aslan, "I don't think I'd ever be able to forget what I heard her say," he will simply respond, "No, you won't" (159). Lucy will *never* forget the painful words she hears here? This seems hard, but Lewis reminds us over and over that choices have consequences. In the moving scene from *Prince Caspian* when the children went down into the treasure chamber, Edmund had no gift from Father Christmas waiting for him. Because of his choices, he will always remain the only sibling without a gift.

Lewis also reminds us that there is redemption for every mistake and that repentance can always lead to some kind of positive outcome. At the end of the first story, Edmund grows into "a graver and quieter man" who is "great in council and judgment" (184). Similarly, it could be argued that Lucy will go through the rest of her life unable to forget the words she heard her friend say here, but this memory will help to transform her into someone wiser and more mature.

### The Spell for the Refreshment of the Spirit

Next Lucy comes to a spell "for the refreshment of the spirit," an incantation that is more story than spell (156). Lucy becomes a part of the spell as she reads it, "living in the story as if it were real."

Coming to the end, she exclaims, "That is the loveliest story I've ever read or ever shall read in my whole life" (156–57). Lucy wants to read the story again, but finds not only that she cannot turn the pages back but also that the details are gradually fading from her memory. Soon all she can remember are its four major elements: "a cup and a sword and a tree and a green hill" (157).

The spell for the refreshment of the spirit works perfectly well simply as a mysterious story, one with vague hints readers are not meant to fully understand. However, three arguments may suggest that the story Lucy reads in the magician's book is the story of Christ's Last Supper, arrest, death, and ascension.

First, the four elements as they are given line up chronologically with the details from the New Testament. The cup can be seen as the one that held the wine at the Last Supper. The sword can be seen as the one Peter draws during Jesus's arrest. The tree can be seen as the cross. The green hill can be seen as the one from which Jesus ascended into heaven.

Second, this is a story that does not seem to belong in Narnia since Lucy forgets all but the four details and the wonderful feeling she is left with. Why should Lucy forget this spell but remember the others? Arguably because Narnia is not its proper place. Aslan promises he will tell Lucy this story of a cup, a sword, a tree, and a hill "for years and years" (160), a time when she will be in England.

But if Lucy forgets the story, or nearly all of it, why include this spell at all? A third reason to link the spell for the refreshment of the spirit with the gospel story is that it comes after Lucy's greatest transgression in the Chronicles—reciting the eavesdropping spell and spying on her friend—and therefore provides the way for her spirit to be made fresh again. As Peter Schakel has observed in *The Way into Narnia*, Lucy's "fall and loss of innocence are quickly followed by grace and redemption" (65).

After Edmund's great wrongdoing in *The Lion, the Witch and the Wardrobe*—his betrayal of his siblings—Aslan supplied a way to atone for this failing through the events at the Stone Table. Since Lucy's offense is linked to this world, not Narnia, it could be argued that the atonement for it—her "Stone Table event"—must take place on Earth.

When Lucy asks, "Have I spoiled everything?" (159), Aslan does not provide an answer. But had Lewis chosen to, he might have had Aslan say something such as, "Be at rest, daughter. I have made a way in your world for anything that has been spoiled to be made right again."

In making one of the magician's spells an actual story, Lewis was drawing on the double meaning of the word *spell*. As Tolkien noted in "On Fairy-Stories," in its Old English roots, *spell* "means both a story told, and a formula of power over living men" (55). We see this other sense in the word *gospel*, which literally means "good story."

### The Spell to Make Hidden Things Visible

Lucy finally arrives at the page she has been looking for. She locates the "spell to make hidden things visible" and recites it, hard words and all (157). Suddenly she hears "soft heavy footfalls coming along the corridor behind her" and remembers that the Dufflepuds had told her "about the Magician making no more noise than a cat" (158). The chief's actual words in the previous chapter were that the magician "always did go about with his bare feet, making no more noise than a great big cat" (140). Lucy turns around and sees not the magician but Aslan himself standing in the doorway.

There are two reasons why Lewis wants to identify the magician with Aslan. First, it is the basis for the dramatic moment seen here. Because Lewis established that the magician walks barefoot like a cat, we—along with Lucy—expect these soft, heavy footfalls coming down the corridor to signal the arrival of the magician. Second, the use of this physical quality serves to associate Coriakin with Aslan. The magician is Aslan's viceroy, his representative or agent here in the land of the Dufflepuds. As readers learn in the next chapter, the Dufflepuds would be frightened "out of their senses" if Aslan were to appear to them, so he has set Coriakin—a smaller, less threatening version of himself—here to govern.

The relationship of the Dufflepuds and Coriakin mirrors the relationship of Coriakin and Aslan. Coriakin committed some fault, and in the magician's best interest, Aslan has given him a corrective punishment: he must govern the Dufflepuds. The Dufflepuds committed a fault, and in their best interest, Coriakin has given them a corrective punishment: they were turned into monopods.

Perhaps Lewis is suggesting here and elsewhere that all of Aslan's followers are ultimately to become like little Aslans themselves. With each passing book, Lucy in particular is becoming more and more like Aslan. Perhaps this was part of the meaning behind Aslan's declaration to her in *Prince Caspian*: "Now you are a lioness" (143). Perhaps one day the Dufflepuds, or at least some of them, will become like Aslan. If so, they will have to start out as cubs.

## Discussion Questions

In this chapter, we see more of the Dufflepuds' propensity for always agreeing with each other. Although it is a silly way to live, Lewis suggests it is better than living a life with no authority higher than self—a life Lewis illustrated first in the White Witch, then in Miraz, and finally in the decrepit, dying dragon.

1. What are some other examples of a self-centered life, both in Narnia and in our world?

2. Why might Lewis have thought it was important to show the consequences of living this kind of life?

In her trip in the magician's house, we again find that Lucy is willing to do what needs to be done despite her fear.

3. Where else in the Chronicles do we find someone getting the job done even though they are afraid?

Aslan takes differing actions in Lucy's temptations, intervening in one spell but not in another. Some readers may be reminded of the promise in 1 Corinthians 10:13 that God will not allow us to be tempted beyond what we can bear.

4. What might be some reasons why Aslan behaves differently on these two occasions?

5. What might Lewis be saying through Aslan's different actions?

In his description of a story that provides refreshment for the spirit, Lewis was not thinking about his own creations. But for many readers past and present, the Chronicles of Narnia have been exactly this. The narrator states, "Ever since that day what Lucy means by a good story is a story which reminds her of the forgotten story in the Magician's Book" (157). Similarly, what many Lewis fans mean by a good story is one that reminds them of their favorite Narnia tale.

6. In what specific ways do the Chronicles of Narnia refresh your spirit?

7. What other stories also serve this purpose in your life?

# ELEVEN

# The Dufflepuds Made Happy

## The Master of This House

Lucy follows Aslan into the hallway, and they are met by "an old man, barefoot, dressed in a red robe" (161). The magician, now visible, has all the traditional wizardly trappings, and in this way Coriakin—with his white hair, long beard, and "a curiously carved staff"—resembles Tolkien's wizard Gandalf.

In chapter fourteen, readers will meet Ramandu, a former star like Coriakin. But Lewis will have Ramandu appear less wizardly and more starlike. Though he will also be barefoot, his robe, hair, and beard will be silver, and light will seem to come from him. In addition, for the first three sentences of chapter fourteen, the narrator will refer to Ramandu as "it," a pronoun that seems to suggest something non-human.

Coriakin is much more manlike. In fact, until Ramandu's statement in chapter fourteen, "You have already met a star" (209), readers have no indication that Coriakin is anything but a magician. The difference may lie in the fact that while Ramandu is "a star at rest" (208), Coriakin "might have shone for thousands of years more" (209). Instead of running low on star power and needing to be made young again, Coriakin has had his light taken from him.

Here in chapter eleven, Coriakin is also depicted with "a chaplet of oak leaves" covering his hair, an element Ramandu does not have. What, if anything, are we to make of this? Paul Ford has suggested that this crown of oak leaves may be related to those worn by both the Druids and the priests of Zeus, but concludes that if this is true, "precisely what Lewis intends to signify by Coriakin's priestliness is not clear" (147). Alternatively, Lewis may have had the Roman Civic Crown in mind, a wreath of woven oak leaves given to someone who has saved the life of a fellow citizen in battle. If Lewis was thinking of the Civic Crown, this would add an interesting element to Coriakin's history before he was assigned to govern the Dufflepuds.

For someone being punished, Coriakin seems quite happy to see Aslan. Clearly they are on good terms. By contrast, the Dufflepuds speak badly of Coriakin and view him as their enemy. In this, Lewis may be suggesting that the further along we are in our growth, the more we welcome the agents of correction in our lives and the opportunity for improvement they bring. At the end of *The Screwtape Letters*, the senior devil talks briefly about the corrective suffering that Wormwood's patient and some of the human spirits may still have to undergo on their journey further into heaven. He explains, "Pains he may still have to encounter, but they *embrace* those pains" (174).

In his essay "Membership," Lewis uses a phrase that could describe the proper position the magician has come to through his penance: "authority exercised with humility and obedience accepted with delight" (338). Rather than growing weary of overseeing the Dufflepuds, Coriakin tells Aslan that he has grown "rather fond" of them (161). His only complaint is that he must use "rough magic" rather than wisdom to govern them—presumably referring to actions like his earlier need to transform the Duffers into monopods when they refused to obey.

The words "this rough magic" may seem a bit out of place in Coriakin's speech, and in fact, Lewis borrowed the phrase from Shakespeare, who has Prospero use it in act five of *The Tempest*. Like Coriakin, Prospero must use magic rather than wisdom to govern the foolish characters on his island. At the end of the play he declares, "This rough magic I here abjure" (5.1.50–51), announcing his intention to give up his supernatural powers and become merely human again. Perhaps Lewis intends to bring to mind not just the day when the Dufflepuds can be governed by wisdom but also the day when Coriakin will give up the magician's role he has been assigned and return to being a star.

Although Aslan promises that this day when the Dufflepuds can be ruled by wisdom will come "all in good time" (161), Lewis never reports to what extent Coriakin is successful with his charges. When we get to *The Last Battle*, Lewis will include monopods in the list of characters who race up to the great doorway where Aslan is standing but does not say what happens to them.

When asked if he intends to show himself to the Dufflepuds, Aslan replies with the hint of a laugh, "Nay, I should frighten them out of their senses" (162). Lewis will revisit this point at the end of *The Silver Chair*. There Aslan will not reveal his full self to the bullies at Experiment House. "They shall see only my back," he explains (241), and even this limited vision of Aslan will be enough to send the headmistress into hysterics. In *The Last Battle*, Aslan *cannot* show himself to the rebellious dwarfs in the stable because they refuse to see him.

In an indication that Coriakin will be at least partly successful with his pupils, Aslan promises that one day after many stars have grown old and have come "to take their rest in the islands" (162), the Dufflepuds will be mature enough, or, as he says, "ripe" for him to appear to them. Evan Gibson sums up the scene in the following way:

> The monopods will eventually develop some intelligence and some courage, but until that time arrives, they must be ruled like children

and disciplined when their foolish stubbornness would do them harm. Lewis seems to be saying that God is no respecter of persons . . . but His dealings with each are tailored to the individual needs of each. Fuller revelations of His nature are withheld until our capacities have been adequately enlarged. (178–79)

Paul Ford points out that Aslan is "always growing bigger with respect to the person who sees him" (55). While this is true in general, we especially see Lucy's perception of Aslan continue to grow as she continues to grow herself.

Aslan abruptly announces that he must "visit Trumpkin the Dwarf where he sits in the castle of Cair Paravel counting the days till his master Caspian comes home" (162). While the Chronicles of Narnia provide a record of only some of Aslan's deeds, this visit would have been a particularly nice one for Lewis to have depicted. We typically see Aslan only at moments of crisis—times of great calamity when he is needed to save the day. Aslan's announcement here makes it clear that he also turns up sometimes just to say hello to a lonely friend. He promises Lucy, who shares his special affection for the dwarf, that he will comfort Trumpkin by telling him "all your story."

## "We Shall Meet Again Soon"

Before vanishing, Aslan tells Lucy not to look so sad and promises her, "We shall meet again soon" (162). Does Aslan know that in a few days the *Dawn Treader* will get lost in the darkness and that Lucy will call on him for help? Does he already know he will appear to her then in the form of an albatross? Does Lewis imply here, or elsewhere in the Chronicles, that Aslan has the ability to foresee the future? There is not a great deal of evidence on this issue, and some of it seems conflicting.

Back in *The Lion, the Witch and the Wardrobe*, Aslan offered Peter "two plans of battle—one for fighting the Witch and her people in the wood and another for assaulting her castle" (146). When Peter pointed out that surely Aslan would be there, the great lion's only response was, "I can give you no promise of that." As Paul Ford observes:

> The fact that the Lion makes two plans with Peter for the course of the coming battle with the witch and her forces and that he cannot guarantee to Peter that he will assist Peter in the battle is an allusion to the "humanness" of the Lion. Lewis is aligning Aslan with what some Christian theologians believe of Christ in his earthly life: that he did not, as man, know the future, that he did not see the resurrection on the other side of his death, and that, therefore, he had to suffer and die like all of his fellow humans, trusting that his Father had a plan even for the dying. (59)

If we are meant to think that Aslan does not know the future, then his comment in this chapter that he and Lucy will meet soon can be seen as more probability than certainty, his attempt to comfort his dear friend before leaving.

In *The Lion, the Witch and the Wardrobe*, Aslan seemed *not* to know the future. Here in *The Voyage of the Dawn Treader*, he *may* know the future. In *The Silver Chair*, Aslan *will* know the future, or at least the part of it that relates to the four signs he tells Jill, which are part instruction and part prediction. Yet even then Lewis will suggest there are things Aslan may not know, as illustrated by Aslan's words in the fourth sign: "You will know the lost prince (if you find him) by this, that he will be the first person you have met in your travels who will ask you to do something in my name, in the name of Aslan" (25).

Lewis seems to have been thinking about the idea of foreknowledge here in *The Voyage of the Dawn Treader*, because he returns to it a mere eight sentences later as he has the magician tell Lucy, "Of course, I knew when I let the Duffers make themselves invisible that you would be coming along presently to take the spell off" (162). How did the magician know that Lucy would be coming? Is he in certain ways omniscient? In the end, Lewis leaves these questions—and the question of Aslan's omniscience—unanswered, and Aslan's and Coriakin's powers remain a mystery both to Lucy and to readers. To further underscore and at the same time complicate this issue of foreknowledge, the magician also tells Lucy, "I wasn't quite sure of the exact day."

When Lucy asks Aslan what he means by soon, his only explanation is, "I call all times soon" (162). The Chronicles indicate that Aslan has great longevity. He was present before Narnia's creation and will be present after its demise—a period that, according to Lewis's notes, spans 2,555 years. Thus the brief time until Aslan sees Lucy again would seem short to him. But this is not quite what he says. Aslan tells Lucy he calls *all* times soon—not just the time until he sees her again. Even the entire time between Narnia's beginning and end is soon from Aslan's perspective.

In Aslan's statement "I call all times soon," Lewis seems to suggest that Aslan is not just someone whose life span extends over several millennia but a being who is outside of time itself. If this is the case, we may find further insights on how Lewis sees Aslan's existence in the chapter titled "Time and Beyond Time" from *Mere Christianity*. There Lewis maintains that while life comes to each of us moment by moment, God does not experience time in this way. We are *in* time, but God, Lewis argues, is *beyond* time and thus sees all moments—both past and future—as the present. Lewis invites us to picture time as a line we travel down. We see one brief part, and only after it has passed do we see the next. God may be seen as the page on which the line is drawn. Lewis concludes that God "contains the whole line, and sees it all" (168).

If Aslan is outside of time, it would explain not only how all times are soon to him but also how he may have knowledge of when he and Lucy will meet again. As Lewis continues in his description of God in *Mere Christianity*, "All the days are 'Now' for Him. . . . He does not 'foresee' you doing things tomorrow; He simply sees you doing them: because though tomorrow is not yet there for you, it is for Him. . . . He is already in tomorrow and can simply watch you" (170).

Almost as if to further complicate this issue again, Lewis makes it clear Aslan must leave the magician's house in order to visit Trumpkin—something we might think would not be necessary if every moment was the present for him. Though Aslan calls all times soon, he does not seem able to be in two places at the same time. This limitation may be one that is an inherent part of his nature, or it may be a limitation he assumes when he visits Narnia. In the previous chapter, when Aslan asked Lucy, "Do you think I wouldn't obey my own rules?" (159), he was referring to obeying the spell of visibility. But there may be other rules in Narnia that Aslan has established and obeys out of principle.

## "Gone!"

"Gone! And you and I quite crestfallen," the magician says to Lucy after Aslan vanishes. "It's always like that, you can't keep him" (162). Here his use of *always* implies that Coriakin has had other experiences with Aslan leaving sooner than desired. Perhaps Coriakin is referring to Aslan's previous appearances on Dufflepud Island, but perhaps he is also remembering his days as a star in the Narnian heavens and Aslan's visits then. In chapter fourteen, Caspian will want to know what the misdeed was that led to Coriakin's punishment, and it is hard not to share his curiosity. Ramandu's rebuke to Caspian, that it is not for him "to know what faults a star can commit" (209), can be applied to inquisitive readers as well. Despite this stipulation, it is possible that Lewis provides some hints about Coriakin's transgression.

In the magician's first words to Aslan, he admitted, "I am a little impatient," and Aslan offered the mild rebuke, "All in good time" (161). Perhaps a lack of patience was Coriakin's downfall, and this is why Aslan set him to govern the Dufflepuds, in order that he might acquire this virtue.

Here after Aslan's departure, the magician points out to Lucy, "You can't keep him" (162). Perhaps when Coriakin was a star, he tried to enforce his own wishes on Aslan in some way—in some way he tried to "keep" Aslan rather than accept his will. Perhaps this is where his acknowledgement comes from—from personal experience trying to do just this. If so, then perhaps an alternate reason Coriakin was set to govern the Dufflepuds was in order to see the role of authority from the side of the one doing the governing.

Despite these hints and the possible connection made earlier about pride and the bearded glass, Lewis never reveals the exact nature of Coriakin's transgression. All we can say for sure is that he was guilty of some fault and was given a corrective punishment. In this sense the magician, although an unworldly being of great power, is no different from other characters in the Chronicles or, Lewis would say, from the readers themselves.

As was noted earlier, Lewis describes the cure for our rebellious nature in *The Problem of Pain*, where he points out, "While what we call 'our own life' remains agreeable we will not surrender it to Him. What then can God do in our interests but make 'our own life' less agreeable to us?" (85). Coriakin's life was made "less agreeable" by being assigned the frustrating and thankless task of overseeing the Dufflepuds.

The magician leads Lucy to a dining room "full of sunlight and flowers" and a bare table that suddenly is set with a "tablecloth, silver, plates, glasses, and food" (163). Earlier in the statement of how Coriakin makes "no more noise than a great big cat" (140), Lewis intended for Coriakin, one of Aslan's agents, to be seen as sort of a smaller version of Aslan—one less powerful, more familiar, and less frightening. In that same vein, the magician here has his own smaller, more ordinary version of Aslan's table and its grand feast that the crew will discover on Ramandu's Island in chapter thirteen.

In contrast with Aslan's table, which will hold "such a banquet as had never been seen" (192), here we are told that Coriakin's modest table is laden with more common, though no less tasty fare: "an omelet, piping hot, cold lamb and green peas, a strawberry ice, lemon-squash to drink with the meal and a cup of chocolate to follow" (163).

As Paul Ford has noted, "Freely given hospitality is a fundamental aspect of Narnia life, bespeaking the Narnian delight in domesticity and attention to courtesy" (257). In *The Lion, the Witch and the Wardrobe*, one of the very first actions in Narnia was Mr. Tumnus's invitation to Lucy to come to his house for "toast—and sardines—and cake" (13). A few chapters later the Beavers provided the children with a homey meal of fried fish, boiled potatoes, and a "gloriously sticky" marmalade roll (74). After his riding accident in the second book, Prince Caspian was immediately offered "a cupful of something sweet and hot" (66). Here through a meal of eggs, lamb, and peas, the magician continues to show the important role Lewis assigns to ordinary hospitality.

Coriakin tells Lucy, "I have tried to give you food more like the food of your own land" (163). Careful readers may note that the magician is the first Narnian character besides Aslan who displays knowledge of Earth. Later in his comments about the stars in our universe, Ramandu will also display a knowledge of our world. By giving these two characters a knowledge of another world besides Narnia, Lewis gives them a further sense of being not of this world, or at least not only of the world of Narnia.

## "They Wouldn't Do What They Were Told"

Soon Lucy and the magician are "chatting away like old friends" (163). Lucy learns that the spell she was sent to read has worked and that the formerly invisible creatures have become visible once more.

Now as the magician's clock strikes three, a host of what look like giant mushrooms or big umbrellas come awake on the lawn, revealing that the invisible creatures are actually a type of dwarf with one large foot. Readers familiar with Pliny's *Natural History* may recognize the source from which Lewis borrowed these creatures. Pliny writes, "Monocoli . . . have only one leg and hop with amazing speed. These people are also called the Umbrella-footed, because when the weather is hot they lie on their backs stretched out on the ground and protect themselves by the shade of their feet" (78).

Although Lucy finds the single-footed creatures so funny she bursts into laughter, critic Kath Filmer has described the magician's punishment of removing one of their legs as "unnecessarily cruel" and "an extreme way by which to effect obedience" (47). Whether readers share Filmer's opinion may depend on whether they think it would be crueler to allow the Dufflepuds to continue on their foolish, disobedient way and never grow to their potential or, alternatively, to administer whatever corrective measures are needed to bring them to maturity. Perhaps Filmer would also argue that Eustace's transformation from a boy to a dragon and back to a boy was unnecessarily cruel and that Aslan should have left him as he was.

As before with Eustace, pain—here the pain of being changed from "common little dwarfs" into monopods (169)—is the only megaphone able to rouse the magician's deaf subjects, the only element they will respond to. That said, this correction does not seem to be overly painful, as it would be if administered to humans in our world. The magician finds the monopods comical, and Lucy—whose compassion and moral compass we have come to trust—does so as well.

Despite the humorous descriptions of the Dufflepuds' antics, Lewis has a serious point to make. The Dufflepuds' relationship to the magician—with their failure to see that his command to mind the garden was for their own good, and their subsequent rebellion against him—in some ways may mirror Adam's and Eve's relationship to God, and our own as well. Lewis suggests that we all go through a Dufflepud stage in life, one characterized by a lack of cooperation and appreciation, a stage that hopefully we grow past. In *The Problem of Pain*, he argues that each of us is "a Divine work of art, something that God is making, and therefore something with which He will not be satisfied until it has a certain character" (38).

From the lowliest Dufflepud to the most majestic star, Aslan has a plan for each. As Paul Ford has observed, he is the "storyteller behind every person's story" (55). In *The Problem of Pain*, Lewis comments that we may wish we were of "so little account to God that He left us alone to follow our natural impulses," but this would be "asking not for more Love, but for less" (39).

Previously Aslan cared enough about the magician to discipline him, doing everything necessary to put him back on the right track.

Now the magician has cared enough to do the same for those whose growth he has been put in charge of. In *The Horse and His Boy*, Aravis will undergo a similar painful but needed correction when Aslan scratches her.

## That Evening and the Next Day

The chapter comes to a close with the Duffers pleased to be visible again and pleased with their new name of Dufflepuds. That evening as the Narnians feast upstairs at the magician's table, we are told Lucy notices "how different the whole top floor looked now that she was no longer afraid of it" (173), a truth for all times and one Lewis explored earlier in his space trilogy.

In *Out of the Silent Planet*, Ransom is initially horrified by the appearance of sorns, one of the three races that inhabit Mars. After he comes to see that they do not want to harm him, his perception of them completely changes. We are told:

> "Ogres" he had called them when they first met his eyes as he struggled in the grip of Weston and Devine; "Titans" or "Angels" he now thought would have been a better word. Even the faces, it seemed to him, he had not then seen aright. He had thought them spectral when they were only august, and his human reaction to their lengthened severity of line and profound stillness of expression now appeared to him not so much cowardly as vulgar. (101)

In *Perelandra*, the next story, Ransom has a similar change in his view of a giant underground beetle. Although Ransom still finds the creature curiously shaped, his emotional response has been altered. Readers are told, "All loathing had vanished clean out of his mind, so that neither then nor at any other time could he remember it, nor ever understand again why one should quarrel with an animal for having more legs or eyes than oneself" (155). Lewis's point is that while an irrational fear of the unknown may be normal, there is another way of seeing things that are strange or different, a way that lies on the other side of fear.

On the next to the last page in this chapter, Coriakin magically produces a map of the *Dawn Treader*'s travels, one that the narrator tells us "still hangs" in Caspian's "Chamber of Instruments at Cair Paravel" (174). When writing *The Voyage of the Dawn Treader*, Lewis envisioned it as the last story in the series. This claim that the map is still hanging in Caspian's castle suggests not only that Narnia is still in existence but also that Caspian is still reigning there—events that do not line up with details in subsequent books. Earlier, after the spell for the refreshment of the spirit, readers were told, "Ever since that day what Lucy means by a good story is a story which reminds her of the forgotten story in the Magician's Book" (157)—a statement that gives the feeling that Lucy is still alive back in England, and a similar indicator that Lewis was at one point planning to end after three books.

Despite being able to draw a detailed map of the places where they have been, Coriakin can tell the crew "nothing about seas or lands further east" (174). He does, however, mend and resupply the ship. In these ways, Lewis's magician resembles Tolkien's Tom Bombadil, who befriends the hobbits during their brief stop in his islandlike country. In *The Fellowship of the Ring*, as Frodo, Sam, Merry, and Pippin are about to take their leave, Tom tells them, "Out east my knowledge fails" (144), a statement quite similar to Coriakin's.

Two chapters later, Caspian will ask Ramandu, "Have you any knowledge of the seas and lands further east than this?" (208). The former star will reply, "I saw them long ago, but it was from a great height. I cannot tell you such things as sailors need to know." Presumably Coriakin also saw these regions when he was a star, but like Ramandu, he was too distant to see helpful details.

## Discussion Questions

It was pointed out that for someone being punished, Coriakin seems quite happy to see Aslan. By contrast, the Dufflepuds see Coriakin as their enemy.

1. How do you interpret the magician's statement that for now he must govern the Dufflepuds by "rough magic" rather than wisdom?

2. Lewis may be suggesting that the further along we are in our growth, the more we welcome the agents of correction in our lives and the opportunity for improvement they bring. Where do you see this principle in your own life?

3. Consider Lewis's phrase "authority exercised with humility and obedience accepted with delight." How applicable do you think it is to the magician's situation? To our own?

It was noted that in *The Problem of Pain*, Lewis comments, "While what we call 'our own life' remains agreeable we will not surrender it to Him. What then can God do in our interests but make 'our own life' less agreeable to us?" (85). He maintains, "We are, not metaphorically but in very truth, a Divine work of art, something that God is making, and therefore something with which He will not be satisfied until it has a certain character" (38).

4. Do you see these statements as relevant here and elsewhere in the Chronicles? If so, how?

5. How would you respond to Lewis's claim that pain can be God's megaphone to rouse a deaf world or rouse an individual who has been deaf to other calls?

In this chapter, when the Narnians attend the magician's feast, we are told that Lucy notices "how different the whole top floor looked now that she was no longer afraid of it" (173).

6. Have you had a similar change in perspective in your own life? If so, how?

## TWELVE

# The Dark Island

### "Do We Go into This?"

The crew sails under a gentle wind for twelve days with nothing more than chess and an occasional whale sighting to pass the time. Then on the thirteenth day out, Edmund sees what at first looks like a "great dark mountain" (176). As the ship gets closer to the strange sight, it is described as a "dark mass" that is "not land at all, nor even, in an ordinary sense, a mist" (177).

In the previous adventure, Lucy's worries proved to be groundless as the magician turned out to be a friend instead of the foe she had imagined. Here in chapter twelve, Lewis revisits the topic of imaginary fears and takes great pains to point out that imaginary fears are sometimes not easily overcome. And if we take the final outcome here as evidence, sometimes they cannot be overcome at all—at least not without help—and so simply should be avoided. Evan Gibson notes that this chapter focuses on "groundless fear—the fear of bad dreams, darkness, and the unknown"

(179), and suggests that Lewis's statement here is that "we should not minimize the terror generated by imaginary evils."

Soon the *Dawn Treader* reaches the edge of the dark mass, an object the narrator notes "is rather hard to describe" (177). As he has at other times, Lewis turns to the use of a simile to suggest more than he merely states. Readers are told:

> You will see what it was like if you imagine yourself looking into the mouth of a railway tunnel—a tunnel either so long or so twisty that you cannot see the light at the far end. And you would know what it would be like. For a few feet you would see the rails and sleepers and gravel in broad daylight; then there would come a place where they were in twilight, and then, pretty suddenly, but of course without a sharp dividing line, they would vanish altogether into smooth solid blackness. It was just so here.

Caspian asks the others for their opinions on whether to proceed. Drinian and Edmund, both brave and experienced adventurers, express reluctance to go on. Lucy and Eustace say nothing but feel "very glad inside at the turn things seemed to be taking" (179). A consensus emerges among the human crew that they should not enter this darkness, and this consensus will be an important part of the point Lewis will make through this episode.

Near the end of *Prince Caspian*, Aslan told Reepicheep, "I have sometimes wondered, friend, whether you do not think too much about your honor" (208). In *The Voyage of the Dawn Treader*—in his longing for something greater than honor at the place where sky and water meet, in his command "Don't fight! Push!" during the sea serpent episode, and in his willingness to allow Lucy to go upstairs alone at the magician's house—readers have seen a more mature Reepicheep. But like all of Lewis's characters, the noble mouse does not become perfect after Aslan's correction, only better. Lewis adds a realistic touch here in chapter twelve, as we find Reepicheep again thinking too much about his honor.

Reepicheep speaks up and wants to know why the others are even considering not continuing. Drinian asks what use it would be to plow on through the blackness, and this allows Reepicheep to make a speech, one of his longest so far, about the fundamental nature of a quest: "Use, Captain? If by use you mean filling our bellies or our purses, I confess it will be no use at all. So far as I know we did not set sail to look for things useful but to seek honor and adventure. And here is as great an adventure as ever I heard of, and here, if we turn back, no little impeachment of all our honors" (179). Reepicheep's claim that their goal is "to seek honor and adventure" is not true but is colored by his own desires. The crew's quest is to find the seven exiled lords, and Reepicheep's quest is to reach the utter east. Sailing into the darkness could actually be antithetical to both these goals. A possible impeachment of their honor is not what should be important here.

In the final chapter of *The Lion, the Witch and the Wardrobe*, the four Pevensies faced a decision similar to the one the *Dawn Treader*'s crew must make. In their hunt for the White Stag, the young kings and queens came upon the lamp-post that marked the boundary near the entrance to the wardrobe. Lucy declared, "It will not go out of my mind that if we pass this post and lantern either we shall find strange adventures or else some great change of our fortunes" (186). Put off by the idea of strange adventures, Susan suggested, "Therefore by my counsel we shall lightly return to our horses and follow this White Stag no further." In words that parallel Reepicheep's statement here, Peter told Susan, "Madam, therein I pray thee to have me excused. For never since we four were Kings and Queens in Narnia have we set our hands to any high matter, as battles, quests, feats of arms, acts of justice, and the like, and then given over; but always what we have taken in hand, the same we have achieved" (186).

Paul Ford has written that in Narnia, "there is no honorable turning away from the adventure, for it is only in leaving the known for the unknown that honor may truly be found" (40). This claim is mostly true, but as will be seen here and at other times in the Chronicles, it has several significant exceptions.

In *The Silver Chair*, Rilian will be tempted to accept the invitation to visit the underground country of Bism and will tell the others, "This is a marvelous adventure and it may be no mortal man has ever looked into Bism before or will ever have the chance again" (205). Puddleglum will then remind him, "If your Highness wants to see your father while he's still alive, which I think he'd prefer, it's about time we were getting onto that road to the diggings" (207). In the end, Rilian agrees and heeds a higher call than mere adventure.

At the end of *The Voyage of the Dawn Treader*, Caspian will face a similar situation when he wants to abandon his responsibilities and sail to the world's end. Reepicheep's stern admonishment— "You shall not please yourself with adventures as if you were a private person" (239)—will fail to move Caspian, and it will take an encounter with Aslan to remind the young king that there are some duties that must come before adventure.

In the episode of the Dark Island, Lewis suggests that this issue of turning away from adventure is not always a simple one. Here the implication is that there may be times when discretion is the better part of valor. In the end, when Caspian commands, "Row, row. Pull for all our lives" (184), Lewis intends for us to hear wisdom, experience, and responsibility, not cowardice or lack of honor. Lewis's point, as will be seen, is that imaginary fears can produce real terror, the kind against which no amount of human courage can prevail.

### "There Are Some Things No Man Can Face"

Still smarting from Reepicheep's rebuke about honor, the crew— for now—rows on into the "lonely darkness" with lanterns lit and weapons drawn (181). After what seems to be a long time of peering vainly into the inky blackness, a cry is heard from somewhere in the distance, a cry of some "inhuman voice" or of someone "in such extremity of terror that he had almost lost his humanity" (181–82). Caspian finds himself unable to speak, so it is Reepicheep—still unaffected by the experience—who shouts out, "Who calls? If you are a foe we do not fear you, and if you are a friend your enemies shall be taught the fear of us" (182). The far-off voice answers back, begging to be allowed to come on board. Soon there is the sound of someone swimming, and then a man with "a wild, white face" appears in the torchlight and is hauled on deck.

The man, as we soon learn, is Lord Rhoop, one of the seven Narnian lords they have been seeking. Lordly no more, he is thin and haggard and dressed only in "a few wet rags" (183). He at once urges the crew to turn the ship about, crying, "Row for your lives away from this accursed shore." When Reepicheep, still undaunted, asks what the danger is, the stranger gasps, "This is the Island where Dreams come true. . . . Not daydreams: dreams."

There is a brief silence as the crew remembers "certain dreams they had had—dreams that make you afraid of going to sleep again" and then realizes what it would mean to land in a place where this kind of dream came true (184). Then they fling themselves on the oars and "row as they had never rowed before."

Readers are told that "only Reepicheep remained unmoved" (184), and he demands to know why this "poltroonery" is being tolerated. This time Caspian ignores Reepicheep's complaint. This is one time that the noble mouse is mistaken: it would be foolhardy, not honorable, to go on. Speaking for Lewis as well as for the rest of the crew, Caspian insists, "There are some things no man can face."

Reepicheep's reply—"It is, then, my good fortune not to be a man" (184)—while humorous, contains a kernel of truth. Reepicheep *is* fortunate not to be human and so to be subject to the terrifying dreams humans have. In this account of the debilitating horror that dreams can produce, Lewis injects another autobiographical element in the Chronicles. In *Surprised by Joy*, Lewis records that one of his earliest memories was the terror of certain dreams and refers to them as a window that opened on what was "hardly less than Hell" (8).

In his essay "On Three Ways of Writing for Children," Lewis provides another clear indication that he took the issue of irrational fears seriously as he addressed the concern that certain stories might overly frighten young readers. He writes, "I suffered too much from night-fears myself in childhood to undervalue this objection.

I would not wish to heat the fires of that private hell for any child" (39). He concludes, "We must not do anything likely to give the child those haunting, disabling, pathological fears against which ordinary courage is helpless." What is the source of these fears? Lewis proposes that "we seem to bring them into the world with us ready made" (40), and that the mind of the young person should, as much as is possible, "be kept clear of things he can't bear to think of" (39).

## "Courage, Dear Heart"

As they row feverishly in what they hope is the direction away from the Dark Island, the crew members begin to be inundated with haunting, disabling, dreamlike fears. Eustace hears "a huge pair of scissors opening and shutting" (185). Someone else reports hearing gongs sounding. Rynelf hears something "crawling up the sides of the ship." Drinian breaks out in a cold sweat, and his hand on the tiller starts to shake. In a statement that recalls Eustace's finding a new layer of dragon skin beneath each one he scratched off, the rowers moan, "We're going round and round in circles."

Suddenly the stranger on the deck bursts out in "a horrible screaming laugh" and yells, "We shall never get out. What a fool I was to have thought they would let me go as easily as that" (186). And this, of course, is Lewis's point: irrational night fears, the fears of bad dreams, do not let go easily. Without external help, perhaps they do not let go at all.

This is arguably the moment of greatest peril on the entire voyage. Not just the dual quest to find the other lords and reach the utter east is at risk of being lost, but so are the very lives of the entire crew. And there is nothing the crew can do. They are trapped inside their darkest nightmares, unable to break free, just as Lord Rhoop was.

Earlier Aslan intervened to do what our characters could not do themselves—to undragon Eustace, to free Caspian and Edmund from the enchantment of Deathwater Island, and to keep Lucy from saying the spell that would have made her beautiful beyond the lot of mortals. Here the entire crew of the *Dawn Treader* is helpless, imprisoned in their private nightmares. Lucy, who has been keeping watch alone in the fighting top, whispers, "Aslan, Aslan, if ever you loved us at all, send us help now" (186).

In response to her prayer, even though nothing external has changed yet, Lucy changes. She begins "to feel a little—a very, very little—better" (186). In *The Last Battle*, Tirian will pray a similar prayer and will experience a similar lightening of heart. Captured, all alone, and tied to a tree, he will call out, "Aslan! Aslan! Aslan! Come and help us now" (49). Then readers will be told, "There was no change in the night or the wood, but there began to be a kind of change inside Tirian. Without knowing why, he began to feel a faint hope. And he felt somehow stronger" (50).

In *Letters to Malcolm*, Lewis describes the effect that prayer has on the petitioner. He writes that by "making known" our requests to God, we unveil ourselves and "instead of merely being known, we show, we tell, we offer ourselves to view" (21). In prayer, Lewis goes on to claim, there is a meeting, and through this meeting a change that takes place in us.

After Lucy's prayer to Aslan, the crew sees first a tiny speck of light and then "a broad beam of light" that falls from the speck down on the ship (186). As Lucy looks along the beam, she sees something in it—something that first appears to be a cross, then an airplane, then a kite, and finally an albatross that circles the ship three times. Lucy alone hears a voice that whispers, "Courage, dear heart" (187)—a voice she feels sure is Aslan's. The strange bird perches briefly on the prow and calls out in a "strong sweet voice" what seem to be words, though no one understands them. After a short time on the prow, the albatross rises up and leads the *Dawn Treader* out of the darkness into a grayness, and finally out into the sunlight.

What, if anything, are we to make of this speck, beam, cross, airplane, kite, and albatross? Does each of these elements have an additional symbolic meaning, or does Lewis intend them to be simply what they are?

Kurt Bruner and Jim Ware point to Melville's "reverential feelings" toward the albatross in *Moby Dick* and to the albatross in "The Rime of the Ancient Mariner," which they claim "in some sense or other" is "a picture of Christ." They conclude, "Lewis must surely have had this kind of symbolism in mind when he introduced an albatross into the story" (93). This interpretation seems overly indirect, since it requires that we tie the meaning of the bird to the associated meaning it takes on in two other literary works. Wayne Martindale asserts that the albatross "evokes biblical imagery associated with the Holy Spirit" (191), a claim that is also problematic since it requires readers to imaginatively link the albatross with a dove. Also, both of their readings suggest a symbolic meaning for only one of the images in the list. If we say the albatross means something else, should we also look for symbolic meaning for the kite or the airplane?

Most critics do not see symbolic meaning in these items. Marvin Hinten simply notes that the albatross is "the traditional good-luck bird of the sea" (43). Similarly, in *A Field Guide to Narnia*, Colin Duriez points to "a long maritime tradition of the albatross as guide and harbinger of good fortune" (167). Sailors lost at sea would have taken an albatross, or any bird, as a sign of land nearby—in this case real land and not the Dark Island—and would have been quick to follow. Here we are told that Drinian steers after it, "not doubting that it offered good guidance" (187).

A similar point can be made for the cross shape in which the albatross first appears. Paul Ford writes, "It is difficult . . . to avoid an allegorical interpretation of the crosslike appearance of the speck in the beam that Lucy first notices when she looks along the beam. Such an interpretation, however, seems to obscure rather than enhance the central experience of the scene" (70).

In an essay titled "The Genesis of a Medieval Book," Lewis himself cautions against seeing extra meanings unless they are supported by the text, writing, "Within any given story any object, person, or place is neither more nor less nor other than what that story effectively shows it to be" (40). In the end, the most sustainable reading is to assume that Lewis has Aslan take the shape of this seabird simply because it is so common and allows Aslan to appear without anyone other than Lucy knowing it.

But why is Lucy the only one to detect Aslan's presence in the albatross? Why should Aslan's voice be heard only by her? Back in *Prince Caspian*, the question of why Aslan appeared only to Lucy was never directly answered, and similar questions remain unanswered here. It is clear that Lewis wants to continue his pattern of having Aslan work more behind the scenes than in them—perhaps to evoke how God often works in our world in a way that may not be apparent to everyone. Lucy is the most spiritually sensitive; she is also the only one who asked for help. If Caspian, Eustace, or Edmund had made a similar request, perhaps they too would have heard a whisper of encouragement from the albatross.

In his book *Into the Wardrobe*, David Downing points out, "Aslan is not a tame lion, and sometimes he is not any kind of lion" (72). In this chapter, Aslan appears as a great bird. Near the end of the story, he will take the form of a dazzling white lamb. In *The Horse and His Boy*, he will comfort and protect Shasta in the form of a cat. Besides the fact that it allows Aslan to work behind the scenes, might there be another reason Lewis has Aslan appear as something other than a lion? Downing observes that "while most other religions usually visualized incarnated gods in human form, the Lord God of the Israelites appears as a burning bush, a cloud of pillar and fire, a voice out of a whirlwind, and a still, small voice. Lewis adopted a similar strategy in the chronicles, depicting Aslan in several forms and in many different roles in order to express the myriad dimensions of God's nature."

In *Letters to Children*, Lewis himself comments on the issue of Aslan's bodily form: "There is one thing Aslan has that Jesus has not—I mean, the body of a lion. (But remember, if there are other worlds and they need to be saved and Christ were to save them as He would—He may really have taken all sorts of bodies in them which we don't know about)" (52).

Christ assumed a human body when he came to earth and appeared to humans. Aslan assumes an animal body when he comes to Narnia, the world of animals. In chapter fourteen, we will learn that the Narnian sun has valleys where fire-berries grow and where large white birds live. It might be tempting to theorize that here in chapter twelve, Aslan has flown to the *Dawn Treader* from the sun, a place where he always assumes the body of a large white bird. This theory becomes a bit more attractive when we note that the albatross speaks words that "no one understood" (187) and the sun birds use a language "which no one knew" (205–6). Did Aslan appear to the sun birds? Did he appear to the sea people that Lucy will see later in the story? If he did, it could be argued, he would appear in a body similar to theirs. However, with nothing else to go on, each of these possibilities remains just that.

## Looking along the Beam

In this chapter, we find the statement, "Lucy looked along the beam and presently saw something in it" (187). This of itself might not seem worth commenting on except for the fact that in Lewis's 1945 essay "Meditation in a Toolshed," we find similar phrasing. There Lewis begins in darkness, much like the crew of the *Dawn Treader* as they near the Dark Island. Lewis writes:

> I was standing today in the dark toolshed. The sun was shining outside and through the crack at the top of the door there came a sunbeam. From where I stood that beam of light, with the specks of dust floating in it, was the most striking thing in the place. Everything else was almost pitch-black. I was seeing the beam, not seeing things by it.
>
> Then I moved, so that the beam fell on my eyes. Instantly the whole previous picture vanished. I saw not toolshed, and (above all) no beam. Instead I saw, framed in the irregular cranny at the top of the door, green leaves moving on the branches of a tree outside and beyond that, 90 odd million miles away, the sun. *Looking along the beam*, and looking at the beam are very different experiences. (212, emphasis added)

In the essay Lewis goes on to make a distinction between someone who directly experiences something, such as a young man in love (who would be looking along the beam), and someone who witnesses the experience from outside, such as a scientist who describes the young man's experience (which would be looking at the beam).

Did Lewis intend for readers of *The Voyage of the Dawn Treader* to make a connection between Lucy's looking along the beam and his essay? Since the essay was written for adults and was rather obscure at the time the Narnia stories were being written, the answer is probably not. However, it seems likely that Lewis made the connection himself, and in writing about Lucy's experience of Aslan, he was thinking of the same point he made in the essay.

In *Not a Tame Lion*, Bruce Edwards elaborates on this idea from "Meditation in a Toolshed." Edwards explains:

> When "looking at" becomes enfranchised as the exclusive way of understanding oneself and the world, or the official genre of knowing and reporting what is true, the unintended and unremarked consequence is to empty both the cosmos and humankind of the supreme spiritual significance each once had. . . .
>
> Lewis is pointing out the ironies of what in our day is common establishment thinking about theological and supernatural phenomena. While our ancestors could speak of God, angels, and the possibility of divine encounters as objective fact, these topics have been reduced to the category of the subjective as wishful thinking. (183–85)

Edwards concludes that the final outcome of this form of "depersonification" is a "disenchanted cosmos" (186).

In her experience of Aslan in this episode, Lucy has a divine encounter. Both literally and in Lewis's metaphorical sense, she looks along the beam. No one else does. While Lucy feels sure that the voice that whispers to her is Aslan's, a scientist looking at Lucy's experience might argue that her conclusion that the albatross is Aslan is merely wishful thinking.

After dismissing the likelihood that the cross in this scene should be interpreted as referring to the cross of Calvary, Paul Ford raises a concern about linking Lucy's experience here with

"Meditation in a Toolshed." Ford maintains, "This 1945 essay is perhaps too distant to form immediate background for *The Voyage of the Dawn Treader*, but the distinction between looking at and looking along is too instrumental to Lewis's epistemology to go unremarked" (70).

## There Was Nothing to Be Afraid Of?

Since 1994, all English-language editions of the Chronicles of Narnia have had the same text, but prior to this time, American editions featured a number of revisions Lewis had made. In *Imagination and the Arts in C. S. Lewis*, Peter Schakel explains how these differences— most of them quite minor—came to be. Schakel writes, "Because of union regulations in the United States, the type of the Chronicles had to be reset for the edition sold in the U.S. That meant Lewis had to read another set of proofs, several weeks or perhaps months after he finished reading proofs for the British edition. As he did so, he occasionally had second thoughts and made changes—usually minor ones, but at least one substantial revision" (35).

The substantial revision Schakel refers to is the modification Lewis made to the ending of the Dark Island episode. In a backwards publishing move, all editions printed after 1994 now revert to the unrevised British text, and in it Lewis treats the irrational fears of the crew lightly. In this text, as the *Dawn Treader* shoots into the sunlight, readers are told, "And all at once everybody realized that there was nothing to be afraid of and never had been" (187). The paragraph ends with, "First one, and then another, began laughing" (188). Rynelf concludes, "I reckon we've made pretty good fools of ourselves."

When Lewis prepared the text for the American version, he addressed this topic of imaginary fears with more compassion and sympathy. He completely cut out these three sentences, so in the revised text there is no claim that there was nothing to be afraid of, no one laughs, and no one is categorized as a fool for being afraid.

In the original text when the crew looks back, readers are told, "The Dark Island and the darkness had vanished for ever" (188). In the revised text for the American edition, the Dark Island does not vanish but instead simply grows smaller and smaller, like a real island would. Paul Ford writes that Lewis's goal in these and other smaller changes to this chapter was "to correct any impression that the original British edition might have given that night fears are unreal and ultimately laughable and that they can be obliterated altogether" (155).

Peter Schakel goes on to observe that the unrevised text risks conveying the message that feelings of fright are "inconsequential or wrong" and that the revisions Lewis made suggest that imaginary fears are "no laughing matter" (37–38). Both Ford and Schakel argue that the revised text better reflects Lewis's real intentions and should have been made the standard. Schakel finds it "regrettable" that "most readers henceforth will read and know only the earlier, less effective original wordings" (38). Perhaps one day the revisions that Lewis made will be restored along with the numbering order used during his lifetime.

Once out of the darkness, the crew sails "all afternoon with great joy" before "a fair wind" (189). The chapter concludes with the comment, "But nobody noticed when the albatross had disappeared," an observation that suggests Aslan's involvement has gone undetected by everyone but Lucy.

In *The Horse and His Boy*, it is only in looking back that Shasta will see the role Aslan played in the critical events of his life. Aslan will explain:

> I was the lion who forced you to join with Aravis. I was the cat who comforted you among the houses of the dead. I was the lion who drove the jackals from you while you slept. I was the lion who gave the Horses the new strength of fear for the last mile so that you should reach King Lune in time. And I was the lion you do not remember who pushed the boat in which you lay, a child near death, so that it came to shore where a man sat wakeful at night, to receive you. (165)

Readers might imagine a scene in Aslan's country where the crew of the *Dawn Treader* will be gathered around the great lion as he explains, "I was the albatross who guided the *Dawn Treader* out of the darkness."

## Discussion Questions

It was noted that one of Lewis's earliest memories was of night fears and the terror of certain dreams.

1. What do you think Lewis is saying in this chapter about the power of imaginary fears? Do you agree with him?

As Lucy looks along the beam of light, readers are told, "At first it looked like a cross, then it looked like an aeroplane, then it looked like a kite, and at last with a whirring of wings it was right overhead and was an albatross" (187). Michael Ward has provided the following commentary on this: "The two-dimensional cross develops motive power as an aeroplane; it then turns from a mere machine into a kite borne aloft on the wind, before becoming something organic, Coleridge's image of Christ, an albatross, the bird with the widest wing-span, which soars the longest and can fly by night" (117).

2. What do you make of the four images Lucy sees? In your opinion, does Lewis intend for one or more of them to have additional symbolic meanings?

Russell Dalton claims that in *The Voyage of the Dawn Treader*, Lewis "follows the mythic pattern of the heroes' quest," on which the heroes "endure a trail of trials on their way to learning their true identity and their place in the world" (134). Dalton concludes, "The role of providence is present in these tales, but it is often a mysterious force that remains deep in the background."

3. Where in the Chronicles or other stories do you see examples of a mysterious force working in the background?

4. What, if any, connections do you see between Aslan's disguised appearance here—which only Lucy is aware of—and the presence of the divine in our own world?

Back in *Prince Caspian*, when Lucy asked Aslan if the others would also see him, his somewhat puzzling response was, "It depends" (143). Lewis never made it entirely clear on what their seeing Aslan depended.

5. What are the factors that allow Lucy, and only Lucy, to be aware of Aslan's presence here in chapter twelve?

6. On what might seeing God's presence in our own world depend?

THIRTEEN

# The Three Sleepers

## "Why, They're Only Asleep"

The voyage the *Dawn Treader* undertakes is a gradual passage from the known to the unknown. At the Lone Islands, the crew encountered a region not much different from the one they left behind in Narnia. Successive stops grew less and less familiar. While the Magician's Island held invisible creatures, at least they were real. The Dark Island moved the journey out of the real world into the world of dreams. The danger the crew encountered there was entirely imaginary. And now having escaped from the land where dreams came true, the crew continues further into the regions of awe.

The wind becomes gentler, the sea smoother. New constellations rise in a sky that seems "to have grown larger" (190). Finally, on "an evening of startling beauty" with a purple and crimson sunset behind them, they arrive at a land with gentle hills and an enticing "dim, purple kind of smell" (191). They have come to Ramandu's Island—the last land before Aslan's country. It is, as Ramandu's daughter will explain, the beginning of the end.

Leaving Lord Rhoop—who "wished to see no more islands"—with the crew on the ship (191), Caspian leads a landing party ashore. They find a mysterious, unroofed space "flagged with smooth stones and surrounded by gray pillars," and inside this space a great table set with an elegant banquet (192). Suddenly Edmund points to the far end of the table, where three previously unnoticed "somethings" are seated (193). Reepicheep quickly threads his way down through the plates and cups to inspect the "mysterious gray mass" and announces it safe (194). The others join him and quickly discover the three hairy mounds are three men—the sleepers of the chapter's title. With three of the missing lords unaccounted for, readers deduce—a little more quickly than our heroes do—that the last of the seven exiles have been found.

Caspian is unable to wake the sleepers. His attempt elicits drowsy murmurings indicating the lords were arguing over whether to turn back to Narnia or continue on to the world's end. Caspian concludes, "I think our quest is at an end" (195).

The second sleeper mumbles, "Weren't born to live like animals. Get to the east while you've a chance—lands behind the sun" (195). His words, as reported by Ramandu's daughter a few pages later, have a similar point: "We are men and Telmarines, not brutes. What should we do but seek adventure after adventure? We have not long to live in any event. Let us spend what is left in seeking the unpeopled world behind the sunrise" (200). These statements sound like something Reepicheep might say, and a less than careful reading might suggest that this second sleeper is expressing Lewis's own opinion about the human need for a quest and to go beyond mere survival. Lewis is pro-adventure, but as was noted earlier, he does not endorse a simplistic adventure-at-all-costs ethic—not in the Dark Island episode, not in Caspian's desire to go with Reepicheep at the end of the book, and not here.

As evidence of the second sleeper's inordinate desire for adventure, Lewis makes him the one who initiated the violence.

Ramandu's daughter will indicate that it was he who "caught up the Knife of Stone . . . and would have fought with his comrades" (200).

In the second sleeper's desire to seek "the unpeopled world behind the sunrise," readers may hear echoes of Tennyson's Ulysses, another character with an overreaching desire for adventure. In Tennyson's poem, Ulysses describes himself as "always roaming with a hungry heart" (line 12) and declares, "I cannot rest from travel" (line 6). He tells his men, "My purpose holds / To sail beyond the sunset" (lines 59–60), and he attempts to rouse them, stating, "Come, my friends, / 'Tis not too late to seek a newer world" (lines 56–57).

In Lewis's depiction of the second sleeper, described as "a very masterful man" (200), readers also can find close parallels to Dante's portrait of Ulysses in the *Inferno*. In Canto 26, Virgil and Dante encounter the aged explorer, who explains how no fondness for his son, reverence for his father, or "due affection" for Penelope, his wife, could overcome his desire for further exploits in the world (line 95). In assertions that echo those of the second sleeper, Dante's Ulysses tells his men to consider the seed they sprang from, and that they "were not made to live like unto brutes" but instead were made to follow after knowledge (line 119).

An examination of the sleepers' signet rings proves that this is indeed Lord Revilian, Lord Argoz, and Lord Mavramorn, though Lewis does not make clear which name to assign to which sleeper. These last three lords were unable to resolve their conflict before coming to blows and were cast into an enchanted sleep. This same conflict—whether to continue on or turn back—will confront the crew of the *Dawn Treader* as well, and Caspian will need to show greater ability as a leader than the three lords did if he is going to resolve it. He will need his crew if he is going to accomplish his mission, but as Ramandu and the example of the second sleeper make clear, he cannot force his will upon them.

Now that we have met all seven lords and know a bit more about them, we might ask whether we are supposed to make anything more of their names. Marvin Hinten has noted that the word *berne* is a sixteenth-century word meaning "warrior" and an appropriate choice for Lord Bern, who helped overthrow the rule of Gumpas and, as Hinten notes, is the only one of the seven "who engages in any sort of warlike activity" (35). Hinten further suggests that Restimar, with its use of the Latin word *mar*, meaning a body of water, is "a playful name" for the lord who "rests in a body of water" (40). Since it is not an exact match, Revilian—the name of one of the sleeping lords here—may or may not be intended to have associations with the French verb *reveiller*, which means "to wake up," and is the word from which we derive the familiar wake-up bugle call. There seem to be no associated meanings for the names Octesian, Rhoop, Argoz, or Mavramorn.

## "I Myself Will Sit at This Table till Sunrise"

When the landing party becomes perplexed by how to wake the sleepers, Rhince suggests, "Why not fall to while you're discussing it? We don't see a dinner like this every day" (196). Caspian has come a long way since he agreed with Lucy's proposal to walk across Felimath, a walk that in their naïveté got the group captured by Pug. There readers were told, "If Caspian had been as experienced then as he became later on in this voyage he would not have made this suggestion" (38). Here in chapter thirteen, we see how this experience has matured Caspian. He swiftly responds to Rhince's hasty suggestion that they partake: "Not on your life!"

Edmund concurs and further points out, "The whole place smells of magic—and danger" (196). In *The Lion, the Witch and the Wardrobe*, it was through enchanted Turkish Delight that Edmund became entangled with the White Witch, and this has given him a heightened awareness of magic and, it might be argued, greater caution about being taken in by magic food. At the start of *Prince Caspian*, it was Edmund who first understood what the strange pulling on the train platform was, and he shouted to the others, "All catch hands and keep together. This is magic—I can tell by the feeling" (5).

Despite agreeing with Edmund's warning, Reepicheep declares that he will sit at the table until sunrise. Unlike Reepicheep's last proposal to continue on toward the Dark Island, this idea is not unduly dangerous, and it is directly connected to the quest of rescuing the three sleepers. Straightaway Edmund, Caspian, and Lucy volunteer to join him. The narrator then reports that Eustace volunteers also, and Lewis uses the opportunity to once again stress the value of reading, as he explains, "This was very brave of him because never having read of such things or even heard of them till he joined the *Dawn Treader* made it worse for him than for the others" (197). A similar point was made in chapter six, where readers were told, "Most of us know what we should expect to find in a dragon's lair, but as I said before, Eustace had read only the wrong books" (87).

In *An Experiment in Criticism*, Lewis argues that reading "admits us to experiences other than our own" (139), allowing us to "see with other eyes" and "imagine with other imaginations" (137). Without a foundation in the kind of reading that would have prepared him for a situation like the one found here on Ramandu's Island, Eustace must overcome an initial shock the others do not experience.

In this section, Lewis suggests that reading the right kind of books and seeing with other eyes can help to overcome fear. In *The Horse and His Boy*, he will point out that reading can also compensate for a lack of experience by supplying a proper amount of caution. There as Shasta waits at the tombs outside of Tashbaan, he will make a plan to steal as many melons as he can carry and make the journey to Narnia alone. There the narrator will comment, "It was a crazy idea and if he had read as many books as you have about journeys over deserts he would never have dreamed it" (93).

At this point, Caspian orders the rest of the landing party, including Drinian, back to the ship. When the captain starts to object, Caspian reminds him, "Your place is with the ship" (197), and here we encounter yet another message from Lewis about the call of duty outweighing the call to adventure.

Now on their own, the five watchers prepare to spend the night. The narrator comments, "They took some time choosing their seats at the perilous table" (197). Back in chapter two, it was noted that Caspian's use of the phrase "for a year and a day" might evoke in some readers a memory of the Grail quest. Here the narrator's use of the expression "the perilous table" may again bring to mind the Arthurian legend, which depicts a number of elements described as perilous—among them the perilous castle, the perilous forest, and the perilous chapel.

In *C. S. Lewis in Context*, Doris Myers points to this parallel, arguing that the magic feast at Aslan's table "is best seen as an attempt to set forth the numinous quality of Celtic horns of plenty and the feasts of Arthurian knights on their way to fulfilling a magic quest" (147). Paul Ford voices a similar opinion, stating that the table with "its medieval setting and grail-like knife" suggests "the spirituality of the ancient Arthurian legends" (101).

## At Last Something Was Happening

After "hours that seemed like ages" (198), the sky begins to show a faint grayness in the east. At that moment a door in the hillside opens and a figure comes out. Gradually this mysterious figure comes to be a tall girl bearing a candle that burns strangely straight. Sensing that this is a "great lady," they all rise to their feet (199).

The stately young woman informs them that they have come to Aslan's table and that the three lords have been cast into sleep, because in their quarrel one picked up the knife of stone, a thing "not right for him to touch" (200). She explains, "As his fingers closed upon the hilt, deep sleep fell upon all the three. And till the enchantment is undone they will never wake."

In *The Way into Narnia*, Peter Schakel maintains that Aslan's table "seems the Narnian equivalent of the Eucharist of Christianity" (67), for it is both "a table of nourishment" and, with the presence of the stone knife, "a table of remembrance." Marvin Hinten also argues that Aslan's table "parallels the Eucharist, sometimes known in Protestant circles as the Lord's table" (44), and sees a connection between the three sleepers and the passage from 1 Corinthians 11:30. There Paul laments the fact that some people had approached the Lord's table improperly and explains, "That is why many among you are weak and sick, and a number of you have fallen asleep."

Other scholars find that Aslan's table and the Christian Eucharist are not similar enough for them to claim a direct parallel. Among the differences, Doris Myers rightly points out, are "the fear and doubt—not faith—with which the travelers approach the table" and "their inability to discern whether the magic is good or bad" (228). The greatest way they are not alike, Myers contends, is "the fact that Aslan is not present." Although the stone knife is on the table, there is no remembering or even any mention of Aslan or his death when the company finally eats and drinks. In fact, Reepicheep declares his intention to drink "to the lady" (201), not to Aslan, giving the feast a very different feel than the eucharistic memorial. Taking his glass, Reepicheep says to Ramandu's daughter, "Lady, I pledge you." The others quickly join him, and in their eating and drinking we find not the slightest reference to Aslan's sacrifice. Our heroes eat solely out of normal, everyday hunger, and all have an "excellent . . . very late supper" (202). Myers concludes that these elements, combined with the statement by Ramandu's daughter that the feast is set only for those who come so far, make it "a poor image of a sacrament 'generally necessary to salvation.'"

In writing about Aslan's table, Evan Gibson holds that while "in some ways it seems to represent the central feast of the Christian faith . . . to say that partaking of the food here enacts a Narnian Holy Communion goes too far" (180–81). Gibson concludes, "It is easy to find more meaning than Lewis intended."

If not a direct parallel to the Eucharist, might there be other parallels in Aslan's table? Paul Ford proposes that a connection may be drawn between the misuse of a sacred object followed by the sleep that fell over the three lords here, and "the Dolorous Stroke, Lord Balyn's seizure of the spear that pierced Jesus' side in the Arthurian legend" (411). After this incident, Sir Balyn (or Balin) is rendered unconscious until, according to some accounts, he is woken by Merlin. In the end, there are probably not enough similarities to know what associations, if any, Lewis drew on in this scene.

## "You Can Only Believe—or Not"

Edmund looks "more and more uncomfortable" as the landing party listens to the mysterious girl. Finally he gives voice to the problem they face, explaining, "I hope I'm not a coward—about eating this food, I mean—and I'm sure I don't mean to be rude. But we have had a lot of queer adventures on this voyage of ours and things aren't always what they seem. When I look in your face I can't help believing all you say: but then that's just what might happen with a witch too" (201).

In these three sentences, Lewis says much about the nature of their predicament. Edmund begins by stating that he is not speaking out of cowardice—or hopes he is not. One way to avoid danger is simply to turn away from all dangerous situations. In Edmund's claim that he hopes he is not speaking out of fear, we can hear Lewis's message that sometimes we may even fool ourselves about our real motivation because the same action can be done for very different motives. Earlier when Caspian ordered the *Dawn Treader* away from the Dark Island, he did so not out of cowardice but out of good judgment, though both motivations could have led to the same action.

Second, Edmund acknowledges that respect and courtesy play an important role in the group's decision. In his statement "I don't mean to be rude" (201), Edmund makes it clear that just as hosts have a duty to offer hospitality to strangers, strangers likewise have a duty to accept this generosity. The one problem with all this, Edmund observes, is that "things aren't always what they seem." What may appear to be hospitality may actually be deception and enchantment—as he knows firsthand.

Summing up their dilemma, Edmund asks, "How are we to know you're a friend?" (201). In response, the mysterious girl simply replies, "You can't know. You can only believe—or not." The statement "You can't know" here should be taken to mean "You can't know for sure" or "You can't know with complete certainty." Lewis is not saying that one choice is just as good as another and that careful discernment and sound judgment are not important. He is not suggesting that wisdom and experience should not be used to carefully weigh whatever evidence may be present.

Edmund has raised a similar question twice before. In *The Lion, the Witch and the Wardrobe*, when the four children found Mr. Tumnus's cave empty and Lucy suggested they follow the robin, Edmund complained privately to Peter, "We're following a guide we know nothing about. How do we know which side that bird is on? Why shouldn't it be leading us into a trap?" (61). In response, Peter offered evidence that the robin was not deceiving them, stating, "Still—a robin, you know. They're good birds in all the stories I've ever read." A chapter later, Edmund asked Mr. Beaver, "How do we know you're a friend?" (67). Mr. Beaver noted it was "quite right" for Edmund to want some indication of his honesty and offered as his token the handkerchief Lucy had give Mr. Tumnus.

A careful, rational examination of all available evidence is Lewis's formula for making difficult decisions in Narnia, and in our world as well. In his essay "On Obstinacy in Belief," Lewis maintains that there is no question of "belief without evidence" (17). Around the time of his conversion in 1930, Lewis wrote to his friend Arthur Greeves, "I learned to dive which is a great change in my life and has important (religious) connections" (*Collected Letters*, Vol. 1, 915). In the end, the diver cannot know for sure that he will be safe but must ultimately take a leap of faith, though not without first checking to make sure the water is deep enough.

So what evidence is there that the tall girl's words are true? They all have the feeling that she is a great lady, but in *The Lion, the Witch and the Wardrobe*, the White Witch also appeared to Edmund as "a great lady" (31). What are the differences?

Ramandu's daughter wears "a single long garment of clear blue" and has nothing on her feet or head (199). Hers is a natural, unadorned beauty. The White Witch, by contrast, appeared in an overly sumptuous white fur and a golden crown. Also, there was something unnatural and not quite right about her complexion, which was "not merely pale, but white like snow or paper or icing-sugar, except for her very red mouth" (31).

Even more distinctive than their appearances is what the two figures say. Both extend invitations to eat, making for another similarity, but when Edmund asks how they can know if the tall girl is a friend, she does not distort the truth or try to tempt the landing party by appealing to their baser natures. The White Witch, by contrast, told Edmund he was "the cleverest and handsomest young man" she had ever met and promised him "whole rooms full of Turkish Delight" if he would bring his siblings to her (38). She also told him he was to be a prince and later the king of Narnia and would have his siblings as courtiers.

As further evidence, Ramandu's daughter acknowledges Aslan as the founder of the feast, a telling indicator of her goodness. In contrast, when the White Witch was told that her enchanted winter was destroyed by "Aslan's doing" (122), she told her dwarf and Edmund, "If either of you mention that name again, he shall be instantly killed." The appearances, attitudes, and words of each of the two great ladies produce an overall sense that there is something about Ramandu's daughter that seems right and something about the White Witch that seems wrong.

In *The Fellowship of the Ring*, the hobbits face a similar decision of whether or not to trust Strider. He also states that they will have to decide without knowing for certain, telling them, "You must make up your mind. I will answer some of your questions, if that will help you to do so. But why should you believe my story, if you do not trust me already?" (163). Frodo tells Strider, "You have frightened me several times tonight, but never in the way that servants of the enemy would, or so I imagine. I think one of his spies would—well, seem fairer and feel fouler, if you understand" (168). Strider responds, "I look foul and feel fair. Is that it?"

Unlike Strider, Ramandu's daughter does not look foul, but she does feel fair in a way the White Witch did not. Reepicheep, after considering the evidence, is the first to reach this conclusion. "Lady,

I pledge you" (201), he says, raising a glass, and then begins to partake from the strange table. Soon everyone follows his lead.

## "He Cannot Kiss the Princess"

Caspian wonders, "What are we to do about the Sleepers?" (202). In a reference to the story of Sleeping Beauty, he tells the mysterious girl, "In the world from which my friends come . . . they have a story of a prince or a king coming to a castle where all the people lay in an enchanted sleep. In that story he could not dissolve the enchantment until he had kissed the Princess." Readers may remember that back in chapter two, Caspian had little interest in the daughter of the Duke of Galma. We now learn that this was not because of a lack of interest in girls, as Caspian clearly has feelings for the daughter of Ramandu.

The tall girl responds, "Here he cannot kiss the Princess till he has dissolved the enchantment" (203). Ramandu's daughter is not being coy. In the following chapter, Lewis will unite Caspian's and Reepicheep's double quests, which up until now have been independent, when Ramandu will explain that the only way to wake the sleeping lords will be to sail to the world's end and then come back having left at least one of their company behind.

The kiss mentioned by both young people here reflects a mutual interest. On the final page of the book readers will be told, "Caspian married Ramandu's daughter and they all reached Narnia in the end, and she became a great queen and the mother and grandmother of great kings" (248). While Lewis includes relatively few married couples in the Chronicles, an understandable decision in a series for young people, he is not opposed to marriage. Besides Caspian and the daughter of Ramandu, the list of great married couples in Narnia includes Frank and Helen, Mr. and Mrs. Beaver, and Shasta and Aravis. Bree and Hwin will also get married, though not to each other.

Readers find a similar scarcity of weddings and married couples in Middle-earth. But Tolkien's central romantic tale—the story of Aragorn and Arwen—shares a number of common elements with the story of Caspian and Ramandu's daughter. In having to accomplish a great feat before being permitted to marry his queen, Caspian mirrors Aragorn, who is told by Elrond, his future father-in-law, that he must unite the divided kingdom and be crowned as king of both Gondor and Arnor before he can wed Arwen. Here Lewis and Tolkien were drawing on an element common in many myths, where the potential suitor must prove his worth by completing a great task that will benefit the kingdom.

Caspian and Aragorn both wed someone who is more than human. The narrator in *The Silver Chair* will tell the story of "Caspian's bride" and will explain how "the blood of the stars flowed in her veins" (58). Readers never learn whether Caspian's mother-in-law, who does not appear in the Chronicles, was human or a star like Ramandu, so it is unclear whether the mysterious girl we meet in this chapter is half human or not. Arwen's mother is an elf who has left Middle-earth by the time of the story. Her father is half elven.

Both Caspian and Aragorn take daughters away from their fathers. Both form unions that combine the blood of mortals and immortals to produce great rulers for generations to come. In addition, Lewis and Tolkien give a distinctively Christian twist to the happily-ever-after formula. Although both of the couples end this life more in sorrow than in joy—Caspian will live alone in grief after the serpent kills his wife, and Arwen becomes a forlorn widow for many years after Aragorn's death—neither relationship ends in hopelessness. In the extra material at the end of *The Return of the King*, Aragorn expresses confidence that he and Arwen will be reunited after death, telling her, "In sorrow we must go, but not in despair. Behold we are not bound for ever to the circles of the world, and beyond them is more than memory" (1038). Caspian will be shown reunited with his wife, "the Star's daughter," at the great reunion scene in *The Last Battle* (205).

Delighted at this point by the promise of a kiss from Ramandu's daughter, Caspian exclaims, "In the name of Aslan, show me how to set about that work at once" (203). "My father will teach you that," the girl says, and she turns and points to the door in the hillside. Lewis ends the chapter on this note of anticipation, telling readers, "The stars had grown fainter and great gaps of white light were appearing in the grayness of the eastern sky."

## Discussion Questions

Here in chapter thirteen, we meet a mysterious figure described as a tall girl and a great lady. Lewis never gives her a name other than "Ramandu's daughter." Paul Ford suggests that not assigning her a personal name is "an indication of the awe with which Lewis wanted to surround her" (156).

1. What reason or reasons do you see in Lewis's decision regarding the name of Ramandu's daughter? Does this add to the awe surrounding her, or does it contribute in some other way? If so, how?

The second sleeper states, "We are men and Telmarines, not brutes. What should we do but seek adventure after adventure? We have not long to live in any event. Let us spend what is left in seeking the unpeopled world behind the sunrise" (200).

2. What is wrong about this declaration? In what ways might this statement be valid?

3. What might Lewis be saying—here and at other times in the Chronicles—about the need for life to be more than mere survival?

In this chapter, Ramandu's daughter makes her famous statement to the landing party: "You can't know. You can only believe—or not" (201).

4. What do you think she is saying in the context of this chapter?

5. What might Lewis be saying here about the adventure of life?

FOURTEEN

# The Beginning
# of the End of the World

## They Began to Sing

The door in the hillside opens again, and another figure emerges, one that the narrator initially refers to only as "it" and, by doing so, hints at the creature's non-human or more-than-human nature (204). Readers are told, "It carried no light but light seemed to come from it." Even when this figure gets close enough to be seen more clearly, the narrator still does not indicate it is a man. Instead we are told, "As it came nearer, Lucy saw that it was like an old man." The creature who appears here in a form "like an old man" is Ramandu, once and future star of the Narnian sky.

In the chapter from *The Discarded Image* titled "The Heavens," Lewis begins by noting, "The question at once arises whether medieval thinkers really believed that what we now call inanimate objects were sentient and purposive" (93). The answer to this question, Lewis states, is "undoubtedly no" except for "one privileged class of objects" to which they "attributed life and even intelligence." This one privileged class of objects was the stars. Lewis urges readers to "go out on a starry night and walk about for half an hour trying to see the sky in terms of the old cosmology" and so "to enter more fully into the consciousness of our ancestors by realizing how such a universe must have affected those who believed in it" (98). Another way to undertake this experience is through reading the Narnia stories, where the stars and planets are given life, intelligence, and purpose.

In *The Magician's Nephew*, Lewis describes the birth of the Narnian stars—presumably Coriakin and Ramandu among them. As Aslan sings Narnia into existence, his voice is suddenly not the only one. Lewis writes:

> Then two wonders happened at the same moment. One was that the voice was suddenly joined by other voices; more voices than you could possibly count. They were in harmony with it, but far higher up the scale: cold, tingling, silvery voices. The second wonder was that the blackness overhead, all at once, was blazing with stars. They didn't come out gently one by one, as they do on a summer evening. One moment there had been nothing but darkness; next moment a thousand, thousand points of light leaped out—single stars, constellations, and planets, brighter and bigger than any in our world. (107)

A moment later, in response to the heavenly chorus, is the first sunrise. Readers have already met two of these singers in a previous book—celestial bodies who came into being in this scene and whose harmony helps sing in the sun. In *Prince Caspian*, Dr. Cornelius brought the young prince to the castle tower to witness the conjunction of the "two noble planets" Tarva and Alambil (48).

Here in *The Voyage of the Dawn Treader*, Ramandu silently takes his place beside his daughter. Raising their arms and facing east, the two join in a song Lucy describes afterward as "high, almost shrill" (204), a "cold kind of song, an early morning kind of song" (205). As the two sing, the eastern sky begins to turn red and then "up out of the sea" rises the sun. The strong similarities between the song sung here on Ramandu's Island and the one sung to welcome the first sunrise in *The Magician's Nephew*—a song sung "far higher up the scale" in "cold, tingling, silvery voices"—suggest that these may be the same song, one that the stars, both those in the heavens and those at rest, sing to welcome, praise, and celebrate every sunrise.

Gradually the air on the island becomes "full of voices"—voices of great, white birds that take up the same song that the lady and her father are singing, but "in far wilder tones" in a language "no one knew" (205–6). As noted earlier, Lewis may intend for readers to make a connection here to the language spoken by the albatross in chapter twelve, when it called out in "what seemed to be words though no one understood them" (187). Given the similarity between the descriptions, perhaps we are meant to think the albatross and these birds are using the same language.

## A Fire-Berry from the Valleys in the Sun

One bird flies to Ramandu and places what looks like "a little live coal" in his mouth (207). The birds then peck the table clean and take flight back toward the rising sun. On the next page Ramandu explains, "Every morning a bird brings me a fire-berry from the valleys in the Sun, and each fire-berry takes away a little of my age" (208).

Critics have seen various associations in this image. Marvin Hinten sees "a striking parallel" to the scene from Isaiah 6 where one of the seraphim touches Isaiah's lips with a live coal (44). Wayne Martindale also sees this scene as "reminiscent of Isaiah" and claims that Ramandu's fiery coal "makes him younger, but more importantly, it symbolizes purification from sin and preparation to meet Aslan" (110). Walter Hooper suggests that, like Isaiah, Ramandu "is unable to speak" until a live coal is laid on his lips (446), a claim that is difficult to support or disprove—Ramandu does not talk until after eating the fire-berry, but it is not clear that this is due to an inability to speak since he is able to sing.

If there is a connection between Ramandu and Isaiah, it is an indirect one. As Paul Ford observes, although the image may be "reminiscent" of the purification of the prophet Isaiah, "the dynamic of Ramandu's rejuvenation is very dissimilar" (365). Three significant dissimilarities are particularly prominent. First, the scene with Isaiah recounts the prophet's initial call from God. In the scene with Ramandu, the star has long ago finished a lifetime of service.

Second and perhaps most important, Isaiah's immediate emotional response to this call is one of shame and anguish as he cries out, "Woe to me! . . . I am ruined! For I am a man of unclean lips, and I live among a people of unclean lips" (6:5). Isaiah's reaction has no parallel in Ramandu's situation. In fact, since Ramandu has faithfully fulfilled his duties to Aslan, his emotional position is the complete opposite of shame and anguish.

Third, Isaiah's coal is a purifying fire that touches his unclean lips and in doing so cleanses them. The seraphim tells Isaiah, "See, this has touched your lips; your guilt is taken away and your sin atoned for" (6:7). By contrast, Ramandu's coal is described as "a little fruit" (207) and a "fire-berry" (208), a thing he actually consumes as we might eat a berry or piece of fruit ourselves. Its purpose is not purification or atonement but rejuvenation.

In this scene, we also learn that the Narnian sun is quite different from ours, as it has valleys on it where fire-berries grow. In addition, birds seem to live there—the large white birds fly "out of the very center of the rising sun" (205). In *The Lion, the Witch and the Wardrobe*, readers learned that the Narnian sun has mountains as well. There Father Christmas told Lucy that her healing cordial was made from "the juice of one of the fire-flowers that grow in the mountains of the sun" (109). In the next chapter, a further distinction between our world and Narnia will be apparent as readers learn that Narnia is flat instead of spherical.

The landing party is told by Ramandu that to undo the enchantment, they must journey to the world's end. Caspian—now a seasoned leader—is eager to learn anything he can that will help him accomplish this task. He asks his future father-in-law, "Have you any knowledge of the seas and lands further east than this?" (208). The retired star reports that he saw the region from "a great height" long ago and so is unable to offer the kind of information "as sailors need to know."

In the chapter "The Heavens" from *The Discarded Image* mentioned previously, Lewis discusses the scene in the *Paradiso* where Dante "looks down from the sphere of the Fixed Stars and sees the northern hemisphere" (100). Lewis notes that according to the model, Dante would have actually been so high that his "talk of seeing any markings on its surface is ridiculous." Here in Ramandu's admission, Lewis corrects Dante's mistake.

## "That Is Not What a Star Is"

Ramandu reveals that the days when he was a star ceased long ago and that when he set for the last time, he was carried "decrepit and old" to the island to be made new (208). In the time since, he has already begun to grow younger. He tells the company, "And when I have become as young as the child that was born yesterday, then I shall take my rising again" (208–9).

Eustace has been redeemed by Aslan, but this does not mean that he has become unrecognizable. Now he inserts himself into the conversation, informing Ramandu, "In our world a star is a huge ball of flaming gas" (209). In chapter one, readers learned that Eustace "liked books if they were books of information" (3). Here Eustace is giving voice to the modern reductionist viewpoint that these books have taught him. The former star gently corrects Eustace's assertion, stating, "Even in your world, my son, that is not what a star is but only what it is made of."

In his essay "Transposition," Lewis argues against materialistic reductionism—the philosophical position that everything can be reduced to, and explained as, the sum of its material components. There Lewis cites several examples of this "merely" or "nothing but" approach (277): the claim that "religion is only psychological, justice only self-protection, politics only economics, love only lust, and thought itself only cerebral biochemistry" (278). Lewis comments that those who look at the world in this way see "all the facts but not the meaning" (277).

In *The Abolition of Man*, Lewis comments further on this topic: "But you cannot go on 'explaining away' for ever. . . . You cannot go on 'seeing through' things for ever. The whole point of seeing through something is to see something through it" (91).

The reductionist position was one that Lewis understood well because before his conversion, he himself believed that everything could be reduced to matter and energy. Tolkien, who played a vital role in Lewis's change of thinking, wrote a long poem titled "Mythopoeia" in which he took on this viewpoint, dedicating it to "C. S. L." The poem begins with a description of Lewis and his limited perspective—as someone who sees trees and labels them "just so" (*Tree and Leaf* 97), someone who sees trees as nothing more than their physical components. In the poem's fifth and sixth lines, we can hear clear echoes of Eustace's statement. There Tolkien describes the reductionist view that Lewis took then, that "a star's a star, some matter in a ball / compelled to courses mathematical."

Lewis seems to have kept these lines his friend wrote about him well in mind. Writing some twenty years after his conversion, he not only made the Narnian stars more than just stars, he also made the Narnian trees more than merely trees, as did Tolkien himself. Here not only is Ramandu considerably more than some matter in a ball, his path across the sky is more than merely a mathematical course that he is compelled to follow by the laws of gravity. Instead, as Ramandu explains, his ordered steps are part of "the great dance" (209).

In his foreword to *Smoke on the Mountain*, a book written by his future wife, Joy Davidman, Lewis notes her humorous litany of the reductionist belief system in which she was raised. He comments:

Joy Davidman is one who comes to us from the second generation of unbelief; her parents, Jewish in blood, "rationalists" by conviction.

This makes her approach extremely interesting to the reclaimed apostates of my own generation; the daring paradoxes of our youth were the stale platitudes of hers. "Life is only an electrochemical reaction. Love, art, and altruism are only sex. The universe is only matter. Matter is only energy. I forget what I said energy is only"; thus she describes the philosophy with which she started life. (7)

Lewis concludes that from the start, this reductionism Joy Davidman was taught "failed to accommodate her actual experience."

Ramandu's statement to Eustace—"Even in your world, my son, that is not what a star is but only what it is made of" (209)—is somewhat enigmatic. Lewis does not have Ramandu elaborate, but in *Letters to Malcolm*, we find this hint: "The night sky suggests that the inanimate also has for God some value we cannot imagine" (55). In *Mere Christianity*, Lewis provides another small clue, writing that everything God has made has "some likeness to Himself" (158).

In *The Discarded Image*, Lewis describes how someone from the Middle Ages who looked skyward saw a universe "filled with music and life" and a "revelry of insatiable love" (119). In his great work *English Literature in the Sixteenth Century*, Lewis points out the spiritual outcome of the new science: "By reducing Nature to her mathematical elements it substituted a mechanical for a genial or animistic conception of the universe. The world was emptied. . . . Man with his new powers became rich like Midas but all that he touched had gone dead and cold" (3–4). Lewis goes on to note that before the dawn of modern science, men and women saw a universe "tingling with anthropomorphic life, dancing, ceremonial, a festival not a machine" (4).

Lewis, a keen amateur astronomer himself, liked to gaze at the heavens through a telescope he placed on the balcony outside his bedroom. In a letter to his poet friend Ruth Pitter on January 2, 1953, shortly after the Christmas season, Lewis provides a small window into what he saw when he looked at the night sky. He writes, "It was beautiful, on two or three successive nights about the Holy Time to see Venus and Jove blazing at one another, once with the Moon right between them: Majesty and Love linked by Virginity—what could be more appropriate?" (*Collected Letters*, Vol. 3, 273).

## The Great Dance

Here in chapter fourteen, Lewis has Ramandu explain that after being renewed, he will "once more tread the great dance" (209). In *Prince Caspian*, when asked if Tarva and Alambil might collide, Dr. Cornelius reassured the young prince, using a similar image: "The great lords of the upper sky know the steps of their dance too well for that" (50). Paul Ford has observed, "Though something of a Trufflehunter at dancing himself, Lewis seems to have been a dancer at heart. He was fond of the Great Dance of the Heavens of the medieval worldview (with its Ptolemaic cosmology full of epicycles and deferents), because it seemed a fitting created reflection of the uncreated Dance within the Trinity itself" (154).

Nine years before *The Voyage of the Dawn Treader* was published, Lewis provided a more detailed description of the great dance. In the last chapter of *Perelandra*, as Ransom stands before the great Oyarsa on Venus, he hears a voice explaining that in the Great Dance, "plans without number interlock," and each one becomes in its time "the breaking into flower of the whole design to which all else had been directed" (186). The voice concludes, "Thus each is equally at the center and none are there by being equals, but some by giving place and some by receiving in, the small things by their smallness and the great by their greatness, and all the patterns linked and looped together by the unions of a kneeling with a sceptred love."

In the Chronicles, Lewis uses the Great Dance to refer to the movements of the heavenly bodies such as Tarva and Alambil or Ramandu. In *Perelandra*, the term is extended to include the participation of all created things. There Lewis describes Ransom's near-mystical vision of the Great Dance:

It seemed to be woven out of the intertwining undulation of many cords or bands of light, leaping over and under one another and mutually embraced in arabesques and flower-like subtleties. . . . Some of the thinner and more delicate cords were beings that we call short-lived: flowers and insects, a fruit or a storm of rain, and once (he thought) a wave of the sea. Others were such things as we also think lasting: crystals, rivers, mountains, or even stars. (187)

In his book *Planets in Peril*, David Downing observes that in the great dance Lewis portrays in *Perelandra*, "Beasts, humans and spirits all find their place; fallen worlds and unfallen ones, ancient ones and new ones, each participate in the pageant" (73).

In *Letters to Malcolm*, Lewis responds to the assertion that his use of the term "the Great Dance" may seem too light or frivolous a metaphor for the part that great spiritual beings play in God's majestic design. Lewis explains:

I do *not* think that the life of Heaven bears any analogy to play or dance in respect of frivolity. I do think that while we are in this "valley of tears," . . . certain qualities that must belong to the celestial condition have no chance to get through, can project no image of themselves, except in activities which, for us here and now are frivolous. . . . Dance and game *are* frivolous, unimportant down here; for "down here" is not their natural place. . . . Joy is the serious business of Heaven. (92–93)

## "That Is Not How Great Unenchantments Are Achieved"

Ramandu turns to the issue of which path Caspian and his crew will take next, a problem the three sleeping lords were unable to overcome. He asks the young king, "Will you sail further east and come again, leaving one to return no more, and so break the enchantment? Or will you sail westward?" (209). The problem, as Caspian points out, is the crew. He explains to Ramandu, "They signed on to seek the seven lords, not to reach the rim of the Earth. . . . I see signs that some of them are weary of the voyage and long to have our prow pointing to Narnia again. I don't think I should take them further without their knowledge and consent" (210).

At the coronation of King Frank in *The Magician's Nephew*, we find some of Lewis's most detailed statements about proper kingship. There Narnia's first monarch is asked by Aslan if he will rule his subjects "kindly and fairly," always remembering that they are not slaves but "free subjects" (151). At the end of *Prince Caspian*, Aslan asked the young prince, "Do you feel yourself sufficient to take up the Kingship of Narnia?" (206), and Caspian replied that he did not think he was. Now with three years of experience as ruler of Narnia and the wisdom acquired on an eventful voyage, Caspian proves that he is able to rule his free subjects kindly and fairly and proves sufficient to be king of Narnia.

Evan Gibson observes, "Caspian confirms our expectations that he will be an able leader of men. Considerate of both his crew and his guests and yet decisive in times of emergency, he shows his mastery of difficult situations in his speech to his men at Ramandu's Island" (173–74). Caspian rises to the challenge here, but as we will see later, he will stumble on the temptation he encounters at the world's end. Like all of Lewis's characters, he too is a work in progress.

So how will Caspian build a consensus among his men to continue on?

Near the time Lewis was writing *The Voyage of the Dawn Treader*, he was also rereading some old favorites by Mark Twain. In a letter written in 1950, Lewis records, "I have been regaling myself on *Tom Sawyer* and *Huckleberry Finn*" (*Collected Letters*, Vol. 3, 67). It is possible that the episode where Tom paints the fence served as an inspiration for Lewis. Readers may see a resemblance between the strategy Tom employs and the one Caspian adopts here. In *The Adventures of Tom Sawyer*, Tom says to Ben, "Does a boy get a chance to whitewash a fence every day?" (16) and asserts, "I reckon there ain't one boy in a thousand, maybe two thousand, that can do it the way it's got to be done" (17). In a similar way, Caspian tells his crew, "It is our pleasure to choose from among such of you as are willing those whom we deem worthy of so high an enterprise" (214).

There is another possible antecedent for Caspian's approach. In an essay titled "Private Bates," published in 1944, Lewis examines how the foot soldiers in Shakespeare's *King Henry V* responded to the king's famous St. Crispin's Day speech. Lewis praises Henry as "a national leader of heroic mould and dazzling eloquence" (46). Comparing his rhetorical skills to Churchill's, Lewis finds Henry to be "as rousing a chief as our present Prime Minister." Lewis concludes, "His 'pep talks' were about as good as Shakespeare could make them, which means they were about as good as that kind of thing can be." The pep talk Lewis includes here in *The Voyage of the Dawn Treader* contains a number of parallels to the one Shakespeare included in *Henry V*, including the principal tactic, seen earlier with Tom Sawyer, that portrays participation not as an obligation but as a privilege.

Rynelf is the first to speak and reminds everyone, "There were some standing on the quay who would have given all they had to come with us. It was thought a finer thing then to have a cabin-boy's berth on the *Dawn Treader* than to wear a knight's belt" (212). Similarly, Shakespeare's Henry claims, "Gentlemen in England, now abed, / Shall think themselves accursed they were not here" (4.3.64–65). He points out that however humble anyone's birth, this day will ennoble him: "Be he ne'er so vile / This day shall gentle his condition" (4.3.62–63). Caspian exclaims, "Aslan's mane! Do you think that the privilege of seeing the last things is to be bought for a song?" (214). Henry declares, "God's will! I pray thee wish not one man more" (4.3.23).

Henry states that anyone who has "no stomach" for the conflict may depart (4.3.35), but after his stirring speech, no one seems inclined to leave, not even those who had just moments before been worrying about the "fearful odds" (4.3.5). Similarly, although anyone from the *Dawn Treader* may choose to stay at Ramandu's Island, we are told, "Soon there were only three left who didn't want to go. . . . And very shortly after that there was only one left. And in the end he began to be afraid of being left behind all on his own and changed his mind" (216). Because of his improper motives, this last man, a sailor named Pittencream, is left behind.

Both Henry and Caspian employ their best rhetorical skills, but in the end each gives his men a free choice. Ramandu tells Caspian that his men must know "where they go and why" and that it would be no use sailing with "men unwilling or men deceived" (210). It is the mark of the good kings and queens of Narnia to govern by consent and a commitment to the truth, just as it is the mark of the evil rulers—tyrants such as the White Witch, Miraz, and Gumpas—to govern by force and deception. Miraz used coercion to send the seven lords into exile. Caspian, if he is to undo his uncle's wrong, cannot use the same means no matter how noble his ends.

The next morning, all but Pittencream and the now peacefully sleeping Lord Rhoop set sail once more, this time for the last leg of the adventure. Lewis closes the chapter with Caspian's parting words to Ramandu's daughter: "I hope to speak with you again when I have broken the enchantments" (217). Ramandu's daughter, we are told, "looked at him and smiled."

## Discussion Questions

While there are many biblical parallels in the Chronicles, not every element has a scriptural antecedent. Though it is helpful and enriches our reading experience to identify these connections, it is also important not to see connections where there are none.

1. Do you see a connection—direct or otherwise—between Ramandu and Isaiah? Why or why not?

Most of the time Lewis guides his readers with an unambiguous hand to his intended meaning, but from time to time he will choose to include a somewhat enigmatic passage that suggests more than it actually states.

2. What do you think Lewis was saying in Ramandu's words to Eustace, "Even in your world, my son, that is not what a star is but only what it is made of" (209)?

3. If, as Lewis suggests, our world has lost something by reductionist thinking, which maintains that everything can be reduced to matter and energy, how can this viewpoint be reversed?

Ramandu announces that after his youth is restored, he will "once more tread the great dance" (209).

4. How effective do you find Lewis's choice of the metaphor of the great dance in evoking the stately, ordered, and yet joyful trek of the stars in the sky? How do you view "the great dance"?

Caspian is not comfortable forcing his crew to continue, and Ramandu explains it would be no use to attempt the last stage of the journey with a crew that is unwilling or has been deceived. Similarly, it has been said that Christians are not supposed to use all means available to accomplish the tasks they are given, but rather all means virtuous.

5. Why is it so important that the crew of the *Dawn Treader* choose freely to sail on?

# FIFTEEN

# The Wonders
# of the Last Sea

## All Was Different

In *Out of the Silent Planet*, Ransom experiences an ineffable sense of wonder as he sails through the vast reaches of outer space. Lewis describes his protagonist's feelings as the unlikely hero looks out on a universe bathed in light:

> The adventure was too high, its circumstance too solemn, for any emotion save a severe delight. . . . Often he rose after only a few hours' sleep to return, drawn by an irresistible attraction, to the regions of light; he could not cease to wonder at the noon which always awaited. . . . Through depth after depth of tranquility . . . he felt his body and mind daily rubbed and scoured and filled with new vitality. (33–34)

Thomas Howard has observed, "This is the language of ecstatic sanctity—the sort of thing we might encounter

THE WONDERS OF THE LAST SEA

in Isaiah, Saint John the Divine, and Saint Teresa. And of course this is the point" (102). Howard explains, "Perhaps the image, discarded by the world now, of the universe as a solemn and rapturous Dance . . . perhaps that image may be useful in a piece of fiction by way of experiment. Let us try it out, Lewis seems to suggest in his fiction. Let us see if this imagery does any sort of justice to our experience."

Here in *The Voyage of the Dawn Treader*, a similar sense of severe delight is experienced by the crew as they journey into the Narnian version of Ransom's regions of light. Shortly after leaving Ramandu's Island, the *Dawn Treader* and its crew reach the uncharted waters of the last sea and the wonders promised in the chapter's title. Here we are told, "All was different. For one thing they all found that they were needing less sleep. One did not want to go to bed nor to eat much, nor even to talk except in low voices. Another thing was the light. There was too much of it" (218). The feeling they all begin to experience here will grow stronger in the following chapter, as they get nearer and nearer to the world's end.

As has been noted, in *Surprised by Joy*, Lewis explains how he himself journeyed "into the region of awe" (221). There he describes how—much like Ransom and the crew of the *Dawn Treader*—he too came to personally understand that "there is a road right out of the self," one that leads to a commerce with something "unknown, undefined, desired."

### She Had Seen People!

Here in the next-to-last chapter, relatively little happens externally as Lewis's prime emphasis is on inner transformation and the deep serenity that gradually comes over the travelers. Evan Gibson has observed, "The final episode, the journey across the last sea, is one not so much of events as of atmosphere" (181).

The first thing that "happens" in the chapter is that Lucy discovers the water has become "beautifully clear" (218), allowing her—as she eventually realizes—to see the shadow of the *Dawn Treader* as it races along the sea bottom beneath them. Lucy notices what looks like a road leading to "a city or a huge castle" and shortly afterward sees an underwater hunting party, "noble and lordly people," mounted on great sea horses (222–23).

Readers have already learned that the Narnian heavens are populated with living, purposeful creatures, and that its stars are not simply huge balls of flaming gas. Here we discover that the Narnian seas tingle with sentient life as well. When Lucy suggests that they knew these sea people in "the old days at Cair Paravel" (226), Edmund points out that these creatures appear to live completely underwater and so must be an entirely different race.

While the plotlines of the later Chronicles may have required that in addition to Narnians there would be Calormenes, Archenlanders, and Lone Islanders, why also include birds that live on the sun, an additional race of sea people, and, as will be seen in the next story, gnomelike Earthmen and mysterious salamanders who live deep underground? Why such overabundance when it could be argued that by adding races so completely peripheral to the Narnians, Lewis may diminish the centrality of the main story?

One answer is that doing so further extends the medieval model of the universe that permeates the Chronicles. In *Spenser's Images of Life*, Lewis points out the belief widely held during earlier times "that aquatic elemental spirits may really exist" (129). In *The Discarded Image*, he refers to the water *nymphae* of Paracelsus, creatures who are "human in stature and talk" (135). He also notes the "principle of plentitude" that Ficino held forth in each of the four primary elements (134). By creating Earthmen, living stars, the mysterious salamanders, and the sea people, Lewis populates Narnia's earth, air, fire, and water.

Along with following the medieval model of the cosmos, a second reason for these extraneous races is that water-breathing sea people and birds from the sun are exactly what we might expect to find among the wonders as we approach the world's end.

But there seems to be more at work than just these two purposes. Interestingly, roughly a decade earlier, Lewis included this same seemingly surplus fecundity in *Perelandra* as Ransom, like Lucy, crosses paths with a sea-dwelling race. While riding on the back of a great fish, Ransom sees a group of underwater creatures whose upper part is so nearly human in shape that when he first sees them he thinks he is dreaming. Later, Ransom has a personal meeting with a single member of this species, much as Lucy will with the solitary fish-herdess. Ransom wakes to find he is staring into "something like a human face," which belongs to a creature swimming alongside him (137). Lewis describes their complete lack of connection: "Each was wholly irrelevant to the other. They met as the branches of different trees meet when the wind brings them together" (138).

Later in *Perelandra*, Ransom travels beneath the planet's surface where he encounters huge insectlike creatures, another race that could be argued to be "wholly irrelevant" to life on the surface. The meeting causes Ransom to conclude, "Assuredly the inside of this world was not for man. But it was for something" (158). In the final chapter, Ransom gives voice to the doubts these experiences have produced, explaining that on Earth the humans who believe in Christ see his incarnation there as "the central happening of all that happens" (183). He laments to Tor, "If you take that from me, Father, whither will you lead me? Surely not to the enemy's talk which thrusts my world and my race into a remote corner and gives me a universe, with no center at all, but millions of worlds."

All his life Ransom has believed that his world and its history were central to the plan of the universe. Now he wonders if there is a center or a plan. He asks Tor:

> "Or do you make your world the center? . . . I do not even see how your world can rightly be called yours. You were made yesterday and it is from of old. The most of it is water where you cannot live. And what of the things beneath its crust? . . . Is the enemy easily answered when He says that all is without plan or meaning? As soon as we think we see one it melts away into nothing, or into some other plan that we never dreamed of, and what was the center becomes the rim, till we doubt if any shape or plan or pattern was

ever more than a trick of our own eyes, cheated with hope, or tired with too much looking." (183)

Here in chapter fifteen, Lucy does not ponder the implications of this separate race of sea people, and this incident passes quickly. However, the existence of this race adds new meaning to Mr. Beaver's statement about Aslan in *The Lion, the Witch and the Wardrobe*: "Of course he has other countries to attend to" (182). Readers may wonder if the stories from the Chronicles—stories about humans, talking animals, dwarfs, and fauns—are as central to the whole world of Narnia as they first seemed to be. If there are created beings that are wholly irrelevant, what might be their purpose?

Lewis provides an answer to this question of abundance in several works. In *The Problem of Pain*, he argues that each of us will "know and praise some one aspect of the divine beauty better than any other creature can" (134). He points out that if everyone experienced God in the same way and returned an identical worship, "the song of the Church triumphant would have no symphony" but would be like an orchestra where "all the instruments played the same note." Similarly, in *The Great Divorce*, one of the heavenly beings explains to the man who was a painter on Earth, "There'll be some things which you'll see better than anyone else. One of the things you'll want to do will be to tell us about them" (79). In *Perelandra*, Ransom is told, "All that is made seems planless to the darkened mind, because there are more plans than it looked for. . . . There seems no plan because it is all plan: there seems no center because it is all center" (186).

Rather than a problem, Thomas Howard sees Lewis's fecundity as essential and reflective of our own tradition. Howard comments:

> Cannot Lewis stay with his story? Must we have these distractions? The answer is that all this is crucial to this particular kind of story. The very pattern of the drama requires that we never forget for long that, awesome and gripping as it is, it is only one of many stories which may or may not touch each other, but which eventually all

form parts of the Whole Pattern. This is one of the prime characteristics of myth, and, it seems, of our own story. Who are the Magi? Who are the seraphim? Who is Melchizedek? . . . The story doesn't tell us. They cross the stage in a moment and go on their way. When will the lines converge? (154)

For readers of the Chronicles, the lines of the until-then distinct stories will converge in the final pages of *The Last Battle*. There all the lands of these formerly separate races will be shown to be "part of a great chain of mountains . . . only spurs jutting out from the great mountains of Aslan" (208–9).

## "Drat That Mouse!"

One of the earliest events of the story was the plunge that Lucy, Edmund, Eustace, and Caspian took into the sea. Lewis now bookends his story with a second plunge—this time by Reepicheep, the only central character who did not get wet the first time.

The sea people have looked up and notice the *Dawn Treader* above them. Readers are told, "The King in the center (no one could mistake him for anything but the King) looked proudly and fiercely into Lucy's face and shook a spear in his hand. His knights did the same" (225). Reepicheep interprets this spear shaking as a personal challenge. And since he views a refusal to accept any challenge as an impeachment to his honor—forgetting about the quest to wake the sleeping lords, about his own quest to reach the world's end, and about Aslan's warning of him thinking too much about his honor—he leaps into the water in response.

In his book *Into the Region of Awe*, David Downing has suggested, "Reepicheep's quest to reach Aslan's country seems the Narnian equivalent of the Grail quest of Arthurian knights. . . . Mere bravery or physical prowess is not enough to achieve the Grail; the quester must also have purity of soul" (137). In the previous chapter, Ramandu explained that to break the enchantment, they must leave one of their company to "go on into the utter east and never return into the world" (207–8). Then Reepicheep responded,

"That is my heart's desire." Despite this statement by the great mouse, as seen here and elsewhere, this is not his only desire nor always his greatest. Reepicheep's desire to reach Aslan's country is not quite pure—not yet.

Drinian complains the mouse is "more trouble than all the rest of the ship's company put together" and concludes, "If there is any scrape to be got into, in it will get!" (226). The Reepicheep we find jumping into the sea here is more like the mouse seen earlier in *Prince Caspian* than the one we will see in the next chapter, the mouse who will fling away his sword and sail over the world's final wave "quivering" with a sublime happiness (244). In *Prince Caspian*, Reepicheep was often more a liability to King Peter than an asset, much as he is here to Drinian. There the overly gallant mouse insisted to the high king that since he had not been sent with the challenge to Miraz, he must be chosen as one of the marshals of the lists. Peter was forced to create a silly excuse just to silence him.

Here in chapter fifteen, the narrator likens Drinian's temporary anger at Reepicheep to that of a mother whose child has run "out into the road in front of a car" (227), a comparison pointing to a maturity that Reepicheep is still lacking at this point.

In his portrait of Reepicheep's failures to keep his longing for Aslan's country ahead of his longing for honor, Lewis was depicting a general truth about spiritual struggles, one he himself was well acquainted with. In a letter written shortly after his conversion, Lewis observes, "I knew that the enemy would . . . try and make me believe . . . that *he* had the fulfillment which I really wanted" (*Collected Letters*, Vol. 1, 898). Lewis then describes his solution to the problem: "Turning my mind to the One, the real object of all desire, which (you know my view) is what we are *really* wanting in all wants" (898–99).

Though from time to time Reepicheep loses sight of it, the real object of his desire is reaching Aslan's country, not his own honor. One evidence of this fact is that no matter how much honor Reepicheep has, he can never have enough and must always be defending it. The smallest suggestion that his honor has been impeached sends him into a heroic frenzy. Lewis would say that this is the way it is when we make second things into first things: we can never get enough.

In "The Weight of Glory," Lewis maintains that we have "a desire which no natural happiness will satisfy" (32). In *Mere Christianity*, he expands on this point, noting that most people, if they truly looked into their hearts, would know that they do want "something that cannot be had in this world" (135). Lewis concludes that there are all sorts of things in the world that claim to satisfy this longing, but these other things "never quite keep their promise."

Lewis was keenly aware of the tendency to turn what should be a secondary desire into a primary goal. While secondary desires may be good in their own way, Lewis argues in *Mere Christianity* that we should never mistake them for the real desire, of which they are "only a kind of copy, or echo, or mirage" (137). In words applicable to man or mouse, Lewis then concludes, "I must keep alive in myself the desire for my true country which I shall not find till after death; I must never let it get snowed under or turned aside: I must make it the main object of my life to press on to that other country and to help others to do the same."

While Reepicheep's pursuit of honor is now sometimes a distraction from his true quest, paradoxically, at the beginning it may have served as a gateway. In his essay "Christianity and Culture," Lewis maintains that "any road out of Jerusalem" may also serve as "a road into Jerusalem" (22). He uses honor as one example of this principle, writing, "To the perfected Christian the ideal of honor is simply a temptation. His courage has a better root, and, being learned in Gethsemane, may have no honor about it. But to the man coming up from below, the ideal of knighthood may prove a schoolmaster to the ideal of martyrdom."

In the next chapter, when Caspian is tempted to turn aside from his quest to wake the three sleepers and return them to Narnia, Reepicheep will tell the headstrong king, "If your Majesty will not hear reason it will be the truest loyalty of every man on board to follow me in disarming and binding you till you come to your senses" (239). Edmund will agree, adding, "Like they did with Ulysses when he wanted to go near the Sirens." Here in chapter fifteen, the excessively gallant mouse has failed to resist his own Siren call, causing Drinian to complain, "It ought to be put in irons" (226).

## "Sweet!"

At the start of the story, readers were told of the prophecy spoken over Reepicheep's cradle:

> Where sky and water meet,
> Where the waves grow sweet,
> Doubt not, Reepicheep,
> To find all you seek,
> There is the utter East. (21)

Now just as he is about to be diverted into seeking after his own honor again, Reepicheep is given a reminder that helps set him back on the right path—the only path that will lead to all he seeks. To everyone's surprise, when he is hauled on board, Reepicheep is "not at all interested in the Sea People" (228). Instead he sputters out, "Sweet, sweet!"

Lewis has already signaled a change in geography with the new clarity of the ocean. Now he further highlights this change to a more sublime location by letting us know that the sea has changed from salt water to freshwater. But there is more to this change than clearness and taste. Drinian lowers a bucket, and when it is drawn up, the liquid in it shines like glass. After Caspian takes the first drink, we are told, "Not only his eyes but everything about him seemed to be brighter" (228).

On the final page of *Surprised by Joy*, Lewis writes about distinguishing between our longing and the object of our longing, noting that signposts are great matters to those who are lost in the woods:

> He who first sees it cries, "Look!" The whole party gathers round and stares. But when we have found the road and are passing

signposts every few miles, we shall not stop and stare. They will encourage us and we shall be grateful to the authority that set them up. But we shall not stop and stare, or not much; not on this road, though their pillars are of silver and their lettering of gold. "We would be at Jerusalem." (238)

Here the crew of the *Dawn Treader* gathers round, and one by one everyone on board drinks. "That's real water," Caspian exclaims (228), adding that it is "like light more than anything else" (229). "Drinkable light," Reepicheep affirms. Lucy concludes, "It's the loveliest thing I have ever tasted." The crew of the *Dawn Treader* has finally reached the place where the waves grow sweet. This is the first signpost that our heroes are nearing the end of their quest. They pause briefly to comment on the water, but not for long. The feeling shared by all is, "We would be at the world's end."

Other wonders take place here on the last sea. The sun grows brighter and larger—it is now "five or six times its old size" (230). Everything shines with a special light—the deck, the sail, their own faces, and even their bodies. The crew finds they can look straight into the sun without blinking. Each wonder is duly noted, and each one adds to the crew's growing sense of awe. At the same time, to use Lewis's own phrase from *Surprised by Joy*, each wonder is valuable only as "a pointer to something other and outer" (238).

As the *Dawn Treader* grows closer and closer to Aslan's country, not only are the crew members able to endure the increased brightness, they also can see far-off items with superhuman accuracy. As the crew stares into the rising sun, we are told they are able to see "the very feathers of the birds that came flying from it" (230). When the Narnians reach Aslan's country in *The Last Battle*, Lewis will use this aspect again as Lucy will find that when she looks at distant objects, they become "quite clear and close as if she were looking through a telescope" (207).

Lewis closes the chapter with another Eustace-ism, another reminder that the cure that began at the end of chapter seven is still ongoing and not complete. As Drinian, Caspian, and Reepicheep deliberate on whether the current they are riding on will spill over the edge of the world or not, it becomes clear that the world of Narnia is flat. At this point, Eustace interjects, in a manner reminiscent of the former know-it-all, "This is all rot. The world's round—I mean, round like a ball, not like a table" (231).

The information about Narnia's shape comes a bit abruptly—it has not been referred to or even hinted at earlier. This may help explain how Pauline Baynes mistakenly includes a round globe, presumably a representation of Narnia, alongside Drinian in the illustration found near the middle of chapter two.

Here, it should be noted, Lewis was not trying to continue his use of the medieval model of the universe. In *The Discarded Image*, Lewis points out the "erroneous notion" that "the medievals were Flat-earthers" and observes that "all the authors of the high Middle Ages" agreed on the fact that "the Earth is a globe" (140–42). So why make Narnia a flat world and not a globe like our own? One reason that Lewis includes this otherwise unused detail here is so that in the following chapter, the *Dawn Treader* can truly be said to come to the world's end, a specific location where sky and water do actually meet, something not possible in a spherical world.

Caspian exclaims, "It must be exciting to live on a thing like a ball. Have you ever been to the parts where people walk about upside-down?" (231). Just as Narnia is a world full of figures from Earth's mythology, our world contains elements of a fairy-tale world from the Narnian perspective. Readers may be reminded of the tea Mr. Tumnus provided in *The Lion, the Witch and the Wardrobe*, where among the books on his shelves Lucy found such titles as *Is Man a Myth?* and *Men, Monks, and Gamekeepers; a Study in Popular Legend*. In this context, Elaine Tixier has commented on another reason that Lewis may have made Narnia flat and the effect Caspian's words here have on the reader. She observes:

Not only does Caspian's wonderment communicate itself to us and cause us to see for a while our "round world" with new, admiring eyes, but the question he asks about our world, however fanciful, also has an important additional function. Episodes of this kind compel us, while we are under the spell of the tale, to forget our immutable certitudes and securities and to reconsider our beliefs from a different angle. (149)

Caspian states his great longing to visit a round world, admitting, "Oh, I'd give anything. . . . If only I had the chance" (231). Lewis will make use of the wanderlust expressed by Caspian here in several ways. Because of this declaration, readers are not very surprised when seven pages later Caspian will be willing to give up his throne to go with Reepicheep to see the world's end. Caspian's desire to travel to new worlds will be seen again at the start of *The Silver Chair*, where he will once more sail east, this time in an attempt to find Aslan to ask who is to be the next king. Shortly after that point in the story, Glimfeather will tell Eustace and Jill, "We're all afraid that, if he doesn't meet Aslan in Terebinthia, he'll go on east" (55).

At the end of *The Silver Chair*, Caspian's Narnian life will end, and he will pass on to Aslan's country, a place most characters have an overwhelming desire to reach and once there never want to leave. Even then, Caspian's longing to travel to new lands will not be diminished. As Eustace and Jill prepare to return home, Caspian will say to Aslan, "I've always wanted to have just one glimpse of *their* world. Is that wrong?" (240). Telling him "You cannot want wrong things any more," Aslan will finally grant Caspian's wish to see a round world, first expressed here in chapter fifteen.

## Discussion Questions

In *The Discarded Image*, Lewis observes, "Whatever else a modern feels when he looks at the night sky, he certainly feels that he is looking *out*—like one looking out from . . . the lighted porch upon dark and lonely moors. But if you accepted the Medieval Model you would feel like one looking *in*. . . . We catch a glimpse of the high pomps within; the vast, lighted concavity filled with music and life" (118–19).

1. How does Lucy's vision of the sea people help advance the view of Narnia as a vast concavity filled with life, and reduce the conception of Narnia's land masses as merely a collection of lighted porches looking out on a lonely moor?

In *Letters to Malcolm*, Lewis argues that we should aim at what St. Augustine calls "ordinate loves" (22). Lewis explains, "Our deepest concern should be for first things, and our next deepest for second things, and so on down to zero—to total absence of concern for things that are not really good, nor means to good at all." In a letter written in 1951, Lewis observes, "Put first things first and we get second things thrown in" (*Collected Letters*, Vol. 3, 111). When Lucy turned around and saw Aslan in chapter ten, readers were told that she "looked almost as beautiful as that other Lucy in the picture" (158). Reepicheep will never have more honor than in the final chapter when he casts away his sword and seeks only to reach Aslan's country. When both characters put first things first, they get second things thrown in.

2. Where else in the Chronicles and in life itself do we see this principle of putting first things first and getting second things thrown in?

In *Mere Christianity*, Lewis claims, "If I find in myself a desire which no experience in this world can satisfy, the most probable explanation is that I was made for another world. . . . Earthly pleasures were never meant to satisfy it, but only to arouse it, to suggest the real thing" (136–37).

3. How has Reepicheep's desire for honor served both to arouse a desire for Aslan's country and also to distract from it?

4. What other desires might serve as both roads away from and roads leading to our true goal?

In *The Way into Narnia*, Peter Schakel offers another possible reason for making the Narnian world flat. Schakel suggests that in this detail, Lewis provides "another instance of what is mythical for us (a flat world) being reality in Narnia, and vice versa" (142). Elaine Tixier sees this element as an example of the "innate capacity of the tale itself to help us conceive the unfamiliar" (148).

5. What effect do you think Lewis might be seeking to achieve here by inserting the detail that Narnia is a flat world? What effect might making the mythical a reality have on readers?

## SIXTEEN

# The Very End
# of the World

### "I See Whiteness"

In his essay "On Stories," Lewis describes two types of readers and the two types of stories they prefer. One type of reader seeks only sheer excitement. The other, and Lewis includes himself among this second group, wants not momentary suspense but "that whole world to which it belonged" (5). A story written for the first type of reader is characterized by a "lack of atmosphere" (7). In it, Lewis complains, there is "no country . . . no weather . . . no feeling that London differs from Paris." In this sort of story, "There is not a moment's rest from the 'adventures': one's nose is kept ruthlessly to the grindstone." This first kind of story produces a "rapid flutter of the nerves" (6). The second, in contrast, "lays a hushing spell." Lewis concludes, "I have sometimes wondered whether the 'excitement' may not be an element actually hostile to the deeper imagination" (10).

Here in the final chapter of *The Voyage of the Dawn Treader*, readers might well feel as though a hushing spell has been cast. Lewis gives us a great sense of country but very little of what may be labeled as excitement in the conventional sense. The pace, already slowed in the previous chapter, becomes even slower as atmosphere becomes Lewis's prime focus.

The chapter opens with the *Dawn Treader* continuing serenely on its journey across the waveless, windless sea. The otherworldly tranquility is punctuated only by a brief glimpse Lucy has of "a little Sea Girl of about her own age" who is herding a flock of fish at pasture (233).

In *The Horse and His Boy*, when Shasta comes upon the Narnian contingent visiting Tashbaan, the narrator will comment, "You could see that they were ready to be friends with anyone who was friendly" (58). Lucy's meeting here with the sea girl further establishes her as the friendliest of the friendly Narnians. The incident also provides another indication that Lewis was thinking this Chronicle would finish the series. Lewis writes of the two girls, "There does not seem to be much chance of their meeting again in that world or any other. But if they do they will rush together with their hands held out" (233). Lewis's shift to present tense in this passage gives the feeling that the two friends are still alive, one living in England and the other beneath the waves of the last sea. The passage also leaves out any suggestion of Aslan's country as a final destination for them, making it clear that at this point, Lewis did not have in mind what was to come.

In "The Weight of Glory," Lewis suggests, "We do not want merely to *see* beauty, though, God knows, even that is bounty enough. We want something else which can hardly be put into words—to be united with the beauty we see, to pass into it, to receive it into ourselves, to bathe in it, to become part of it" (42). Here in the final chapter of *The Voyage of the Dawn Treader*, Lewis provides a moving account of what passing into beauty and becoming part of it might actually be like. Readers are told:

Every day and every hour the light became more brilliant and still they could bear it. No one ate or slept and no one wanted to, but they drew buckets of dazzling water from the sea, stronger than wine and somehow wetter, more liquid, than ordinary water, and pledged to another silently in deep drafts of it. And one or two of the sailors who had been oldish men when the voyage began now grew younger every day. Everyone on board was filled with joy and excitement, but not an excitement that made one talk. The further they sailed the less they spoke, and then almost in a whisper. (233–34)

Commenting on the writing style Lewis employs here, Donald Glover has observed, "When elaborate phrasing and verbal ornaments might be used to heighten the effect, Lewis uses the simple and direct. The hush of Joy, the quality of light and air, are described as a child would experience them, uncomplicated by sophisticated distinctions and evaluations" (156). Glover concludes, "One false step, one lurch into sentiment, and the whole aura would have collapsed. . . . It is a tribute to Lewis's mastery of prose that he can make the last chapter moving without making it mawkish" (155–56).

Back in chapter four, readers were told that after being "victualed and watered" (63), the *Dawn Treader* could sail for twenty-eight days, allowing for "a fortnight's eastward sailing." Perhaps now that the water they are sailing on provides both food and drink, the exact count of days since leaving Ramandu's Island becomes vague and not very important. After many days of this tranquil sailing, a "whiteness" appears, stretching "all along the horizon from north to south" (234). What this whiteness is caused by or made of is impossible to say. Drinian wisely cautions that they "get men to the oars and hold the ship back" lest they crash into the unknown substance. Even after they turn out of the swift current and slowly draw near, they are still unable to make out what the "white stuff" is, so a boat is lowered to investigate more closely.

A team led by Rynelf and Lucy soon returns with lilies that appear to be the same "as in a pool or a garden at home" (236), but as Eustace characteristically points out, they cannot be quite the same, as these are able to live in deep water. Having determined there is no danger in sailing on, the ship is turned into the flowers, where it is once more caught into the current and sent toward the east.

The narrator reports that now "the strangest part" of their already strange travels begins (236). Behind them the open sea becomes "a thin rim of blue on the western horizon," and whiteness "shot with faintest color of gold" spreads all around them, save for a narrow lane of open water at the stern where their passage has pushed the mysterious lilies apart. For mile after mile and day after day, they glide on what they call the Silver Sea. From the flowers comes "a fresh, wild, lonely smell" (237), one that we are told "seemed to get into your brain and made you feel that you could go up mountains at a run or wrestle with an elephant."

In *The Last Battle*, the Narnians who pass through the stable door will find that they are able to run "faster and faster" without getting "hot or tired or out of breath" (197). As they reach the golden gates to Aslan's country, they will dash up a great hill with a slope "nearly as steep as the roof of a house" without the slightest fatigue (202). Here in the invigorating smell of the flowers that mark the boundary of Aslan's country, Lewis provides a foretaste of what is to come.

## "There's a Queer Look in His Eyes"

After several days on the sea of lilies, the time comes when the *Dawn Treader* can sail no further east as the water becomes shallower and shallower. Caspian calls for the small boat to be lowered and orders the crew to gather for an announcement. It is Eustace—perhaps because he for so long lived a life of doing only what he pleased—who notes the "queer look" in Caspian's eyes (237), a look that causes the young king to appear, as the narrator will point out, "not unlike his uncle Miraz" (239).

Caspian tells the crew that with the seven lords accounted for and Reepicheep sworn to remain and thus undo the sleepers' enchantment, they have now fulfilled the quest. He instructs Drinian to bring the ship and crew safely back to Narnia and once there to have Trumpkin pay out the rewards he has promised. Finally, should he himself not return, Caspian asks that Trumpkin, Cornelius, Drinian, and Trufflehunter select a new king of Narnia—presumably one of the good Telmarines who decided to stay at the end of the last adventure, since the monarch of Narnia must be human.

Drinian interrupts to ask if the king is abdicating. Caspian announces, "I am going with Reepicheep to see the World's End" (238). Technically, we could say Caspian is not abdicating here. His statement "if I come not again" suggests that it is his plan to see the world's end and then to return to Narnia if he can. He is, as Rynelf correctly observes, deserting—if only temporarily. Reepicheep points out the error in Caspian's decision to ignore duty and jump ship. The mouse tells the young king, "You break faith with all your subjects, and especially with Trumpkin" (239).

Caspian has always been a reluctant monarch. In *Prince Caspian*, when his Uncle Miraz, who was childless at the time, asked Caspian how he would like being king one day, the young prince's unenthusiastic reply was, "I don't know, Uncle" (42). Eleven chapters later, with Miraz now dead, Aslan asked Caspian if he felt "sufficient to take up the Kingship in Narnia" (206). Again we find hesitancy in Caspian's response. He tells Aslan, "I—I don't think I do, Sir." Both of these scenes reveal a certain ambiguity about Caspian's desires. Up until this point readers might have interpreted Caspian's tentativeness initially as an appropriate response to the model of kingship Miraz presented and then later as an indication of his own humility. Now we can see it as a result of other factors at work as well: perhaps he simply does not have the same passion for the day-to-day responsibilities of kingship as he does for faraway lands.

From the start, Caspian has been characterized by his longing for other worlds, a trait he shares with Lewis himself. Among his first words recounted in *Prince Caspian*, we find his declaration to Miraz, "I wish—I wish—I wish I could have lived in the Old Days" (42). Here in *The Voyage of the Dawn Treader*, Caspian has announced he would "give anything" to visit a round world

(231). In retrospect, we can see Caspian's oath to find the seven lords—an oath he swore on his coronation day—as an indicator of not only a proper desire to right Miraz's wrong but also of his wanderlust.

Caspian's announced intention of going with Reepicheep to see the world's end is not a terrible desire. So exactly what is it that causes Caspian for a moment to look "not unlike his uncle Miraz" (239)? Paul Ford suggests that Caspian's resemblance to his uncle stems not from his desire to see the world's end but from the fact that here briefly Caspian "will not be told he can't do something he wants to do" (135). In words reminiscent of both his uncle and of his earlier quarrel with Edmund on Deathwater Island, Caspian complains, "I had thought you were all my subjects here, not my schoolmasters" (239).

From the start of the series, Lewis has presented rival conceptions of what it means to govern. One group of rulers—the White Witch in the first story, Miraz in the second, Gumpas here in the third, and the Queen of Underland in the next—sees being king or queen or governor as simply a means to dominating others and getting whatever they want. Aslan's idea of a ruler has always been quite different. In *The Magician's Nephew*, Aslan will instruct Narnia's first monarch that his duty is to protect, do justice, and rule "kindly and fairly" (151). In *The Horse and His Boy*, upon hearing the news that his brother Cor is the rightful heir to the throne, Corin will cry out "Hurrah! Hurrah!" (223). Why such happiness? As Corin declares from firsthand experience, "It's princes have all the fun." King Lune explains that a true king must be "first in every desperate attack and last in every desperate retreat." Here in *The Voyage of the Dawn Treader*, Reepicheep states this general principle to Caspian this way: "You are the King of Narnia. . . . You shall not please yourself with adventures as if you were a private person" (239).

In *Letters to an American Lady*, Lewis writes, "Each must do his duty 'in that state of life to which God has called him'" (53). The brief passage quoted here by Lewis comes from the catechism in *The Book of Common Prayer*, which in Lewis's time would have been learned by every person before confirmation. At this point in his maturation, Caspian has not fully accepted the state of life and the service to which Aslan has called him.

In his speech to the crew, Caspian seems to feel he has taken care of his responsibilities. He argues that he has fulfilled his oath to find the seven lords. Then he provides for the crew to be paid once they reach Narnia. Finally, in the event he does not return, Caspian establishes the procedure to choose his successor.

Back on Ramandu's Island, Caspian had properly reminded Drinian, "Your place is with the ship" (197). What King Caspian is unable or unwilling to see here is that even in peacetime, even when all is well and "there's no trouble at all" (20), as he stated in chapter two, his own place is with his subjects.

## "I'm to Go Back"

The question of obedience in the Chronicles has always been nuanced, making the series less a simple fairy tale and more reflective of the complex world we live in. It goes without saying that subjects are not bound to obey unlawful monarchs. Thus in the first book, Mr. Tumnus's refusal to follow the command of the White Witch—that he catch and hand over any son of Adam or daughter of Eve—was seen not as insubordination but as heeding his proper duty. The same could be said for the defiance of Miraz by Caspian and the old Narnians in the second book. But even when the monarch is lawful, the issue of obedience is not without qualification.

In *Prince Caspian*, Trumpkin gave voice to a simplistic, black-and-white view of duty when the question arose of whether to follow Lucy. Trumpkin told the four children, "If you all go, of course, I'll go with you; and if your party splits up, I'll go with the High King. That's my duty to him and King Caspian" (148). However, in *The Silver Chair*, Trumpkin's one-dimensional view of obedience will become a liability as Jill and Eustace must meet with the owls without the dwarf's knowledge. As Glimfeather will explain, "Trumpkin will stick to the rules. . . . You could never make him see that this might be the time for making an exception" (54–55). Readers are meant to think Trumpkin's real duty was to disobey rather than obey the king's command prohibiting anyone from seeking the lost Prince Rilian.

In *Prince Caspian*, Lucy was told that she must follow Aslan alone if need be, with or without the consent of the high king. Here in *The Voyage of the Dawn Treader*, Lewis adds a further complexity to the issue of obedience, as the crew members are called not only to go against the king's wishes but to physically restrain him from doing what he himself seeks to do. As Reepicheep explains to Caspian, "If your Majesty will not hear reason it will be the truest loyalty of every man on board to follow me in disarming and binding you till you come to your senses" (239).

Edmund concurs with Reepicheep and adds, "Like they did with Ulysses when he wanted to go near the Sirens" (239). Edmund's comparison of their situation to this episode from *The Odyssey* is accurate in one way and not quite accurate in another. In Homer's tale, the Sirens tempt Odysseus (Ulysses) with the promise of extraordinary knowledge that would make him a wiser man. Caspian too is tempted with the extraordinary knowledge of the world's end. Both kings find their temptations too great to bear without restraint. However, Odysseus *commands* his men to bind him to the mast and to ignore any later commands he might make to free him until they are past the danger. Caspian issues no such orders, making the issue of duty and obedience more complicated.

Caspian's hand is on his sword hilt, threatening violence, when Lucy intervenes to remind him that he "almost promised" Ramandu's daughter he would go back (239). Even then Caspian is still "in a temper" and declares, "Well, have your way. The quest is ended. We all return" (240). This is no solution, for if they leave no one behind, the sleepers' enchantment will not be broken. Again Reepicheep defies the king, stating, "We do not *all* return." In an outburst that Paul Ford finds "reminiscent of Henry II's frustration over Thomas Becket" (135), Caspian cries, "Will no one silence that Mouse?" and storms into his cabin and slams the door (240).

When the others join the young king a short time later, they find him changed. Through his tears, Caspian explains that Aslan has appeared, "a bit stern at first" (240), and has told him that Reepicheep, Edmund, Lucy, and Eustace are to go on alone and the others must turn back "at once" (241).

Earlier, a passage from *The Screwtape Letters*—"The Enemy will be working from the center outwards, gradually bringing more and more of the patient's conduct under the new standard" (11)—was cited as an accurate description of Eustace's ongoing transformation. Here the same passage can be said to reflect Caspian's development as well. In *Mere Christianity*, Lewis elaborates on this principle, writing, "'Make no mistake,' He says, 'if you let Me, I will make you perfect. The moment you put yourself in My hands, that is what you are in for. Nothing less, or other, than that. You have free will, and if you choose, you can push Me away. But if you do not push Me away, understand that I am going to see this job through'" (202).

Although Caspian is compared to Miraz in this scene, his intentions here are not evil like his uncle's. Caspian does not want to kill a king and take his crown; he only wants to see the world's end. But while it might be good for Caspian to see the world's end, it is not good now—it is not the highest good. Lewis points out in this section from *Mere Christianity* on being made perfect that when people turn to Christ, God will push them "on, or up, to a higher level" and will place them in situations where they will have to be "very much braver, or more patient, or more loving" than they ever dreamed of being before (205), a description that matches Caspian's experience, particularly here in the final chapter.

Finally the boat is lowered, and Reepicheep, Lucy, Edmund, and Eustace pull away "to row through the endless carpet of lilies" (241). Though readers will be given a short summary of Caspian's return to Narnia on the book's final page, this will be the last time we actually see him. At this last moment, Lewis provides what may be a brief indication of Caspian's contrite attitude. The four in the landing boat watch as the *Dawn Treader* turns and the men "begin rowing slowly westward." Caspian might have been tempted to watch longer, perhaps until the four were out of sight, but Aslan has commanded that he go back at once. Alternatively, it might be argued that Caspian simply could not bear to watch anymore.

## What They Saw Was a Range of Mountains

On and on the current draws the four remaining voyagers and their small boat steadily to the east. No one eats or sleeps, for no one needs to. Then just before dawn on the third day, they spy in the early morning dimness yet another wonder, this time a "greenish-gray, trembling, shimmering wall" on the horizon (242). As the sun rises with extraordinary brightness, the wall becomes filled with "wonderful rainbow colors," and they realize it is a wave "endlessly fixed in one place."

After months of travel and many adventures, Edmund, Lucy, Eustace, and Reepicheep have at last come to the end of the world. Suddenly beyond this great wave, which is described as being about thirty feet high, the travelers see a range of mountains located not only behind the wave but "behind the sun" and thus "outside the world" (243). Readers find a number of special mountains or mountain ranges in the Chronicles, so much so that from this story onward, we can say that whenever Lewis needs to endow a place with spiritual significance, we might expect to find a mountain marking a boundary between one world and another.

We have already visited one of Narnia's special summits back in chapter seven, when Eustace was led to the top of a mountain he had never seen before and was transformed back into a boy. Lewis will start the next book, *The Silver Chair*, right where he left off by bringing Jill and Eustace out of England to "the top of a very high mountain" (13). Later the narrator will make it clear that this is "the Mountain of Aslan, high up above and beyond the end of that world in which Narnia lies" (237). In *The Horse and His Boy*, Shasta will meet Aslan "right at the top" of the mountain pass between Archenland and Narnia (161). In *The Magician's Nephew*, Digory's quest for an apple to protect Narnia will take him to what he calls "terribly big mountains" and a mysterious garden on top of "a steep, green hill" (155). At the great reunion in *The Last Battle*, Mr. Tumnus will explain that they are on one of the spurs that juts out "from the great mountains of Aslan" (209).

Lewis also has a mountain peak serve as a transcendent location at the end of *Perelandra*, as Ransom ascends a "great mountain" where he meets the two planetary archangels (164). In this use of mountains as a place of contact with the divine, Lewis follows a pattern seen in the Bible with such summits as Mount Sinai, the Mount of Transfiguration, and the Mount of Ascension. Lewis's use of mountains also reflects his own personal experience. In *Surprised by Joy*, he describes the view across the plain of Down to the Mourne Mountains as a vision into a different world. In words that sound like they could have come straight from *The Voyage of the Dawn Treader*, Lewis concludes that this view allows one to see "the way to the world's end, the land of longing" (155).

Lewis provides another glimpse into his feelings for geographical heights in *Letters to Malcolm*. He writes that although he loved the mountains he saw during his walking trips, he considered himself one of the "people of the foothills" (63), both in the physical sense as he did not have "the head" for soaring altitudes, and in the spiritual sense that he did not feel personally called to scale "the crags up which the mystics vanish."

Here in *The Voyage of the Dawn Treader*, readers are told that the mystical mountains, though so high that they "ought to have had ice and snow on them" (243), are "warm and green and full of forests and waterfalls however high you looked." In *The Silver Chair*, Lewis will return to this point as Jill wonders "why a mountain so huge as that was not covered with ice and snow" (28).

Lewis himself liked winter. In a 1955 letter, he writes, "We had our first frost last night—this morning the lawns are all grey with a pale, bright sunshine on them: wonderfully beautiful. And somehow *exciting*. The first beginning of the winter always excites me: it makes me want adventures" (*Collected Letters*, Vol. 3, 659). Despite Lewis's own love for the season of ice and snow, winter must be the time of year associated with the White Witch, while spring must be

Aslan's season, just as it is the season associated with Christ. At the end of his 1945 sermon "The Grand Miracle," Lewis provides a stirring portrait of this last association, using words we can find echoed in the final pages of *The Voyage of the Dawn Treader*:

> In the natural spring the crocus cannot choose whether it will respond or not. We can. We have the power either of withstanding the spring, and sinking back into the cosmic winter, or of going into those 'high mid-summer pomps' in which our Leader, the Son of man, already dwells, and to which He is calling us. It remains with us to follow or not, to die in this winter, or to go on into that spring and that summer. (88)

In *Miracles*, Lewis makes a similar observation, writing, "The Captain, the forerunner, is already in May or June, though His followers on earth are still living in the frost and east winds of the Old Nature" (187).

Suddenly from the warm, green mountains of Aslan's country comes a mysterious breeze that lasts only a moment but brings "a smell" and "a musical sound" (243), aspects we are told the three children never talked about later but never forgot. Lucy will say only that the sound, though not sad, "would break your heart."

This is not the first time Lewis has associated a fleeting smell and musical sound with Aslan. Readers may be reminded of Susan's response to the very first mention of Aslan's name in *The Lion, the Witch and the Wardrobe*. There we were told, "Susan felt as if some delicious smell or some delightful strain of music had just floated by her" (68).

The narrator says no more here about what comes to Edmund, Lucy, and Eustace on the breeze. For elaboration we might turn to "The Weight of Glory," where Lewis expands on this experience of longing, pointing out that the things that stir longing are not what we are in fact longing for. He explains:

> The books or the music in which we thought the beauty was located will betray us if we trust to them; it was not *in* them, it only came *through* them, and what came through them was longing. . . . For

they are not the thing itself; they are only the scent of a flower we have not found, the echo of a tune we have not heard, news from a country we have never yet visited. (30–31)

## "This Is Where I Go On Alone"

In *That Hideous Strength*, Merlin tests Ransom with a number of questions, among them, "Where is the ring of Arthur the King?" (271). Ransom answers that the ring is still on Arthur's finger; for as Ransom explains, "Arthur did not die; but Our Lord took him, to be in the body till the end of time . . . with Enoch and Elias and Moses and Melchisedec the King." In the end, Lewis gives Ransom himself this same translation from life to life. Here in *The Voyage of the Dawn Treader*, Reepicheep will likewise be treated to the same fate.

The landing boat runs aground, and the valiant mouse tells the others that he must go on alone, so they lower the coracle scavenged from Burnt Island. Then in another similarity with Arthur, whose last action is to have Excalibur cast into the water, Reepicheep flings his sword "far away across the lilied sea" (244). Arthur's sword is caught by a mysterious hand that rises out of the water—presumably the hand of the Lady of the Lake who first gave him the blade. Reepicheep's sword is described as landing upright, "the hilt above the surface." While Arthur's action was intended to keep Excalibur from enemy hands, Reepicheep's final action here has a very different meaning and may be seen as his final renunciation of his quest for honor, making him now, and only now, ready to find what he really seeks.

Here in the final pages of *The Voyage of the Dawn Treader*, Reepicheep completes the character arc he began in the previous book. In *Prince Caspian*, Reepicheep told Peter, "My life is ever at your command, but my honor is my own" (186). The valiant mouse has now come to a point where he no longer reserves his honor as something that must be his own and not offered up in service and sacrifice. In *Prince Caspian*, Reepicheep held that a tail was "the honor and glory" of a mouse (208). Now he has a higher honor and a greater glory.

On Ramandu's Island, Reepicheep stated his single-minded intentions:

> My own plans are made. While I can, I sail east in the *Dawn Treader*. When she fails me, I paddle east in my coracle. When she sinks, I shall swim east with my four paws. And when I can swim no longer, if I have not reached Aslan's country, or shot over the edge of the world in some vast cataract, I shall sink with my nose to the sunrise and Peepiceek will be head of the talking mice in Narnia. (213)

Reepicheep is finally ready to single-mindedly carry out these intentions.

After losing his tail near the end of *Prince Caspian*, Reepicheep was "confounded" because of his appearance and confessed to Aslan, "I am completely out of countenance. I must crave your indulgence for appearing in this unseemly fashion" (208). In restoring the mouse's tail, Aslan made it clear that he did not do this for the sake of Reepicheep's "dignity." Here in a final indication that, along with his sword, Reepicheep has flung away any last concerns about his dignity and maintaining an honorable appearance, he allows Lucy to do "what she had always wanted to do" (244)—she takes him in her arms and caresses him, an action that back in chapter one "would have offended him deeply" (16).

We are not told what happens to Reepicheep on the other side of the great wave. The narrator simply reports, "The coracle went more and more quickly, and beautifully it rushed up the wave's side. For one split second they saw its shape and Reepicheep's on the very top. Then it vanished, and since that moment no one can truly claim to have seen Reepicheep the Mouse. But my belief is that he came safe to Aslan's country and is alive there to this day" (244). The concluding statement, like the one made earlier about Lucy and the sea girl, is another indication that Lewis thought this would be his final Narnia story.

Jonathan Rogers has described Reepicheep's final voyage in these words: "Forgetting himself, forgetting the world, forgetting everything that lies behind, he goes up, up, up, to be welcomed into the heart of things" (74). In *The Last Battle*, Lewis will have Reepicheep waiting as keeper of the golden gates to welcome Lucy and the rest. In that scene and Pauline Baynes's delightful illustration that accompanies it, Reepicheep will have his left paw "resting on a long sword" (203), one we may assume Aslan has given him to replace the one he has left behind here—making this another time where Lewis seems to suggest that if we put first things first, we get second things thrown in.

## It Was a Lamb

As the sun rises into the sky, readers are told that "the sight of those mountains outside the world faded away" (244–45). From the landing boat, Edmund, Lucy, and Eustace can see the great wave, but now behind it is "only blue sky." Reepicheep and the momentary vision of Aslan's country are gone—for now. The three children are alone at the end of their journey, as they were at the start.

With their boat grounded, the three wade in the shallows southward, away from the wall of water. We are told, "They could not have told you why they did this; it was their fate" (245). Lewis made use of similar language a page earlier when Reepicheep departed, writing, "They did not even try to stop him, for everything now felt as if it had been fated or had happened before" (244). In these brief references to fate, Lewis is certainly not evoking the impersonal, irrational, and inescapable determinism found in classical mythology, the fate decreed to humankind by the uncaring gods or some other indifferent force. In writing that "everything felt *as if* it had been fated," Lewis may be hinting that there is actually something else at work.

In a letter written a decade after his conversion, Lewis states that what others may see as fate, he saw as "providence," or the principle that everything, including "the fall of a sparrow," is "in the hand of God" (*Collected Letters*, Vol. 2, 511). As was noted earlier, in *The Silver Chair*, when Caspian arrives at Aslan's country, Aslan will explain to him, "You cannot want wrong things any more" (240). Here as Edmund, Lucy, and Eustace come to the very edge of Aslan's country, Lewis, in a glimpse of what is to come on the other side, may be suggesting that the formerly separate strands of divine will and free will become intertwined.

Splashing out of the warm sea, Edmund, Lucy, and Eustace step onto a vast plain of grass, completely level and "spreading in every direction" (245), a place where "at last the sky did really come down and join the earth." Waiting there is a dazzling white lamb who invites them to a breakfast of roast fish. As they speak, suddenly the lamb's snowy white turns into tawny gold, and he becomes "Aslan himself, towering above them" (246).

In his observations about *The Wind in the Willows* found in "On Stories," Lewis asks, "Does anyone believe that Kenneth Grahame made an arbitrary choice when he gave his principal character the form of a toad, or that a stag, a pigeon, a lion, would have done as well?" (13). Readers might pose the same question about Aslan's appearance here as a lamb. If this choice was not arbitrary, what might Lewis be hoping to convey?

Back in chapter twelve, Aslan appeared as an albatross. In *The Horse and His Boy*, he will appear as a cat. Some readers may take Aslan's appearance here as a lamb simply as yet another example of the diverse forms the great lion temporarily chooses to appear in. Perhaps just as the lion is an appropriate form for the country-side of Narnia, an albatross for the Narnia seas, and a cat for the outskirts of Tashbaan, so a lamb is a particularly apt form for the grassy plain here at the world's end.

But Lewis seems to have more in mind than just this. In the final paragraph of *The Last Battle*, the narrator will tell how, as Aslan speaks to the great reunion, suddenly he "no longer looked to them like a lion" (210). What form does Aslan assume in the very end? The narrator will say only, "The things that began to happen after that were so great and beautiful that I cannot write them." The implication is that the great being who has taken on the form of a lion, an albatross, a lamb, and a cat is in reality none of these creatures but something indescribably different.

In *Imagination and the Arts in C. S. Lewis*, Peter Schakel observes that "part of the imaginative appeal of the Chronicles is Aslan in his rich complexity of forms and moods" (67). He maintains that the fact that Aslan appears primarily as a lion is "no coincidence" (66), for through this form Lewis coveys the "greatness and grandeur of the divine." Schakel suggests that the form of a lamb conveys the qualities of "meekness and vulnerability." So is Aslan intended to be great and grand or meek and vulnerable? Having described this set of opposite qualities, Schakel concludes, "Lewis, in fact, wants both."

Marvin Hinten has pointed out that in appearing here as a lamb, Aslan echoes "numerous biblical descriptions" of Christ as the Lamb of God and points to John 21, where "Christ prepares a fish breakfast for the apostles" (45). In Lucy's question about Eustace's return, Hinten sees a parallel to the question Peter asks about what will happen to John. Aslan asks Lucy, "Do you really need to know that?" (248). Jesus asks Peter, "What is that to you?" (John 21:22). Paul Ford follows a similar line, suggesting that the scene is "too reminiscent" of the breakfast the risen Christ prepares for his apostles "for Lewis not to have intended the association" (70).

Why would Lewis make such a deliberate association between Aslan and Christ now when previously Aslan has been more of a Christ-figure with more indirect associations? As has been mentioned, when Lewis penned *The Voyage of the Dawn Treader*, he thought it might be his final Narnia story. Perhaps in writing what he thought could be his last words about Narnia, he wanted to make the parallels harder for readers to miss. Additionally, since Aslan will tell the children that they must come to know him in their world as well, where he goes by another name, his appearance as a lamb here may be intended as a clue for Lucy and Edmund as well.

In *Letters to Children*, we find one of the rare times Lewis explains his fiction. He writes, "At the very *edge* of the Narnian world Aslan begins to appear more like Christ as He is known in *this* world. Hence, the Lamb. Hence, the breakfast—like at the end of St. John's Gospel" (93).

## "This Was the Very Reason Why You Were Brought to Narnia"

Just before his transformation into a lion, the lamb tells Lucy, "For you the door into Aslan's country is from your own world" (246). Now in his lion form, Aslan further explains, "I will not tell you how long or short the way will be; only that it lies across a river" (247). The river Aslan refers to is physical death, a requirement for all creatures except Reepicheep and those who are alive at the end of time in *The Last Battle*.

Next, as he did with Peter and Susan in the previous story, Aslan explains to Edmund and Lucy that they are too old to return to Narnia. In response to Lucy's sobs, Aslan promises that they will meet him in their own world, though under a different name. He concludes, "This was the very reason why you were brought to Narnia, that by knowing me here for a little, you may know me better there" (247).

In *The Last Battle*, Edmund, Lucy, and the others will be killed in a railway accident without even knowing it and will pass over the river of death to Aslan's country, where they will finally be allowed to remain for good. For them the waiting will not be too long, for according to Lewis's notes, seven years of English time will pass between this scene, when Edmund and Lucy are sent back to England, and the episode in *The Last Battle*, when they return to Aslan's country to stay.

Lewis never tells us how or to what extent Edmund and Lucy get to know Aslan better in England during this time. In *The Last Battle*, Eustace will explain to Tirian that during those seven years, the friends of Narnia—Professor Kirke, Polly, Peter, Edmund, Lucy, Eustace, and Jill—get together to "have a good jaw about Narnia" (58), but Lewis chooses not to say anything about the Pevensies' Christian faith. Perhaps Aslan would tell the curious reader who wants to know whether they were ever baptized or went to church the same thing he tells Lucy when she wants to know if Eustace will return: "Child, do you really need to know that?" (248).

Having said this, Lewis may have provided us with a hint. It will be seven years before we see Lucy again. When she and her siblings arrive at the stable in *The Last Battle,* Lucy's first words will be the only direct reference to Christianity found in the Chronicles. She will point out, "In our world too, a stable once had something inside it that was bigger than our whole world" (161). In Lucy's statement that alludes to the story of Christ's birth, we can see her belief that in the Bethlehem stable, the divine truly came to dwell among us.

Here on the final page of *The Voyage of the Dawn Treader,* suddenly there is a "rending of the blue wall" and a "terrible white light" as Aslan opens a door in the sky (248). The children briefly feel Aslan's mane and "a Lion's kiss on their foreheads," and then they find they are in Aunt Alberta's back bedroom in Cambridge, where they started.

In the very last paragraph, the narrator reports "only two more things need to be told" (248). Caspian and his men make it safely back to Ramandu's Island, and the three lords wake from their sleep. Caspian and Ramandu's daughter marry, and we are told, "They all reached Narnia in the end." The other item has to do with Eustace's ongoing improvement, which is good news to everyone except Aunt Alberta, who finds her miraculously transformed son now to be "commonplace and tiresome," a reaction that allows Lewis to end the story on a light note as he had the previous two.

We could say that in Aslan's statement to Lucy and Edmund, "This was the very reason why you were brought to Narnia, that by knowing me here for a little, you may know me better there" (247), Lewis is speaking to his readers as well. In an often quoted passage from "Sometimes Fairy Stories May Say Best What's to Be Said," Lewis explains that during his childhood, ideas associated with God and Christ took on negative "stained-glass and Sunday school associations" (47), causing his own faith to become "paralyzed" for many years. In writing the Chronicles of Narnia, Lewis sought to cast "all these things into an imaginary world," where they could "for the first time appear in their real potency," completely free from any off-putting connections. As Stephen Smith has proposed, through these stories, Lewis intends "to awaken in us a hunger" and "to open our hearts to the reality of God as the one in whom power and goodness, majesty and compassion meet" (170).

In his essay "When the Science Is Fiction but the Faith Is Real," David Downing comments on Lewis's decision to "recast" essential Christian truths in the stories of Narnia in an attempt to steal past the watchful dragons of "enforced reverence or tedious religious lessons" (100). Downing concludes, "By enlisting the unfettered powers of imagination, Lewis hoped to recapture the original beauty and poignancy of the Good News. In this strategy, Lewis has been brilliantly successful in the hearts and minds of millions of readers."

As they look back on the effect Lewis's writing has had on their own hearts and minds, fans of *The Voyage of the Dawn Treader* would heartily agree: Lewis truly has been brilliantly successful.

## Discussion Questions

Lewis's description from "On Stories" of two types of readers and the two types of stories they prefer was a topic in this chapter. One type of reader seeks only excitement. The other seeks not just momentary suspense but "that whole world to which it belonged" (5).

1. The Narnia tales are filled with excitement and also give us a "whole world." Would you say that one element is more prominent or more important to Lewis? Which is more important to you? To younger readers?

It was pointed out that in "The Weight of Glory," Lewis suggests we do not want merely to *see* beauty, we want to be united with it, pass into it, receive it into ourselves, bathe in it, and become part of it.

2. To what extent does this final chapter allow you not only to see beauty but to become part of it? Which aspects or elements were the most effective?

Readers may feel like they have known Caspian for a long time. Here in the final chapter, the young king attempts to abandon his men and continue on with Reepicheep.

3. Did Caspian's action seem in line with what we know of him? In what ways?

4. What do you think Lewis is saying about duty through this episode?

5. Caspian's temptation fits in with the other conflicts in the book's second half, where Lewis focuses more on the enemy within. Earlier our heroes faced external foes like Gumpas and the sea serpent. What might Lewis be saying through this shift in antagonists?

Here in the final pages, Reepicheep comes to the place where sky and water meet, and the prophecy spoken over his cradle is fulfilled as he leaves behind his sword and sails over a great wave to find all he has been seeking.

6. To what extent could we say the spell of heaven has been on us all our lives, even if we—like Reepicheep—have sometimes confused it with lesser desires?

Lewis's aim in writing the Chronicles was to recast truths from our world in an imaginary world, where they would be freed from any negative associations and thus be presented in their full power.

7. What do you make of Lewis's choice of having Aslan appear as a lamb?

8. In *Mere Christianity*, Lewis outlines this principle: "If you let Me, I will make you perfect" (202). How do the stories of Caspian, Lucy, Edmund, Eustace, and Reepicheep align with this idea?

9. What, if anything, do you think Lewis implies about what happens to Edmund and Lucy after they return to our world?

10. Near the end of this chapter, Aslan says, "This was the very reason why you were brought to Narnia, that by knowing me here for a little, you may know me better there" (247). How does this statement resonate with your own experience of being brought to Narnia through the act of reading?

In his celebrated essay "On Fairy-Stories," J. R. R. Tolkien writes of the "consolation" that fairy tales hold, the "catch of the breath," the "lifting of the heart," and the "fleeting glimpse of Joy" they provide, a joy "beyond the walls of the world" (85–86).

11. Do you agree with Tolkien's statement? How would you describe what *The Voyage of the Dawn Treader* and the other Chronicles offer their readers?

# Reference List

Adey, Lionel. *C. S. Lewis: Writer, Dreamer and Mentor*. Grand Rapids: Eerdmans, 1998.

Austen, Jane. *Pride and Prejudice*. New York: Scribner's, 1918.

Boethius. *The Consolation of Philosophy*. Mineola: Dover, 2002.

Bruner, Kurt, and Jim Ware. *Finding God in the Land of Narnia*. Wheaton: Tyndale, 2005.

Collodi, Carlo. *Pinocchio*. Hertfordshire, England: Wordsworth Editions, 1995.

Dalton, Russell W. "Aslan Is On the Move: Images of Providence in The Chronicles of Narnia." In *Revisiting Narnia: Fantasy, Myth and Religion in C. S. Lewis' Chronicles*, edited by Shanna Caughey. Dallas: Benbella, 2005.

Dante. *The Divine Comedy*. Translated by Henry Wadsworth Longfellow. New York: National Library Company, 1909.

Dickens, Charles. *A Tale of Two Cities*. New York: Allyn and Bacon, 1922.

Downing, David. *Into the Region of Awe: Mysticism in C. S. Lewis*. Downers Grove, IL: InterVarsity Press, 2005.

———. *Into the Wardrobe: C. S. Lewis and the Narnia Chronicles*. San Francisco: Jossey-Bass, 2005.

———. *Planets in Peril*. Amherst: University of Massachusetts Press, 1992.

———. "When the Science Is Fiction but the Faith Is Real." In *Mere Christians*, edited by Mary Anne Phemister and Andrew Lazo. Grand Rapids: Baker, 2009.

Duriez, Colin. *A Field Guide to Narnia*. Downers Grove, IL: InterVarsity Press, 2004.

———. *Tolkien and Lewis: The Gift of Friendship*. Mahwah, NJ: HiddenSpring, 2003.

Edwards, Bruce. *Not a Tame Lion*. Wheaton: Tyndale, 2005.

Filmer, Kath. *The Fiction of C. S. Lewis: Mask and Mirror*. New York: St. Martin's Press, 1993.

Ford, Paul F. *Companion to Narnia*. Rev. ed. New York: HarperSanFrancisco, 2005.

Foster, Richard. *Celebration of Discipline: The Path to Spiritual Growth*. New York: HarperSanFrancisco, 1988.

Gibson, Evan. *C. S. Lewis: Spinner of Tales*. Grand Rapids: Christian University Press, 1980.

Glover, Donald. *C. S. Lewis: The Art of Enchantment*. Athens, OH: Ohio University Press, 1981.

Hinten, Marvin. *The Keys to the Chronicles*. Nashville: Broadman & Holman, 2005.

Hooper, Walter. *C. S. Lewis: A Companion and Guide*. New York: HarperCollins, 1996.

Howard, Thomas. *C. S. Lewis: Man of Letters*. San Francisco: Ignatius, 1987.

Jacobs, Alan. *The Narnian: The Life and Imagination of C. S. Lewis*. New York: HarperSanFrancisco, 2005.

King, Don. "The Wardrobe as Christian Metaphor." *Mythlore*, Autumn 1987, 25–27, 33.

Kinghorn, Kevin. "Virtue Epistemology: Why Uncle Andrew Couldn't Hear the Animals Speak." In *The Chronicles of Narnia and Philosophy*, edited by Gregory Bassham and Jerry Walls. Chicago: Open Court, 2005.

Kipling, Rudyard. *Puck of Pook's Hill*. Charleston: Bibliobazaar, 2007.

Lewis, C. S. *The Abolition of Man*. New York: Collier, 1955.

———. *All My Road Before Me: The Diary of C. S. Lewis*. Orlando: Harcourt, 1991.

———. "Answers to Questions on Christianity." In *God in the Dock*. Grand Rapids: Eerdmans, 1970.

———. "Christianity and Culture." In *Christian Reflections*. Grand Rapids: Eerdmans, 1995.

———. *The Collected Letters of C. S. Lewis: Books, Broadcasts, and the War 1931–1949*. Vol. 2. Edited by Walter Hooper. New York: HarperSanFrancisco, 2004.

———. *The Collected Letters of C. S. Lewis: Family Letters 1905–1931*. Vol. 1. Edited by Walter Hooper. New York: HarperSanFrancisco, 2004.

———. *The Collected Letters of C. S. Lewis: Narnia, Cambridge, and Joy 1950–1963*. Vol. 3. Edited by Walter Hooper. New York: HarperSanFrancisco, 2007.

———. *The Discarded Image*. Cambridge: Cambridge University Press, 2004.

———. *English Literature in the Sixteenth Century*. New York: Oxford University Press, 1954.

———. *An Experiment in Criticism*. New York: Cambridge University Press, 1992.

———. "Foreword." In *Smoke on the Mountain*, by Joy Davidman. Philadelphia: Westminster, 1954.

———. "The Genesis of a Medieval Book." In *Studies in Medieval and Renaissance Literature*. New York: Cambridge University Press, 1998.

———. "The Grand Miracle." In *God in the Dock*. Grand Rapids: Eerdmans, 1970.

———. *The Great Divorce*. New York: Touchstone, 1974.

———. *A Grief Observed*. New York: HarperSanFrancisco, 1961.

———. *The Horse and His Boy*. New York: Harper Trophy, 1994.

———. *The Last Battle*. New York: Harper Trophy, 1994.

————. *Letters of C. S. Lewis*. Edited by W. H. Lewis and Walter Hooper. New York: Harvest, 1993.

————. *The Letters of C. S. Lewis to Arthur Greeves*. Edited by Walter Hooper. New York: Collier, 1986.

————. *Letters to an American Lady*. Grand Rapids: Eerdmans, 1971.

————. *Letters to Children*. Edited by Lyle W. Dorsett and Marjorie Lamp Mead. New York: Touchstone, 1995.

————. *Letters to Malcolm: Chiefly on Prayer*. New York: Harvest, 1992.

————. *The Lion, the Witch and the Wardrobe*. New York: Harper Trophy, 1994.

————. *The Magician's Nephew*. New York: Harper Trophy, 1994.

————. "Meditation in a Toolshed." In *God in the Dock*. Grand Rapids: Eerdmans, 1970.

————. "Membership." In *C. S. Lewis Essay Collection: Faith, Christianity and the Church*. London: HarperCollins, 2002.

————. *Mere Christianity*. New York: HarperSanFrancisco, 2001.

————. *Miracles*. New York: Touchstone, 1996.

————. "Miserable Offenders." In *God in the Dock*. Grand Rapids: Eerdmans, 1970.

————. "On Obstinacy in Belief." In *The World's Last Night and Other Essays*. New York: Harvest, 1988.

————. "On Science Fiction." In *On Stories and Other Essays on Literature*, edited by Walter Hooper. New York: Harvest, 1982.

————. "On Stories." In *On Stories and Other Essays on Literature*, edited by Walter Hooper. New York: Harvest, 1982.

————. "On Three Ways of Writing for Children." In *On Stories and Other Essays on Literature*, edited by Walter Hooper. New York: Harvest, 1982.

————. *Out of the Silent Planet*. New York: Scribner, 1996.

————. *Perelandra*. New York: Scribner, 2003.

———. "Preface to the 1961 Edition." In *The Screwtape Letters*. New York: Macmillan, 1982.

———. *Prince Caspian*. New York: Harper Trophy, 1994.

———. "Private Bates." In *Present Concerns*. New York: Harvest, 1986.

———. *The Problem of Pain*. New York: Touchstone, 1996.

———. *The Screwtape Letters*. New York: Touchstone, 1996.

———. *The Silver Chair*. New York: Harper Trophy, 1994.

———. "Sometimes Fairy Stories May Say Best What's to Be Said." In *On Stories and Other Essays on Literature*, edited by Walter Hooper. New York: Harvest, 1982.

———. *Spenser's Images of Life*. Edited by Alastair Fowler. New York: Cambridge University Press, 1967.

———. *Surprised by Joy*. New York: Harvest, 1955.

———. *That Hideous Strength*. New York: Scribner, 2003.

———. "Transposition." In *C. S. Lewis Essay Collection: Faith, Christianity and the Church*. London: HarperCollins, 2002.

———. *The Voyage of the Dawn Treader*. New York: Harper Trophy, 1994.

———. "The Weight of Glory." In *The Weight of Glory and Other Addresses*. New York: HarperSanFrancisco, 2001.

Malory, Thomas. *Malory's Le Morte D'Arthur*. Translated by Keith Baines. New York: Mentor, 1962.

Manlove, Colin. "'Caught Up into the Larger Pattern': Images and Narrative Structures in C. S. Lewis's Fiction." In *Word and Story in C. S. Lewis*, edited by Peter Schakel and Charles Huttar. Columbia: University of Missouri Press, 1991.

———. *The Chronicles of Narnia: The Patterning of a Fantastic World*. New York: Twayne Publishers, 1993.

Martindale, Wayne. *Beyond the Shadowlands*. Wheaton: Crossway, 2005.

Mills, David. "The Writer of Our Story: Divine Providence in *The Lord of the Rings*." *Touchstone*, January/February 2002, 22–28.

Myers, Doris T. *C. S. Lewis in Context*. Kent, OH: Kent State University Press, 1994.

Pliny. *Natural History: A Selection.* New York: Penguin, 2004.

Rogers, Jonathan. *The World According to Narnia: Christian Meaning in C. S. Lewis's Beloved Chronicles.* New York: Warner Faith, 2005.

Ryken, Leland, and Marjorie Lamp Mead. *A Reader's Guide Through the Wardrobe.* Downers Grove, IL: InterVarsity Press, 2005.

Sayer, George. *Jack: A Life of C. S. Lewis.* Wheaton: Crossway, 1994.

Schakel, Peter. *Imagination and the Arts in C. S. Lewis.* Columbia, MO: University of Missouri Press, 2002.

———. *The Way into Narnia: A Reader's Guide.* Grand Rapids: Eerdmans, 2005.

Shakespeare, William. *King Henry V.* New York: Cambridge University Press, 1994.

———. *The Tempest.* New York: Cambridge University Press, 2005.

Smith, Stephen. "Awakening from the Enchantment of Worldliness: The Chronicles of Narnia as Pre-Apologetics." In *The Pilgrim's Guide: C. S. Lewis and the Art of Witness*, edited by David Mills. Grand Rapids: Eerdmans, 1998.

Tennyson, Alfred Lord. "Ulysses." In *The Classic Hundred Poems*, edited by William Harmon. New York: Columbia University Press, 1998.

Tixier, Elaine. "Imagination Baptized, or, 'Holiness' in the Chronicles of Narnia." In *The Longing for a Form: Essays on the Fiction of C. S. Lewis*, edited by Peter Schakel. Grand Rapids: Baker, 1979.

Tolkien, J. R. R. *The Fellowship of the Ring.* Boston: Houghton Mifflin, 1994.

———. *The Hobbit.* Boston: Houghton Mifflin, 1994.

———. *The Letters of J. R. R. Tolkien.* Edited by Humphrey Carpenter. Boston: Houghton Mifflin, 2000.

———. "On Fairy-Stories." In *The Tolkien Reader.* New York: Del Rey, 1966.

———. *The Return of the King*. Boston: Houghton Mifflin, 1994.

———. *Tree and Leaf*. Boston: Houghton Mifflin, 1989.

———. *The Two Towers*. Boston: Houghton Mifflin, 1994.

Twain, Mark. *The Adventures of Tom Sawyer*. New York: Harper and Brothers, 1920.

Ward, Michael. *Planet Narnia*. New York: Oxford University Press, 2008.

Yandell, Stephen. "A Narnian Atlas." In *Companion to Narnia*, by Paul Ford. Rev. ed. New York: HarperSanFrancisco, 2005.

**Devin Brown** is a Lilly Scholar and professor of English at Asbury University. His books *Inside Narnia* (Baker, 2005) and *Inside Prince Caspian* (Baker, 2008) have been widely successful and have gone through several printings. His novel for young people, *Not Exactly Normal* (Eerdmans Books for Young Readers, 2005), was named as one of Bank Street College's "Best Children's Books of the Year." In summer 2008, Devin served as scholar-in-residence at the Kilns, C. S. Lewis's home in Oxford. He and his wife, Sharon, live in Lexington, Kentucky, with their fifteen-pound cat, Mr. Fluff.

# Don't miss Devin Brown's insightful guide on the book that started it all!

"Highly recommended." —*Library Journal*